PREACHING IN THE SPANISH GOLDEN AGE

A STUDY OF SOME PREACHERS OF THE
REIGN OF PHILIP III

HILARY DANSEY SMITH

OXFORD UNIVERSITY PRESS
1978

Oxford University Press, Walton Street, Oxford OX2 6DP

OXFORD LONDON GLASGOW
NEW YORK TORONTO MELBOURNE WELLINGTON
IBADAN NAIROBI DAR ES SALAAM LUSAKA CAPE TOWN
KUALA LUMPUR SINGAPORE JAKARTA HONG KONG TOKYO
DELHI BOMBAY CALCUTTA MADRAS KARACHI

British Library Cataloguing in Publication Data

Smith, Hilary Dansey
  Preaching to the Spanish Golden Age. – (Oxford modern
  languages and literature monographs).
  1. Preaching – History – Spain – 17th century
  I. Title   II. Series
  252'02'46   BV4208.S/   78-40246

  ISBN 0-19-815532-8

*Set by Hope Services, Wantage
and printed in Great Britain by
Billing & Sons Ltd.,
Guildford, Worcester & London*

**FOR
MY PARENTS**

PREFACE

The structure of this study is the result of an attempt to combine a certain amount of historical documentation on preachers and preaching in early seventeenth-century Spain with a degree of internal analysis or evaluation of representative sermons. I have tried to survey the field as a whole, to indicate the intellectual background and training of the preachers, the range of subject-matter of the sermons, the manner in which they were preached, the reception they met with, and the course whereby they came to be printed. Since sermons at this period were not, as a rule, written out in full *before* they were preached, we are entitled to suspect that the printed text that has reached us differs in some degree from what was spoken in the pulpit, and I have tried to take this fact into consideration.[1] However, for the purposes of this study, a certain amount of 'overlap' is assumed, and the sermon is considered both as an event, seen through the eyes of contemporaries,[2] and as a printed text,[3] since my main interest in preaching is summed up in Lanson's definition: 'la source vive de la parole publique'.[4]

I chose the reign of Philip III because all the major literary figures of the Spanish Golden Age were writing (or at least reading and hearing sermons) then and also because it offered the chance to examine the preaching scene before and after the advent of Paravicino. In order to make my task easier I then chose to concentrate on the career and works of ten preachers, from five different religious congregations and two

[1] See Chapter II.

[2] In letters, travellers' diaries, biographies of individual preachers, and accounts of important religious ceremonies.

[3] I have chosen to ignore the manuscript sermon since printed sermons are themselves so numerous. As I explain in Chapter II, it is difficult enough to discover what the public actually heard from the pulpit, but at least the printed sermon gives us what they *read*, although not always in the exact form intended by the preacher. Only three Spanish preachers are in twentieth-century editions (see List of Works Consulted under Cabrera, Santiago, and Vázquez).

[4] G. Lanson, *Histoire illustrée de la littérature française* (Paris and London, 1923), i. 422.

different generations, whose names occurred frequently in
the writing of contemporaries and whose printed work was
accessible.[1] The preachers are:

Fray Cristóbal de Avendaño, O. Carm. (c. 1570–1628)
Padre Jerónimo de Florencia, S.J. (1565–1633)
Fray Cristóbal de Fonseca, O.S.A. (c. 1545–1621)
Fray Diego Murillo, O.F.M. (1555–1616)
Fray Agustin Núñez Delgadillo, O. Carm. (1570–1631)
Fray Basilio Ponce de León, O.S.A. (1570–1629)
Fray Tomás Ramón, O.P. (?1569–1640)
Fray Luis de Rebolledo, O.F.M. (1549–1613)
Fray Pedro de Valderrama, O.S.A. (1550–1611)
Fray Diego de la Vega, O.F.M. (?1558–?1622)

I have supplemented my observations on the preacher's life
and work with reference to some of the preaching manuals of
the period, particularly those by Don Francisco Terrones del
Caño[1] and Fray Diego de Estella.[3] They have guided me
considerably in the organization and sub-division of the subject by indicating the preacher's frame of reference and scale
of priorities, both of which need to be taken into account
when one attempts to evaluate the degree of artistic awareness
of individual preachers, or the right emphasis to be given to
particular passages in their sermons. In few other literary
genres (and I believe that the sermon is a genre as well as a
religious function) is the personal voice so difficult to distinguish from the persona: but it is possible and, I think,
advisable to measure the sermons of preachers within a
limited historical period against the yardstick of contemporary
preaching theory. This approach seems to me to be further
justified when we find the same precepts on preaching and
prescriptions for the character of the preacher restated within
the sermons themselves. The *sermonarios* of the early seventeenth century are themselves *artes praedicandi*, containing
not only preachable material and model sermons but also

[1] The Oxford D. Phil. thesis from which the present book has developed
contains as an Appendix bio-bibliographies of all the preachers, some of which
will be published separately.
[2] *Instrucción de predicadores* (1st edn., Madrid, 1617; ed. F.G. Olmedo,
Madrid, 1946).
[3] *Modo de predicar y Modus concionandi* (1st edn., Salamanca, 1576; ed. P.
Sagüés Azcona, 2 vols., Madrid, 1951).

rules governing decorum and delivery in the pulpit. I therefore
believe that the nature of my subject, because it includes the
spoken word and the sacramental, or liturgical, activity as well
as the written word, requires a *mixed* approach, to supply those
dimensions which have disappeared with the passage of time.
Studies on English and French preaching from the Middle Ages
to the eighteenth century, particularly the works of Owst,
Gilson, Blench, and Fraser Mitchell (see List of Works Consulted), suggested a wide range of approaches to deal with the
'phenomenon', some of which I have adapted and appropriated.

Finally, I should like to acknowledge a debt of gratitude to
the friends and colleagues who have made this book, and the
doctoral thesis from which it derived, possible. I have received
help from many quarters, but my special thanks go to the Revd.
Quintin Aldea, S.J., the Revd. Bede Edwards, O.C.D., Professor
Nigel Glendinning, the Revd. David Gutiérrez, O.S.A., the
Revd. M.B. Hackett, O.S.A., the Revd. Juan Meseguer, O.F.M.,
Mr. Richard Pearce, the late Revd. Geoffrey Preston, O.P., Miss
G.M. Robinson, Mr. Eric Southworth, and the late Professor
E.M. Wilson. A whole legion of librarians have made an invalu-
able contribution to the research which produced this book
and I am especially grateful to the Librarians of Emmanuel
College, Cambridge; Wadham College, Oxford; Milltown Park,
Dublin; the Franciscan house of studies at Dun Múire, Killiney,
and, of course, the staffs of the Taylorian Institute, Bodleian
Library (Duke Humphrey), and British Library. Mr. A. Wilson,
formerly of the National Library of Scotland, made consul-
tation of certain rare volumes possible at a distance. In Spain
I am indebted to canons D. José Dominguez (Toledo), D. Pedro
Rubio (Seville), and D. Francisco Serrano (Saragossa) for
granting me access to the chapter records of their respective
cathedrals. Nearer home, Mrs. Margery Macnaught has proved
an excellent and reliable typist of the revised version of the
thesis.

My guide and mentor in Spain was the Revd. Vicente
Gómez Mier, O.S.A., who was unfailingly patient and helpful,
and my supervisor at Oxford was Dr. R.W. Truman, who
watched over the progress of the thesis in its early stages.
Lastly, I must thank my examiners, Professors Gareth Davies
and Peter Russell, for their encouraging words and valuable
suggestions which prompted and informed this book.

ABBREVIATIONS

AHN	Archivo Histórico Nacional, Madrid
A I–A	*Archivo Ibero-Americano* (Franciscan)
AV	Authorized Version
BAC	*Biblioteca de Autores Cristianos*
BAE	*Biblioteca de Autores Españoles*
BH	*Bulletin Hispanique*
BHS	*Bulletin of Hispanic Studies*
BL	British Library, London
BNM	Biblioteca Nacional, Madrid
BNP	Bibliothèque Nationale, Paris
Bodl.	Bodleian Library, Oxford
BRAE	*Boletín de la Real Academia Española*
BRAH	*Boletín de la Real Academia de la Historia*
C de D	*Ciudad de Dios* (Augustinian)
HR	*Hispanic Review*
MLR	*Modern Language Review*
NBAE	*Nueva Biblioteca de Autores Españoles*
PL	*Patrologiae cursus completas: series latina*, ed. J.P. Migne (Paris, 1844)
RFE	*Revista de Filología Española*
R y F	*Razón y Fe* (Jesuit)
RH	*Revue Hispanique*
RLC	*Revue de Littérature Comparée*
Sp	*Speculum*
ST	*Summa Theologica* of St. Thomas Aquinas
TCD	Trinity College Library, Dublin

In my quotations I have, wherever possible, modernized spelling and punctuation and expanded contractions, in order to facilitate the reader. The Bible is quoted in the Authorized Version for the most part, but in the Vulgate where it seemed most appropriate for the sense of a particular reading.

INTRODUCTION

When we turn to the corpus of critical works on Spanish preaching we find, not a comprehensive survey of the field, nor a detailed critical assessment of any one aspect of it, but a motley collection of articles, *discursos leídos*, and prefaces to individual works in modern editions, like the two preaching manuals mentioned in the Preface. Most of the writers who attempt to take stock of the state of sermonizing in Spain during the Golden Age (and no other period is even so well documented) begin by bemoaning the fact that it is virtually an unploughed field, or 'una mina de todo punto inexplorada'.[1] While patriotically hoping to find therein the 'gold' of a Bossuet or a Fénélon, especially in an age of so many great mystics and theologians, they are rather dismayed when they turn up the baser metals of Fray Gerundio and his prototypes. There is a *leyenda negra* of Spanish preaching, promulgated by the eighteenth century and re-diffused by nineteenth-century Protestant scholars unsympathetic to the floridity and extravagance of what may loosely be termed 'Spanish religious Baroque'[2] in all its manifestations, and this *leyenda* has persisted into the twentieth century, despite a revival of interest in Góngora, Quevedo, and the whole question of *conceptismo*. It would appear that, whereas it is quite legitimate for a poet, dramatist, or novelist to aim at *admiratio* through the cunning deployment of tropes and fine-sounding phrases, the preacher must always be a severe and plain speaker whose message is simple and unchanging. Since most of those critics who have undertaken research into the sermon literature of the Golden Age have been clerics it is

[1] M. Mir, *Predicadores de los siglos xvi y xvii* (Madrid, 1906), p. xvii. Since these words were first published the studies of Herrero García, Alarcos, and Olmedo have appeared, together with a handful of articles on individual preachers, but the authoritative study which should put them all into perspective is still lacking. Unpublished material, collected before their deaths by Herrero García and Olmedo, is allegedly being worked on with this aim in view.

[2] E.C. Dargan, *A History of Preaching* (New York, 1905–12), ii, belongs to what I would call 'the school of Ticknor' (whom he quotes extensively on Spanish preaching) and writes that 'Decadent Spain and distracted Italy wither under the blight of triumphant bigotry' (p. 26).

understandable that they should judge the sermons by their own standards of pastoral activity and find them wanting. However, it is unrealistic to expect a sermon written for one age to speak effectively to another. The Word of God is timeless, but its preaching belongs to history, and that is why the ministry of preaching must continue and renew itself continually. A large part of its attachment to history consists in the particular sensibility it expresses and the cultural language through which it communicates.

I would suggest that the chief defect of the works written on Spanish pulpit oratory in the Golden Age is their unanimous assumption that the subject must be seen in terms of a 'decline' or 'decadence', following a Golden Age of 'Apostolic' preaching,[1] and which begins around 1611 (the emergence of Paravicino) or at least by the 1630s. This decline is seen as being peculiar to Spain, although there are similar complaints voiced in France and England by the mid-seventeenth century,[2] and is given a variety of explanations that are also specifically Spanish: Spain's economic and moral 'decline';[3] the pernicious influence of Góngora and/or Paravicino;[4] the Jesuit *Ratio Studiorum*, helped by that rogue Jesuit Baltasar Gracián's treatise on *agudeza*, which spread the vogue for *conceptista* writing.[5] What is more,

---

[1] The 'Apostolic' preachers are understood to be San Juan de Avila, Sto. Tomás de Villanueva, the Beato Alonso de Orozco, Fray Luis de Granada, and others of that generation. Cf. G. Mayans y Siscar, *El orador christiano* (2nd edn., Valencia, 1786), p. xiii, and works by R. Ricard, D. Gutiérrez, and M. Herrero García.

[2] La Bruyère, 'De la chaire' in *Les Caractères* (1687), ed. R. Garapon (Paris, 1962), p. 445: 'Le discours chrétien est devenu un spectacle'. See also Furetière, *Nouvelle Allégorique ou Histoire des derniers troubles arrivez au Royaume d'Eloquence* (Paris, 1658). For England see R.F. Jones, 'The Attack on Pulpit Eloquence in the Restoration', in *The Seventeenth Century* (Stanford, 1951), pp. 111–42, which deals with South, Glanvill, and Tillotson and their campaign for plain preaching.

[3] A. de Capmany, *Teatro histórico-crítico de la Eloquencia Española* (Madrid, 1786–94), iv.4; F.G. Olmedo, 'Decadencia de la oratoria sagrada en el siglo xvii', *R y F* xlvi (1916).

[4] G. Ticknor, *History of Spanish Literature* (3 vols., London, 1849), iii. 127. E. Alarcos Llorach, 'Los sermones de Paravicino', *RFE* xxiv (1937), 162–197, 249–319, claims that Paravicino developed his peculiar mixture of *conceptismo* and *culteranismo* independently of Góngora and before the publication of the ode 'A la toma de Larache' (1612).

[5] A.M. Martí, 'La retórica sacra en el Siglo de Oro', *HR* xxxviii (1970), 294–8. His presentation of the question is not entirely convincing.

all these critics quote roughly the same texts,[1] and these texts are for the most part literary.

However, the closer one looks at literary 'evidence' of this kind the less convinced one becomes that it can be taken altogether 'literally'. In my first chapter I advance the suggestion that all these passages, so painstakingly quoted, belong to a single topos (see below, pp. 7–9), and that so far from marking a clear watershed in the development of Spanish preaching they in fact occur from Fray Luis de Granada (1576), and even Sta Teresa de Avila[2], to Gracián (1657),[3] as well as in every preaching situation there has ever been.[4] Moreover, in some cases the myth of the decline from the lost Golden Age is inverted and we find (in 1589) the Jesuit P. Juan Bonifacio inveighing against 'aquellos sueños y delirios de la antigua predicación de que todavía quedan entre nosotros algunos vestigios, no sólo en los pueblos sino aun en las ciudades'.[5] Of course there are 'fashions' in preaching, as in any other human activity, and the student of sermon literature would do well to take this into account, but a much more comprehensive study is required before these fashions can be judged objectively. Perhaps the most illuminating article on preaching in Spain so far published is one which reports, in some detail, a controversy carried on in 1628 between P. José de Ormaza, S.J. (under the pseudonym

---

[1] Otis H. Green, *'Se acicalaron los auditorios*: an aspect of the Spanish literary baroque', *HR* xxvii (1959), 413–22 is hardly more than a conflation of F.G. Olmedo's and Alarcos' articles cited above. More original, but on the same lines, is M. Baselga y Ramírez, 'El púlpito español en la época del mal gusto', *Revista de Aragón* iii (1902), esp. 212–14.

[2] *Libro de la vida* (c. 1564–5), cap. xvi, in *Obras completas* (2nd rev. edn., *BAC*, Madrid, 1967), p. 79: 'hasta los predicadores van ordenando sus sermones para no descontentar'. A similar complaint made by José de Sigüenza in 1589 is recorded by M. Bataillon in *Erasmo y España* (2nd Spanish edn., Mexico, 1966), p. 743.

[3] *El criticón III*, crisi x, in *Obras completas*, ed. Arturo del Hoyo (Madrid, 1960), p. 974: 'Ya echándolo todo en frasecillas y modillos de decir, rascando la picazón de las orejas de cuatro impertinentes bachilleres, dejando la sólida y substancial doctrina. . .'. See below, p. 8.

[4] Dargan, *History of Preaching*, ii. 7–8 talks of 'culminations of interest and power', followed by periods of decline, as being a constant pattern of Christian preaching. However, another constant factor is that, in any preaching situation, the preacher sees himself as being in the trough rather than at the crest of the wave: 'qualquier tiempo passado fue mejor'.

[5] *De sapiente fructuoso, III*. iii, in F.G. Olmedo, *Juan Bonifacio, 1538–1606* (Madrid and Santander, 1938), p. 187.

of Dr. D. Gonzalo Pérez de Ledesma), and P. Valentín
Céspedes, S.J. (under the pseudonym of Juan de la Enzina).[1]
This controversy stretches back to the first two decades of
the century and is a *Querelle des anciens et des modernes* in
which two different schools of thought coexist and periodically
confront each other, without either having the mastery. This
article is useful in that it avoids making absolute value-
judgements and at the same time categorizes each school
according to its salient features, which include many of the
aspects of preaching that I hope to discuss in the chapters
that follow. One becomes aware, on reading López Santos'
article, that what is old-fashioned in the 1580s, namely the
use of scholastic logical argument in sermons, is once more
the height of fashion in the 1630s, and so the wheel keeps
turning.

[1] L. López Santos, 'La oratoria sagrada en el seiscientos', *RFE* xxx(1946),
353–68.

I
THE SERMON AS EVENT

Was the seventeenth century really addicted to the sermon? The same phenomenon is reported all over Europe at this period: large congregations sitting (or standing) spellbound at the feet of a preacher who, by the sheer power of his eloquence and personal magnetism, was able to hold their attention for an hour or possibly longer.[1] Catholics and Protestants seem to have been possessed of an equally voracious appetite for sermons, to judge by the numbers of them to appear in print as the century progresses, and by the persistent homiletic strain which runs through contemporary prose fiction, particularly in Spain.[2] While Spanish sermon-going is not as well documented as English— Spain seems to lack diarists of the calibre of Pepys, Evelyn, and Manningham[3] to chronicle the small details of everyday life—there are none the less many references to fashionable Court preachers in letters, particularly those of Lope de Vega to the Duque de Sessa, which suggest a commensurate interest.[4] Preachers' letters, when they can be found, are invaluable, as are reports on missions.[5] *Relaciones de fiestas* at this period, the first quarter of the seventeenth century, accord considerable

[1] '...chi può ripensare al Seicento senza rivedere in fantasia la figura del *Predicatore*, n.-ovestito come un gesuita, o biancovestito come un domenicano o col rozzo saio cappuccino, gesticolante in una chiesa barocca, innanzi a un uditorio dai fastosi abbigliamenti', B. Croce, *I predicatori italiani del Seicento e el gusto spagnuolo* (Naples, 1899), p. 9.

[2] In his 'Nueva interpretación de la novela picaresca', *RFE* xxiv (1937), 343–62, M. Herrero García advanced the theory that the structure of the picaresque novel was modelled on that of the *sermón de santos*, without, however, producing any very precise documentation from the sermon side. Many critics have flirted with this theory, latterly E. Cros in *Protée et le gueux* (Paris, 1967), esp. pp. 137–50, 166, where he relates the *Guzmán de Alfarache* to sacred rhetoric. See also R. Ricard's chapter, 'Los vestigios de la predicación contemporánea en el Quijote', in *Estudios de la literatura religiosa española* (Madrid, 1964), which draws attention to the divulgation of preacherly commonplaces.

[3] *The Diary of John Manningham*, ed. John Bruce (Camden Society Texts, 99, London, 1868). This covers the year 1602–3 and contains almost daily accounts of sermons with detailed resumés of what was preached.

[4] *Epistolario de Lope de Vega*, ed. A. González de Amezúa (Madrid, 1935–43), iii and iv. Letters 61, 62, 306, 503, and 562 are of special interest.

[5] *Obras del P. Jerónimo Gracián de la Madre de Dios*, ed. Silverio de Santa Teresa (Burgos, 1933), iii: *Epistolario*. See also A. Domínguez Ortiz, *Crisis y decadencia de la España de los Austrias* (Barcelona, 1969), pp. 13–71, for ministry of P. Pedro de León, S.J.

importance to the sermon, among the welter of hieroglyphs, triumphal
arches, and poetic contests, while Dámaso Alonso testifies to the theory
that preaching was an 'hecho social apasionante en el siglo xvii' by quoting
a number of satirical sonnets on Court preachers from Villamediana and
the *Cancionero Antequerano*, as well as from Góngora and Lope.[1]

These reflections of interest in sermons are scattered throughout the
Golden Age, and yet do not afford us any precise information as to how
popular sermon-going really was at this time. On the one hand, we read
that, at the very end of the sixteenth century, the popularity of the
Carmelite preacher Fray Luis de la Cruz was such that:

empleándose en predicar era tanto el concurso de su auditorio que, si
era por la mañana, antes de amanecer ya estaban esperando a la puerta
de la Iglesia, y si por la tarde, comían tan temprano para oírle que a las
once estaban tomando lugar.[2]

P. Arriaga writes of the famous Dominican preacher Fray Agustín
Salucio that 'cuatro cuaresmas continuas predicó en Sevilla y, a las tres
y a las cuatro de la mañana, no cabía la gente en las iglesias, que eran
muy capaces',[3] and this is also the case with Fray Pedro de Valderrama,
according to his biographer Luque Fajardo:

en la Iglesia Parrochial de Santiago el Viejo, otro día de Conversión, estuvo
puesta escalera levadiza en la calle, para que subiese por las bóvedas de
ella, porque de ninguna manera hubo orden de abrir las puertas, según
lo que el auditorio había mañaneado y el aprieto en que estaban.[4]

On the other hand, these anecdotes might be dismissed as the stock-in-
trade of hagiographers and therefore not a true report. Moreover, they
all occur very early in the period and by 1605 we find P. Jerónimo
Gracián complaining to the Discalced Carmelite nuns at Avila that 'yo
estaba en Madrid con algún asiento, aunque no con satisfacción de
henchir mi ministerio y ejercitar mis talentos, porque había más
predicadores que oyentes'.[5] The underlying suggestion is that the

---

[1] *Del Siglo de Oro a este siglo de las siglas* (Madrid, 1962), pp. 95–104.
[2] Francisco Pacheco, *Libro de descripción de verdaderos retratos de illustres
y memorables varones. . .En Sevilla, 1599* [in fact it must be after 1627] (reproduction in photochromotype, 1881–5). This contains Pacheco's own portrait-
sketches, engraved by F. Heylan, of several preachers including Luis de León,
Pedro de Valderrama, Luis de Rebolledo, and Agustín Núñez Delgadillo, together
with short biographies.
[3] *Historia del Colegio de San Gregorio de Valladolid*, ed. M. de Hoyos, ii
(Madrid, 1920), 149. Salucio died in 1601 and from the *Actas Capitulares* of
Seville Cathedral it emerges that he was nominated to preach in 1580 and 1581.
[4] *Razonamiento grave y devoto que hizo el padre M.F. Pedro de Valderrama
. . .con más un breve Elogio de su vida y predicación* (Seville, 1612), fo. 9ᵛ.
[5] Silverio de Santa Teresa, op.cit., p. 392. Góngora writes to Paravicino (19
Dec. 1623) about a certain preacher that 'tuvo. . .más oyentes que autoridades de
santos, que no quiero decirlo al revés por la suya' (ed. Millé, *Obras completas*, n.d.,
108 [39] p. 1105), which probably means the sermon was well attended, but is
deliberately ambiguous.

public was tired of the unremitting barrage of sermons from all sides and growing blasé, but since Manningham in England at the same period often records two sermons he has heard on the same Sunday it is not always the case that sermons taken in large quantities produce satiety. However, it is an oft-repeated explanation for a cooling of devotional fervour. For example, during the debate on the use of the vernacular in books dealing with spiritual matters which was held at Salamanca in 1601, the Dominican Fray Alonso Girón blames the 'poca devoción que hay el día de hoy en oír los sermones' on the fact that so many of them are in print and may be read by the laity in their own homes,[1] to which the canon Francisco Sánchez makes the rejoinder that it is due rather to the numbers of sermons being preached. He continues:

La multitud de las mercadorías, dice Aristóteles, las hace baratas. Cuando había menos predicadores eran al vulgo más preciosos los sermones, aunque no tuviesen flores, pero ya que la caridad se va resfriando y la estimación de la palabra de Dios no es tanta, por ser tanta y tan frecuente, ¿qué han de hacer los pobres predicadores sino alcorzar y llenar de flores sus sermones para que los quieran oír?[2]

Fray Diego de la Vega tells preachers not to be discouraged by 'el poco fruto que se hace con los sermones, y que siendo así que se exercitan tanto las redes'.[3] A similar comment by Fray Cristóbal de Avendaño is closely bound up with a commonplace of *desengaño*, coming as it does at the end of a long gloss on *video mundum senescentum*, and therefore seems even less appropriate as sociological evidence:

Cuando considero el día de hoy tantos predicadores y tantos libros devotos, tantas congregaciones, tantas fiestas, tantos jubileos; ¡o qué llenos debéis de tener esos corazones de espíritu! Antes no, padre mío, que son como vaso quebrado, que todo cuanto en el echa nuestra madre la Iglesia y sus predicadores se sale y se pierde.[4]

A rhetoric of this passage is a traditional topos, used by preachers since St. Paul, to complain about poor attendances and lack of zeal on the part of their congregations, and thus is not a very reliable barometer of the spiritual climate of the age. It represents basic presuppositions of the preaching situation and assumes a certain formal relationship

---

[1] Fray Agustín Núñez Delgadillo, in the prólogo to *De la Victoria de los Justos* (Granada, 1618), sig. ¶3, says 'hay tantos sermonarios que me parece no ser los míos necessarios'.

[2] The debate is quoted in full in Pedro Urbano González, 'Documentos inéditos acerca del uso de la lengua vulgar en libros espirituales', *BRAE* xii (1925), 485. The same argument is used by Fray Tomás Ramón, *Cadena de oro* (Barcelona, 1612), fo. 49ᵛ.

[3] *Parayso de la Gloria de los Santos* (Medina del Campo, 1604), i.19.

[4] *Sermones de Adviento* (Madrid, 1617), pp. 79–80. See below, pp. 131–2.

between preacher and congregation, which is understandable in rhetorical
and theological terms rather than in a strictly historical perspective.
Such topoi of decadence and decline are used almost as a preacher's
code language, and a single text, 2 Timothy 4:3–4, is evoked frequently
by two catch-phrases: *prurientes auribus* and 'los gustos están estragados'.[1] For example, when Fray Basilio Ponce de León speaks of the
bad preacher 'rascando y haciendo cosquillas en las orejas sarnosas'[2]
and Fray Tomás Ramón in turn says 'que les rascó valientemente las
orejas, *Prurientes auribus*, que floreó y deleitó los oídos',[3] both are
referring to the same text, although both use it in condemnation of
those preachers who over-adorn their sermons with *humanidades*.
Therefore, although Ramón specifically attacks *culto* language in the
pulpit I do not think that it is as indisputable a sign of a historically
attested 'decline' of pulpit oratory as do Félix G. Olmedo, M. Herrero
Garcia, and Otis H. Green.

To bear this out, let us look at a text which two of the above-
named critics quote as 'sociological' documentation for their theory
of decline. It occurs in a sermon by Fray Diego de la Vega and even
has a marginal note beside it: *locus pro negligentia audiendi verbum Dei.*
. . .pues habiendo tanta sobra de predicadores y de sermones en este
tiempo, hay a veces tanta falta de oyentes que es menester alquilarlos
. . . Ahora lloran los de las Iglesias, por ver quán pocos son los que con
devoción Christiana acuden a los sermones. Que si se corren toros, si
se juegan cañas, si se representa una comedia, desde el caballero hasta
el pobre oficial, y desde la que arrastra telas hasta la que viste buriel,
no queda nadie que no vaya a verlo. Y si se predica la palabra de Dios,
apenas hay quien la oiga. Para lo uno faltan ventanas compradas y para
lo otro sobran asientos dados de balde.[4]

The second sentence is an echo of Lamentations 1:4—*Viae Sion lugent,
eo quod non sint qui veniant ad solemnitatem*—and the very same text
is glossed in a similar context, and with the same sense of immediacy,
by Fray Alonso de Cabrera in his sermon on St. Sebastian in his Advent
collection (Barcelona, 1609, ii) which must have been preached some
time before 1598, the date of Cabrera's death. If there is a specific

[1] The Vulgate gives: 'erit enim tempus cum *sanam doctrinam non sustinebunt*,
sed ad sua desideria coacervabunt sibi magistros *prurientes auribus*, et a veritate
quidem auditum avertunt ad fabulas autem convertentur' (my italics). See Green,
'*Se acicalaron los auditorios*', 413–22.
[2] *Discursos para diferentes Evangelios del año*, i (Salamanca, 1608), p. 174.
See also D. de la Vega, *Discursos predicables [Quaresma]* (Alcalá, 1611), prólogo.
[3] *Nueva premática de Reformación, contra los abusos de los afeytes, calçado,
guedejas, guardainfantes, lenguaje crítico, moños, trajes y exceso en el uso del
tabaco* (Saragossa, 1635), p. 326.
[4] *Empleo y Exercicio Sancto sobre los Evangelios de las Dominicas de todo
el año* (Vallodolid, 1608), ii. 97. Quoted in Félix G. Olmedo, 'Decadencia de la
oratoria sagrada en el siglo xvii', *Razón y Fe* xlvi (1916), 310–21.

decline in congregations it is difficult to place in time, if we have only the evidence of the sermons to go on, and I would therefore suggest that we treat such evidence as literary rather than historical. Furthermore, we should perhaps distinguish between what the preacher says about sermon attendance *from the pulpit* and what he says in a treatise or prologue to his fellow, although there, too, a certain rhetoric obtains. Vega's statement that 'hay a veces tanta falta de oyentes que es menester alquilarlos' does acquire a certain amount of historical validity, however, by being echoed by Cristóbal Suárez de Figueroa,[1] who was not himself a preacher, as well as by Fray Cristóbal de Avendaño. The latter describes a preacher:

solicitando el auditorio, violentando los ánimos de los deudos, parientes y amigos para que le oyan; hace visitas a Señores con este fin, y tal vez le es fuerza buscar coches y escuderos para llenar de acarreo el auditorio. Estos turban la Iglesia, pues comparándose ella a nave la truecan en galera, metiendo en ella forzados.[1]

In some theorists there seems, on the other hand, to be an injunction to cultivate popularity of a visible kind. Terrones del Caño, himself a well-known preacher, is ready to admit that:

No es mala regla, la que decía un amigo mío, para conocer un predicador si predica bien o mal, ver si le sigue mucha gente o poca, porque, en viendo que huyen de donde predica, si es cuerdo, había de dejar el oficio. Verdad es que el vulgacho suele seguir de tropel a algunos predicadores, no tan exactos, pero, por lo menos, tienen alguna excelencia de hablar, o prepresentar, o hacer llorar o reír.[2]

There is, in fact, *no* way of knowing how popular sermons were in the Spanish Golden Age, unless we simply study the number of times certain preachers were invited to preach in cathedrals which still have chapter records, or if we count the number of editions, official and pirated, of their printed sermons. These could be quite numerous and in 1629 Fray Cristóbal de Avendaño could claim that his works 'han pasado muchas veces a las Indias Orientales y Occidentales; hanse extendido por toda la Italia y Reinos de Nápoles;[3] en Francia los han traducido en su lengua,[4] y finalmente estoy cierto que han llegado a Polonia y Hungría'.[5] He gives the number of his Spanish editions as

---

[1] *Libro intitulado Otro tomo de sermones, para muchas festividades de los Santos* (Valladolid, 1629), Prólogo, sig. ¶¶7, See also same author's *Sermones de Santos* (Valladolid, 1628), fo. 169. Ticknor treats it as fact in his *History*, iii. 127.

[2] *Instrucción*, ed.cit., pp. 10–11.

[3] He is probably referring to the *Sermones del Adviento* which was published in Italian at Venice in 1629, although Spanish versions would be read in Naples. All his other sermon collections were translated into Italian in the late 1630s.

[4] Translator was Barthélemy Milet and the Advent sermons were published at Paris in 1628 by G. Methuras, who also produced a 1636 edition, as did C. Rouillard (all in Bibliothèque Nationale).

[5] *Otro tomo de sermones*, Prólogo, sig. ¶¶4[V].

thirteen or fourteen, but I can only confirm half that number between 1617 and 1630 for the *Sermones del Adviento*. Nevertheless, Avendaño does better than either Fray Agustín Núñez Delgadillo or Fray Tomás Ramón on this popularity count, although Fray Pedro de Valderrama and Fray Diego de la Vega can also boast of being 'best sellers' and translated into French, Italian, and Latin shortly after their first appearance in Spanish. Fray Diego Murillo tells us that his Lenten sermons were reprinted four times in two years.[1]

Spanish church-going habits are often described by travellers in Spain at the period, but the custom of hearing mass daily does not extend to sermons, as they were usually only preached on Sundays and feast-days, or in the afternoons of Lent and during retreats and novenas. In the first decade of the seventeenth century Spaniards have the reputation of being devout, according to the Portuguese traveller Pinheiro da Veiga, writing about a journey made in 1605 or thereabouts:

Hombres y mujeres, todos oyen misa cada día, y sacados los de fiesta en que por razón de las apreturas de la gente hablan quizás demasiado, los demás días la oyen toda entera con mucha devoción y recogimiento, lo más cerca que pueden del sacerdote oficiante, y no fuera de la iglesia o a la puerta, como en Portugal, donde no se oye casi nada.[2]

The same writer also emphasizes the importance of the church as a social centre, commenting on those who attend simply to see and be seen, and perhaps to carry on a discreet flirtation with a *tapada*. Church and playhouse are often contrasted in popularity by disgruntled preachers—'una hora de sermón parece un año de martirio, y tres de una comedia, un cuarto de hora'[3] —while in fact it is the similarities between the two which are most likely to strike us. Miguel Herrero García was perhaps the first to put forward the idea that 'el sermón y la comedia eran entonces [in the Spanish Golden Age] los únicos centros de reunión de la sociedad culta y los únicos cauces de la literatura oral en España'.[4] Rodríguez-Moñino goes further and posits an 'adoctrinamiento', both theological and stylistic, which springs from a mutual interaction between preacher and congregation, similar to that which might be built up between a popular dramatist and his audience:
. . .la oratoria sagrada pone a veces su vehículo expresivo al nivel del lenguaje popular para que llegue a todos el adoctrinamiento y la censura.

[1] *Discursos predicables* [*Adviento*](Saragossa, 1610), sig. *8^V.
[2] In *Viajes de extranjeros por España y Portugal* (Madrid, 1959), ii. 140.
[3] Fray Miguel de Almenara, *Pensamientos literales y morales sobre los Evangelios de las Dominicas después de Pentecostes* (Valencia, 1619), p. 322. When a preacher enjoys unusual popularity, however, he is accused by his peers of being a 'farsante' or 'representante', Cf. R.A. Preto-Rodas' article on the Jesuits Anchieta and Vieira in *Luso-Brazilian Review* vii (1970), 100.
[4] *Sermonario clásico* (Madrid. . .Buenos Aires, 1942), p. xviii.

Hay, pues, una corriente de mútua influencia constante: el público
determine ciertas características de la obra teatral o del sermón, y a su
vez recibe el impacto de ellos sin intermedio alguno.[1]
Something similar is suggested by Arnold Reichenberger, when he
speaks of the Spanish *comedia* as a collective enterprise.[2] Certain
conventions are held in common by the playwright and his audience,
and this enables countless variations to be played within a constant
tradition. If we are to discover whether this applies equally to the
preacher and his congregation, we must examine in some detail the
circumstances within which he operates and discover what are the
conditioning factors of a sermon, before it reaches the printed page.

ACCOMMODATION TO A CONGREGATION

The context of a sermon and the precise circumstances of its preaching are an essential part of that sermon, and cannot be ignored without
serious misrepresentation of its meaning. As Etienne Gilson has said of
the medieval sermon: 'On voit immédiatement que nous ne sommes
pas ici devant un œuvre littéraire à composer, mais devant une fonction
religieuse à remplir.'[3] This is fundamentally true of all preaching,
whatever degree of literary sophistication it may appear to adopt, and is
a fact which must be taken into consideration when reading any sermon:
a preacher is addressing a *congregation*, real or imagined, in the hope of
speaking to them individually—one might say 'sacramentally'—at a very
deep level. This function is a particular and temporal one, however
often repeated, and however dependent on the extra-temporal, universal
dimension. Therefore preachers tend to adopt the convention that a
particular congregation is being preached to, even when the sermon is
phrased in quite general terms.

In the seventeenth century Fray Diego de Arce appears to be aware
of the need to represent this aspect of his sermons when he publishes
them:

En los principios de algunos sermones pongo el nombre de la ciudad, o
pueblo donde los prediqué, y de la persona a cuya devoción se predicaron, para que así se entiendan mejor algunas cosas, que en ellos se
dicen, y la obligación que tuve para poner más cuidado en el estudio,
pues no todas las cosas son para todo auditorio, ni con igual trabajo
hemos de predicar en cualquier parte.[4]

Fray Diego de Arce is presenting his sermons to apprentice preachers,

[1] 'Construcción crítica y realidad histórica en la poesía española de los siglos
xvi y xvii', *Acta of the 9th Congress of FILLM* (2nd edn., Madrid, 1968), pp.
18–19.
[2] 'The uniqueness of the *comedia*', *HR* xxvii (1959), 304–5.
[3] *Les Idées et les Lettres* (Paris, 1932), p. 98.
[4] *Miscelánea Primera de Oraciones Eclesiásticas* (Murcia, 1606), Al Predicador,
sigs. A5^V–A6.

not merely to the interested reader, and therefore it is relevant to
remind them of the principle of 'accommodation', which has been an
enduring feature of preaching theory since St. Paul's 'I am made all
things to all men, that I might by all means save some' (1 Corinthians
9:22).[1] 'Accommodation' is seen in both social and intellectual terms,
as well as in the rhetorical sense of *decorum*. Not only are all states
and conditions of men to be addressed, but the preacher must also
ensure 'ut ea quae concipit possit convenienter auditoribus proferre'
(*Summa Theologica*, 1–2, q. 111, iv).[2] In the Golden Age there is much
mention of the 'capacidad' of the hearers, and the image most frequently used in this context is that of the *maestresala* or *trinchante*,
who parcels out the food at the feast according to the teeth and digestive
capacity of those whom he serves.[3] Thus the preacher should try to
allot 'lo sútil y dificultoso que tiene hueso que roer, a los que tienen
mejor dentadura, más sabiduría, más alto entendimiento'.[4] Fray Basilio
Ponce de León points out that 'lo que puede el Papa, no lo puede en
los estrados de las señoras, y salas de mesas de Trucos', and the same
is true of moral exhortations, which should be both particular and
pertinent. It is mistaken to attempt to

. . .reprehender la ambición, trajes, y coches en una triste aldea, donde
no oyen sino labradores, llenas de callos las manos, que no saben más
que estar en el campo arando o segando, y su común pecado es maliciar
y murmurar, como ellos dicen, y arrojar dos pares de pullas al que
pasa, en fin no acomodar las doctrinas a lo que corre en el tiempo, ruín
Maestresala.[5]

If the sermon is to be seen as a banquet of the Word of God, it ought to
be a banquet to which all are admitted (*para todos*—a popular catch-
phrase of the secular literature of the age)[6] and from which all receive
sustenance fitting to their needs: the idea is echoed over and over

---

[1]   The idea recurs in the Pastoral Constitution *Gaudium et Spes* (7 Dec. 1965):
'Quae quidem verbi revelati accomodata praedicatio lex omnis evangelizationis
permanere debet' (in *BAC* edn. of 1968, p. 326, para. 44). Here accommodation
to regional and cultural differences within the universal Church is being counselled.

[2]   St. Thomas Aquinas was pre-eminent as a theological authority at this
period, following his proclamation as Doctor of the Church in 1567, reiterated
by Pius V in 1570. His teachings had been followed closely by the Council of
Trent in the formulation of its decrees, particularly on justification.

[3]   This derives from an alternative reading of 2 Timothy 2: 15: *recte tractantem
verbum veritatis*, whereby *secantem* is substituted for *tractantem*. The *maestresala*
was a distinctly Spanish figure, remarked upon by Bartholomé Joly in his travels
in the Peninsula, *RH* xx (1909), 473.

[4]   Fray Pedro de Valderrama, *Exercicios espirituales para todas las festividades
de los santos* (Barcelona, 1607), p. 236.

[5]   *Discursos para diferentes Evangelios*, ii (Salamanca, 1609), p. 171.

[6]   Juan Pérez de Montalbán's miscellany *Para Todos* (Madrid, 1632), día v
contains a 'Discurso del predicador'.

again by our preachers.[1] Often a preacher will gloss the text which sums up the Council of Trent's concern for renewed efforts of evangelization: 'Parvuli petierunt panem, et non erat qui frangeret eis' (Lamentations 4:4).[2] Not only the nourishing quality of the bread is at stake, but also its effective breaking and distribution.

Fray Tomás Ramón goes even further when he uses the simile of 'madres que mascan primero el manjar y lo convierten en leche, y dan a mamar a los niños lo que les basta y cumple, y no los dejan comer el pan porque aun no tienen dientes para ello. . .'[3] to describe preachers whose mission is to the intellectually and spiritually illiterate. The Pauline dictum which is here invoked is 1 Corinthians 3:1–2: 'And I, brethren, could not speak unto you as unto spiritual, but as unto carnal, even as unto babes in Christ. I have fed you with milk and not with meat.' Moreover, Ramón is specifically concerned with the newly converted, who cannot be fed 'strong meat', by which he understands not only speculative theology but the Scriptures in anything except predigested form (*Cadena*, fo. 49^V).

It is not merely the difference in their states of life and their theological competence which accounts for the most important distinction between congregations, although these are both fundamental and insuperable, but the plain fact of their education, or the lack of it, in rhetoric and dialectic. The most important distinction, inherited from the Middle Ages and which could not be ignored, was that between sermons preached to the clergy (*ad clerum*) and those to the laity (*ad populum*). Quite apart from the more advanced counsels of perfection which might be preached to a community of religious, it was also customary, at least up to the end of the seventeenth century in Spain, for sermons to religious or clerks to be preached in Latin and to be constructed on the principle of *divisio intra*.[4] This is a rhetorical model, based on the categories of Aristotelian logic and Ciceronian topics, which extracts 'points' from within the text and submits them to dialectical investigation and proof rather than to confirmation with other 'authorities'. It often led to *divisio per verba*, founded on assonance and etymologies, and could frequently become pedantry and

---

[1] Vega, *Parayso*, i. 516–19; Murillo, *Discursos predicables [Quaresma]*, i. 722–3.
[2] Sess. V, cap. ii, and preface to *Catechism of the Council of Trent for Parish Priests* [1566](New York, 1949), p. 8.
[3] *Cadena*, fo. 50^V.
[4] Gilson, *Les Idées et les Lettres*, pp. 113–15. Also A.D. Deyermond, *The Middle Ages*, vol. i of *A Literary History of Spain*, ed. R.O. Jones, (London, 1971), p. 62. Janet A. Chapman, 'Juan Ruíz's learned sermon', in *Libro de Buen Amor Studies*, ed. G.B. Gybbon-Monypenny (Tamesis, 1970), pp. 29–51. Nuns were addressed in the vernacular and with *divisio extra*, but there would still be a high scriptural content. Such sermons, in Spanish, were known as *pláticas*.

obscurantism.[1] The *ad clerum* sermon was one preached at the university and as such was one of the exercises (*legere, disputare, praedicare*) required for the degree of Master of Theology.[2] A formal sermon was also one of the tests in the *oposiciones* for canonries in Toledo Cathedral, and presumably others in Spain.[3]

The *divisio extra* sermon was preached in the vernacular and was based on analogies, which included not only passages from the Fathers and scriptural cross-references of a typological nature but also *exempla* and similes drawn from everyday life.[4] An entry for 1 April 1602 in the *Actas Capitulares* of Toledo Cathedral (xxiii. fo. 19) requests an inquiry into whether the *sermón del Mandato*, which has traditionally been preached in Latin in the Cabildo, may henceforth be preached in Spanish 'entre los dos coros'.[5] This alternative term for a sermon *ad populum* draws attention to the fact of a certain degree of physical separation between clergy and laity during the delivery of sermons at this period—a legacy of the massive, enclosed choir of so many Gothic cathedrals and collegiate churches in Spain. Most often sermons to priests or to religious would be given inside the *coro* or in the Chapter House (*cabildo* or *sala capitular*). On occasions when both the laity and the chapter were present at a sermon, the canons would come down from their stalls and occupy benches (*bancos*) inside the *coro* and facing the preacher.[6] Between 1599 and 1610 in the *Autos Capitulares* of Seville Cathedral there are repeated injunctions that the laity shall not be allowed to enter the *coro* while a sermon is being preached, and that the doorkeepers are to be given instructions to exclude them. There are also many attempts to prevent people, other than 'ministros o pajes del Arzobispo', sitting on the altar steps, or on the 'sillas bajas' under the pulpit.[7] The space 'entre los dos coros', which corresponds to that between the *reja* of the sanctuary and that of the centrally placed *coro* (canons' choir stalls), is very restricted in most Spanish cathedrals, and it must frequently have been the case that a large part of the congregation would have been in the side-aisles

[1] See below, pp. 44–5.
[2] G.R. Owst, *Preaching in Medieval England* (Cambridge, 1926), pp. 155, 259–62 and C. Smyth, *The Art of Preaching* (London, 1940; rev.edn., 1964), pp. 19–54.
[3] Three Gospel texts were selected at random ('abrió un niño con un cuchillo por tres partes de los Evangelios') and the candidate had to preach on one of them, in *Actas Capitulares*, xxii (1599), fo. 184[V], and entries for following five days.
[4] Deyermond, *The Middle Ages*, pp. 96–7, 152.
[5] Reiterated by the Dominicans in 1604 (fo. 159) and approved by canons. 'Entre dos coros' was noted as a place of rendezvous for *damas* and *galanes* in Spanish Cathedrals.
[6] Seville, *Autos Capitulares* (1610), fo. 58.
[7] Saragossa [Seo] *Actas* (1601), fo. 118.

and transepts.[1] In medieval times the word *pulpitum* was usually, but by no means invariably, applied to the substantial screen shutting off the nave from the choir in monastic, minster, and collegiate churches, and the Gospel was read from the north end and the epistle from the south. Pulpits attached to the screen in front of the sanctuary are found in Spanish churches of the early Renaissance, and in Seville Cathedral there are a pair of secondary pulpits fixed to the rear wall of the *coro*.[2] Sermons were customarily preached from the 'lado del Evangelio'. In Barcelona Cathedral the pulpit is attached to the end of the north side of the *coro*, at right angles to the *reja*.[3]

Franciscan and Dominican churches, particularly those built in the early years of the fourteenth century, are better adapted for preaching to large congregations than are many Spanish cathedrals, as they have long, wide naves and fewer aisles or side-chapels.[4] In Jesuit churches, too, the emphasis was on instruction and there was therefore a single, wide nave with both altar and pulpit in full sight of the congregation.[5] The choir is generally in a raised gallery at the rear of the church, as in the Dominican churches of San Esteban (Salamanca), San Pablo and San Gregorio (Valladolid), and San Pablo (Seville).[6] The basilica of El Escorial has a fine example of an upper choir facing pulpit and altar, built between 1578 and 1581. Any gallery would give a greater sense of intimacy with the preacher, particularly in a small church.

Preaching was not, however, confined to the churches. San Carlo Borromeo justifies the custom of preaching in unconsecrated places by appealing to the example of Christ and his apostles:

Praedicationis munus nullo, neque tempore, neque loco sibi Christus Dominus praefinuit, neque Apostoli item, qui omni loco, omnique tempore sacrosanctum Evangelium disseminarunt...non solum in Ecclesia, qui locus praedicationis proprius est, sed vbique omnique tempore sacra concione populus Dei pascendus erit.[7]

Bartolomé Ximénez Patón, rather grudgingly, admits that sermons may be delivered anywhere, provided that it is a public place:

[1] L. Bouyer, *Liturgy and Architecture* (Univ. of Notre Dame, Indiana, 1967), p. 79.
[2] A.N. Prentice, *Renaissance Architecture and Ornament in Spain*, ed. H.W. Booton (London, 1970), p. 18 and Pl. 18, also photo 130.
[3] G.E. Street, *Some account of Gothic architecture in Spain* (London, 1865), Pl. xvi.
[4] N. Pevsner, *An Outline of European Architecture* (1943; Harmondsworth, 1963), pp. 141–2. P. Anson, *The Building of Churches* (London, 1964), pp. 973–5.
[5] A. Biéler, *Architecture in Worship* (London, 1965), p. 56.
[6] The last is exceptionally wide, perhaps as a consequence of alterations in 1608 and 1724.
[7] *Instructiones Praedicationis Verbi Dei* (Barcelona, 1588), p. 21.

El lugar es la Iglesia acomodado para este santo ministerio. Aunque
también se puede predicar en las plazas, y campos, y en otros lugares
públicos. . . Así que no se ha de predicar en secreto, en algunas casas
particulares, porque no nazca sospecha de doctrina herética.[1]
At the back of his mind may be the scandal surrounding lay *alumbrado*
preachers at the ducal palace of Escalona in the 1520s, which Marcel
Bataillon has described to us.[2] Only the Pope, or the King of Spain,
might have sermons preached to them in private, being presumably
above suspicion. Fray Hernando de Santiago is reported to have preached
to Philip II when that monarch was confined to bed with gout, and only
four hearers were present.[3] Don Francisco Terrones del Caño admits to
having had to perform the same ministry, with some trepidation.[4]

The Jesuit theologian, Francisco Suárez, goes even further towards
an unrestricted place of preaching: not only is it 'nec malum, nec
indecens esse in plateis et locis publicis populo praedicare', but since
preaching

neque etiam ordinatur ad aliquam mysticam significationem sed solum
ad moralem et spiritualem fidelium utilitatem, ideoque ex ratione sua
non postulat sacrum locum, in quo fiat, sed tantum accommodatum, et
opportunum ad vtilitatem et aedificationem audientium.[5]

He is here principally defending the original practice, followed by both
friars and Jesuits, of preaching in the streets. This extended, in the
seventeenth century, to delivering sermons in the galleys[6] and in the
mancebía at Seville.[7] Lent courses were customarily preached in the
hospitals, the most famous on the preaching circuit being the Hospital
General de Nuestra Señora de Gracia, otherwise known as the Hospital
Real at Saragossa. Baltasar Gracián, in the *Dedicatoria* to the third part
of *El criticón*, calls it the 'palenque de los mayores talentos' and it
certainly attracted the leading preachers of the day, including (in our
period) Lanuza, Valderrama, Avendaño, and Núñez Delgadillo. Founded
in 1425 by Alonso V of Aragon, by 1599 when Philip III paid it a royal
visit the hospital had about six hundred patients with every kind of
infirmity. It was supported financially from the proceeds of a public

---

[1] *El perfecto predicador* (Baeza, 1612), fos. 80 and 81. Also 41[V]:
[2] *Erasmo y España*, p. 182 and Ch. iv *passim*.
[3] Quintín Pérez, S.J., *Fray Hernando de Santiago* (Santander, 1929), p. 22,
where he quotes BNM MS. 8, 293, fragmento 16.
[4] *Instrucción de predicadores*, ed. cit., p. 97.
[5] *Operis de Religione pars segunda* (Lyons, 1625), iv. 670a–671a.
[6] P. Pedro de León's ministry to convicts is recorded by Pedro Herrera Puga
in *Sociedad y delincuencia en el Siglo de Oro* (Granada, 1971), where pp. 196–8,
278-85 relate specifically to preaching. Herrera bases himself on León's own
account of 1619.
[7] F. Rodríguez Marín refers to sermons preached to prostitutes in *el Compás*,
Seville, in his 'Discurso preliminar' to Cervantes's *Rinconete y Cortadillo* (2nd
edn., Madrid, 1920, pp. 114–15.

theatre, the Coliseo del Coso.[1] Fray Cristóbal de Avendaño describes the hospital thus:

...lugar donde se curan todas enfermedades, y se albergan en el todos los desválidos del mundo, hasta niños expuestos, locos de todos los Reinos de España: y extiéndese a tanto su caridad, y grandeza, que hasta los que son de Reinos muy estraños, fuera de España, a todos cura con gran regalo, cuidado de grandes Médicos, y excelente botica... varias y diversas redes, para los menguados de juicio, que yo soy testigo haber visto en aquella santa casa, más de ciento y cincuenta locos, y locas, unos convaleciendo, otros detrás de las redes.[2]

The hospital was famed for its humane treatment of madmen, which may have extended to letting them hear sermons!

Preachers regularly visited hospices for the poor and sermons were also preached in the Consejo de Italia and the Consejo de Indias (by Fray Hortensio Félix Paravicino), various *audiencias* and *cabildos*, both ecclesiastical and secular, and the Casa de Contratación at Seville (by Fray Pedro de Espinosa, O.P.). I have found a copy of a sermon by the Jesuit Juan de Pineda entitled *Sermón a Jueces y otros ministros de Justicia... último día de Pascua de Navidad, haciendo fiesta votiva del Espíritu Santo la congregación de su avocación* (Seville, 1612), which would, however, probably have been preached in the church of their confraternity.[3] We should not forget the pulpit in the *patio de los naranjos* of Seville Cathedral, where SS. Vicente Ferrer, Francisco Borja, and Juan de Avila all preached open-air sermons. Processions of flagellants and *autos-de-fe* were also accompanied by sermons,[4] which are often printed as *extravagantes* at the end of a collection of sermons for saint's-days or *Santoral.*

The magnetic attraction exercised by the Court and the provincial capitals meant that in the mid-sixteenth and early seventeenth centuries many small towns and villages in remote, and not so remote, districts seldom saw a preacher.[5] Frei Bartolomeu dos Mártires produced a *Catecismo, o Doctrina Christiana y Pláticas Espirituales, ordenado... para que se leyese en los lugares adonde no llegan Predicadores* (Lisbon, 1594), which was translated into Spanish in 1653. However, in the second half of the seventeenth century, all over Europe there was a great increase in parochial missions of five to six weeks, encouraged

[1] *Privilegios de la antigua Fundación del Hospital Real y General de Nuestra Señora de Gracia de Zaragoza*, Comunicación III, Semana de Estudios de Derecho Aragonés (Jaca, 1944).

[2] *Marial* (Valladolid, 1629), fos. 30^v–31.

[3] In the Obispado, Cordoba. Sermons addressed to specific 'states' or 'walks of life' are discussed in Ch. V, pp. 118–29.

[4] 'Cuando se ofrece hacer alguna Fiesta, o procesión votiva por alguna necesidad, hay sermón, *Regla del coro y cabildo de...Sevilla* (Seville, 1658), p. 128.

[5] Fadrique Furió Ceriol, *Bononia, sive de libris sacris in vernaculam linguam convertendis* (Basle, 1556; Leyden, 1819), p. 126.

18 THE SERMON AS EVENT

by the example of S. Vincent de Paul.[1] In Spain, the Jesuits PP. Jerónimo
Dutari (Navarre and Galicia), Jerónimo López (Aragon), and Tirso
González were extremely active and there were also many missions
sent by Jesuits and Franciscans to the townships of Castille and
Andalusia.[2] The sermons preached tended to be *sermones de aparato*
with visual aids for emotional effect, and not many survive in printed
form. Baltasar Gracián, himself a preacher on missions in the 1640s,
published the mission sermons of P. Jerónimo Continente (the nephew
of his former superior) as *Predicación fructuosa* (Saragossa, 1652).[3]
His own famous 'sermón del infierno' dates from December 1644 in
Valencia. In my study I have disregarded both home and foreign
missions, although some sermons from the latter can be found in
print.[4]

WHO PREACHED THE SERMONS?

According to Aquinas, the duty of preaching to the faithful belongs,
by virtue of his office, to the bishop ('Praedicare est principalissimus
et proprius actus episcopi', *Summa Theologica*, 3, q. 65, 1 ad 1), whereas reading the Gospel at the mass or addressing catechumens has
traditionally been considered separately and sometimes performed by
a deacon.[5] In practice, however, it has long been the custom for the
priest to combine these three functions and to deliver a short homily
at each mass he celebrates. Nevertheless, the traditional distinction
of roles remains an inevitable commonplace in sixteenth- and seventeenth-century treatises on preaching, reinforced by the determination
of the Fathers of the Council of Trent to draw attention to the special
obligation (*munus praecipuum*) of the bishop to preach regularly to
his flock.[6]

[1] J. Delumeau, *Le Catholicisme entre Luther et Voltaire* (Paris, 1971), pp.
274–80. A. Gemelli, *Il Francescanesimo* (Milan, 1932; trans. H. Hughes, London,
1934), p. 146.
[2] A. Domínguez Ortiz, *La sociedad española en el siglo xvii*, ii (Madrid, 1970),
176–80.
[3] See M. Batllori and C. Peralta, *Baltasar Gracián en su vida y en sus obras*
(Madrid, 1969), p. 157.
[4] The works of Fray Alfonso Herrera y Molina, printed first in Seville and
later in Lima, and the works of the redoubtable Bishop Palafox in Mexico.
[5] Women and the laity were officially excluded from the ministry. Ximénez
Patón, *El perfecto predicador*, fos. 40 and 48ᵛ–50. Carolus Regius, S.J., *Orator
Christianus* (Cologne, 1613), pp. 5–6.
[6] Sess. v, cap. 2 (17 June 1546) and Sess. xxiv, cap. 4 (11 Nov. 1563) in
J. Tejada y Ramiro, *Colección de canones de la Iglesia española* (4 vols., Madrid,
1849–53), iv, 47–9 and 342–3. Also H. Jedin, *History of the Council of Trent*,
ii (London, 1961), 123 and Ch. 9 *passim*. This is linked to the vexed question of
episcopal residence which, to judge by a letter written by Clement VIII to Philip
III in 1599, was not particularly popular in Spain: 'Señor, lo que nuestro corazón
siente el considerar que muchos de los Obispos de España viven y pasan la vida

However, even the most conscientious bishop might find some difficulty in preaching in person throughout the whole of his diocese, except perhaps once or twice a year, and he was therefore expected to appoint substitutes and to guarantee their competence and orthodoxy. Bartolomé Ximénez Patón points out that the bishop delegates his apostolic role 'a cualquier Prelado de las Iglesias, como son los que llamamos curas, y en el Reino de León, y Valencia Retores, y en Andalucía Priores, y en otras partes con otros nombres'.[1] Almost any cleric might find himself in the pulpit at some stage in his career. Nevertheless, in theory, it was not admission to holy orders in itself which entitled a man to preach, but rather the authoritative charge of souls (ratio prelationis). If others—monks, friars, graduates in theology, vicars, or chaplains—wished to preach in public they must be commissioned to do so by the apostolic authority of the Church (missio canonica), which generally meant obtaining a licence from the local bishop.[2]

Los frailes no prediquen en el obispado de algún obispo, siéndoles por él contradicho. Y ninguno dellos de todo sea osado a predicar al pueblo si por el Ministro general desta Fraternidad no fuere examinado, y aprobado; siéndole por él concedido el oficio de la predicación.[3]

Religious engaged in preaching were granted permits, renewed annually, by their superiors—either Provincial or Difinidor—after an initial examination, and were subject, under the conditions of the bull Dum intra mentis arcana (19 December 1516), to the visitation and approval of their Ordinary.[4] In addition, special authorization was required from the prelatus of the place where the sermon was to be delivered when it was a case of friars preaching in churches not belonging to their order. This formality, although modified by the privileges conferred on the Mendicant orders by Boniface VIII (reconfirmed by Pius V in the bull Etsi Mendicantium ordines, 16 May 1567) and on the Jesuits by Gregory XIII, in the bull Ad perpetuam rei memoriam (1575), which allowed greater scope to their missionary activities, still proved a cause of

---

como Príncipes del siglo, no como Ministros de Christo, y dispensadores de sus misterios, desestimando lo que es propio de Obispos; de aquí procede el celebrar raras veces, asistir poco a sus Divinos Oficios, no predicar a sus ovejas, no administrar Sacramentos, no celebrar Ordenes para la milicia de Christo. (G. González Dávila, Historia de la vida y hechos de. . .D. Felipe Tercero [1619], posthumously published in Salazar de Mendoza, Monarquía de España (Madrid, 1770–1), iii. 71).

[1] El perfecto predicador, fo. 21.

[2] Owst, Preaching in Medieval England, pp. 4–5.

[3] Un tractado muy provechoso llamado Manual de las cosas essentiales a que son obligados los frayles menores por su regla (Coimbra, 1571), 'Regla de los predicadores', cap. ix (no fos.).

[4] H. Jedin, History of the Council of Trent, i (London, 1957), 136.

friction between regulars and seculars at the end of the sixteenth century.[1]

Although anxious to retain as much control as possible over the evangelization of their dioceses, only a few Spanish bishops ever took a very active part in the preaching ministry.[2] They would delegate the task to 'professional' preachers, especially in the great preaching seasons of Lent and Advent, when, in addition to the homily preached at mass, sermon courses were also preached in the afternoons.[3] Special preachers were engaged, occasionally, for novenas, retreats, and to preach a sermon to launch the *Bula de la Santa Cruzada*. Funeral sermons would also fall outside the normal preaching routine, or *tabla*, which was drawn up by the *canónigo magistral* in every cathedral and collegiate church as a means of distributing 'pulpit-time' among the canons. Certain sermons were the prerogative of the *magistral* himself, although he was not permitted to preach in both Lent and Advent of the same year,[4] and a distinction was made between sermons which were 'de tabla' (i.e. reserved for the *cabildo*, or a specific religious order) and sermons which were 'de convidar'. A list of such sermons, throughout the Church's year, may be found in the book of ceremonies of each cathedral and varies according to local custom. In Toledo it would appear that the rivalry between the Dominicans and the Franciscans manifested itself, between 1612 and 1613, in alternate visits to the *cabildo* to petition for more 'de tabla' sermons.[5]

When preachers were invited to deliver sermons during Lent or Advent in a cathedral church they would previously have been submitted to quite a lengthy selection procedure several months before (usually in December or January). The names of various candidates, some of whom might live quite a distance away, would be proposed at a chapter meeting and inquiries would be made about them. Then a secret ballot would be held, either with *habas* (bean counters) or *papeles secretos*, whereupon the *magistral* (or *quaresmero*) would begin negotiations to 'book' the successful candidate, or candidates.[6]

[1] Tejada y Ramiro, *Colección*, iv. 50–1.

[2] At the end of their careers famous preachers like Diego de Arce, Jerónimo Lanuza, and Plácido de Todos Santos obtained bishoprics.

[3] These frequently took the form of a 'serial story', based on one of the Psalms or the Book of Job, cf. Cristóbal González, *Consideraciones sobre el Psalmo ciento y treinta y tres. Para los seis Domingos de Quaresma en la tarde* (Madrid, 1609) and works by Vega, Núñez Delgadillo, and Semple de Tovar (see List of Works Consulted).

[4] Saragossa [Seo], (1606), fo. 209^V.

[5] *Actas Capitulares*, 12 and 13 Feb. 1612 and also 1611 (no fos.).

[6] Toledo, *Actas Capitulares* (1599), vol. xxii, fo. 146^V, speak of five preachers 'los quales han de predicar por antigüedad, volviendo el turno'. In Seville there were three different preachers for each of the three *ferias* of Lent: *Autos* (1580), fo. 4^V.

If the chosen preacher was unable to accept, or had to withdraw owing to illness, the whole process of nomination, investigation, and ballot had to begin again.

Preachers had their expenses paid, *lo común* (daily ration of food), and a further *limosna* or *stipendio*, which might be 100 *libras* for a Lent cycle and 10 for Advent, if he were the only preacher.[1] Ximénez Patón points out that, 'Un sermón no se puede regatear, ni vender, mas atarse a un púlpito un Letrado, como cosa muy diversa de la palabra divina, se puede poner muy bien en precio.'[2] Nevertheless, we read of Padre Jerónimo de Florencia, S.J., being paid the sum of 1,300 *reales* by the town of Madrid for the funeral sermon he preached for Queen Margarita in Sta María on 19 December 1611, although this purported to cover the cost of its eventual printing as well.[3] A few years earlier the Seville chapter had rewarded Padre Martínez for his 'buen servicio' in the *sermones del Sagrario* with 'mil reales de ayuda de costa'.[4]

There are several mentions of payment for sermon courses in the letters of P. Jerónimo Gracián, O.C.D., among them this one from Valencia, addressed to the Prioress and Carmelite nuns at Consuegra in December 1604:

En lo de predicar aquí la Cuaresma aun no estoy del todo resuelto, porque el Patriarca y Marqués de Malpica, su sobrino, me han importunado que no dé la palabra a ninguna parte, y aunque dan 500 o 600 reales aquí a quien la predica, mas eran 200 ducados que daban en Consuegra y quizás mayor provecho de almas, aunque aquí no falta.[5]

However, in these same letters, Gracián tells the nuns that: 'He predicado este Adviento desde que aquí llegué cuarenta entre pláticas y sermones, con provecho, a mi parecer. . .' (p. 386). This included a set of afternoon sermons on the *Paternoster* 'con mucho concurso'.

Funeral sermons, of course, would be commissioned and paid for by the bereaved family, who would probably also see to it that the text of the sermon was printed as a *pliego suelto* and circulated among their friends. More details of the transmission and publication of sermons will be found in the following chapter.

The preachers appointed for such occasions would usually be members of religious orders. We are told that:

En España, como en los demás países donde hay regulares, antes de la estinción de éstos, casi ellos solos se ocupaban de la predicación; y los

---

[1] Entry referring to payment of Fray Martin Peraza (27 Mar. 1598) in *Actas Capitulares de la Seo* (Saragossa), 1593–1610, fo. 72. The *libra* was an Aragonese currency.

[2] *El perfecto predicador*, fo. 55.

[3] León Pinelo, *Anales de Madrid. . .en el reinado de Felipe III*, ed. R. Martorell Téllez-Girón (Madrid, 1931), p. 100.

[4] *Autos Capitulares* (8 Jan. 1593), fo. 49.

[5] *Obras*, iii. 384. A *ducado* was equivalent to 11 *reales de plata*.

párrocos y rectores, según la diversidad de costumbres locales, y la
mayor o menor vigilancia o cuidado de los obispos, suelen tener sólo en
ciertos días festivos algunas pláticas entre misa mayor en estilo sencillo
y familiar.[1]

That idea that 'preaching was regarded as the prerogative of monks'[2]
is borne out by Padre José de Isla in the 'Prólogo con morrión' to his
satire *Fray Gerundio de Campazas* (first published in 1758), where he
justifies the name and designation of his preposterous hero:

No me negarás que es mucho mayor el número de los predicadores que
se honran con el nobilísimo, santísimo distintivo de *fray*, que el de
los que se reconocen con el título de padre o con el epiteto de *don*. . .
los que en el clero secular ejercitan el ministerio de predicar, claro está
que en el número no pueden compararse con los que ejercen el mismo
ministerio en el estado religioso.[3]

We need only examine the section 'Concionatoria' at the back of the
second volume of Nicolás Antonio's *Bibliotheca Hispana Nova* (1783-
8) to be persuaded that this state of affairs is equally typical of the
sixteenth and seventeenth centuries. Franciscans, Dominicans, Jesuits,
Augustinians, Carmelites, all regularly appear as the authors of printed
sermons, followed by Benedictines, Mercedarians, Trinitarians, Hierony-
mites, and even Cistercians.

Numerical superiority alone does not account for the preponderance
of the regulars on the preaching scene in Spain at this time, although it
has been calculated that there were twice as many religious as secular
priests, and that during the twenty-three years' reign of the pious Philip
III seventeen new religious houses were founded in Madrid alone.[4] It
might be argued that members of religious orders had certain advantages
over the secular clergy which enabled them to excel at preaching and
to exercise a greater influence still by their published sermons. For
instance, the opportunities for serious study and scholarship were
greater within the orders, and even the most remote convent or priory

---

[1] Tejada y Ramiro, *Colección*, iv. 51.
[2] R. Trevor Davies, *The Golden Century of Spain* (London, 1937), p. 288.
'Monks' here includes friars and means regulars.
[3] *Clásicos Castellanos*, ed. Russell Sebold (1960), i. 15-16. Here *fray* designates all mendicant friars, *padre* probably refers to the Jesuits, and *don* to secular
priests and (perhaps) Benedictines. Joly [1603]: 'C'est en ce pais que les moines
ont trouvé leur element. Ils sont appellés partout *padres* . . . Les autres s'appellent
frayles, sçauoir les Mendians', in *RH* xx (1909), 554.
[4] Pedro de Texeira, *Topographia de la Villa de Madrid*, 1st edn. 1656 (facsimile reprint Madrid, 1965), p. 16. F.C. Sainz de Robles says 14 in *Madrid,
crónica y guía de una ciudad impar* (Madrid, 1962), p. 147, whereas Gil González
Dávila writes: 'En este año [1619] que iba escribiendo esta historia tenían las
Ordenes de Sto. Domingo y San Francisco 32,000 religiosos, y los obispados de
Calahorra y Pamplona 24,000 clérigos; . . .sacerdote soy, pero confieso que somos
más de los que son menester' (*Historia*, iii. 215).

was likely to possess a better-stocked library than any to which a
parish priest or curate would have access. Although theological faculties
had since the thirteenth century been widely scattered throughout
Spain, they were almost without exception under the aegis of one or
other of the Mendicant orders. However, it has been claimed that
internecine strife and bickering between Dominicans and Franciscans,
Dominicans and Augustinians or Jesuits, reduced their efficiency and
probably made them training-grounds for professional controversialists
rather than apostolic preachers of the Gospel.[1]

Even so, the religious was generally better served than the secular
priest, despite the Cathedral schools, the colleges for diocesan clergy,
founded by San Juan de Avila in the 1540s, and even the conciliar
seminaries which began to proliferate in Spain during the last quarter
of the sixteenth century.[2] Pedro Urbano González de la Calle quoted
from a discussion held in 1601: '. . .los curas y beneficiados de aldeas. . .
son de ordinario poco doctos y no oyeron sino gramática. . .de los
libros latinos no saben sacar ni ordenar.'[3] The basic instruction for
seminarians was as follows:

. . .aprenderán gramática, canto, computo eclesiástico, y otras facultades
útiles y honestas; tomarán de memoria la sagrada Escritura, y las
fórmulas de administrar los Sacramentos, en especial lo que conduce a
oír las confesiones, y las de los demás ritos y ceremonias.[4]

None of the Mendicant orders was obliged to contribute financially
to the Tridentine seminaries when they were established, since 'eorum
domos, non minus quam ea, quae per ordinarios erecta sunt, seminaria
vocari posse'.[5] According to the Constitutions of the Franciscan General
Chapter of 1553, each province was to have at least one house of
studies, and by 1639 the Franciscans had twenty Spanish provinces.[6]

In a Dominican document of 1612 it is proposed that centres be set
up by the order in each province specifically for the training of future
ministers of the Word, who are to be selected carefully from the start:
. . .in singulis provinciis in quibus commode observari poterit, instituatur
unus ex praecipuis conventibus pro instruendi fratribus in officio
praedicationis. In quo conventu semper vigeat lectio sacrae scripturae
et moralis theologiae in quo assignantur fratres ex sua vel aliena provincia,

---

[1] M. Andrés Martín, *Historia de la teología en España, 1470–1560*, i (Rome,
1962), 257.

[2] Council of Trent, sess. XXIII, cap. xviii (15 July 1563) in I. López de Ayala,
El Sacrosanto y ecuménico concilio de Trento (Madrid, 1785), pp. 357–66. Also
F. Martín Hernández, *Los seminarios españoles* (Salamanca, 1964).

[3] 'Documentos inéditos. . .' *BRAE* xii (1925), 480.

[4] López de Ayala, *El Sacrosanto. . .concilio de Trento*, p. 359.

[5] L. Pastor, *History of the Popes*, xvii, trans. R.F. Kerr (London, 1929),
270 n. 6. This refers to a ruling by Pius V (3 Oct. 1567).

[6] Andrés Martín, *Historia*, 256.

de scitu tamen et consensu reverendissimi magistri ordinis qui sunt insignes in officio praedicationis ut possint studentes de modo praedicandi ac conciones componendi instruere et non mittant ad eos conventus, nisi fratres quos invenerunt idoneos ad officium praedicationis laudabiliter exercendum.[1]

The Society of Jesus, too, was concerned with the formation of competent and effective preachers, and in a letter of 14 August 1599 the Master General, Aquaviva, reminds the Provincials of the Society:

Et quoniam bonos praedicatores habituri non sumus, nisi ad eos formandos instruendosque operam conferamus, eas illis studendi et praeparandi commoditates praebendo, quae necessariae sunt ut solidam utilemque doctrinam acquirunt.[2]

Special encouragement in the form of additional theological instruction in relevant areas was to be given to prospective preachers, according to the *Regulae Provincialis*, paragraph six:

Quod si forte iis, qui concionandi facultatem habent, biennium non sufficiat ad eas Theologiae materias in scholis audiendas, quae necessariae videntur, ut toto, et sine errore suum munus exequantur cuiusmodi sunt, quae in summa Divi Thomae in prima parte docentur ante disputationem de Angelis, in tertia de Incarnatione, et Sacramentis et in prima secundae de Gratia poterit tunc illis tertius Theologici studii annus ad eam rem concedi.[3]

They should also become versed in the Scriptures and compile their own notebook of suitable quotations and commonplaces:

(4) Lectioni sacrae Scripturae, ac Patrum praecipue incumbant. Conferet etiam peculiari studio vidisse evangelia toto anno currentia, et in eis ea, quae usui esse possunt, adnotasse: itemque compendium fecisse explicationis rerum ad fidem et christianam vitam necessariarum.[4]

As to the student's practical exercises in preaching, it should be noted that in the first Jesuit colleges, each day during meals or at least once a week, the students of Rhetoric took turns in giving declamations, and the students of philosophy and theology in preaching, either in Latin or in the vernacular.[5] Many a future preacher, before joining the noviciate of his chosen order, would begin his formal education with Jesuits: Fray Pedro de Valderrama is one example. However, his own

---

[1] A.M. Walz, *Compendium Historiae Ordinis Praedicatorum* (Rome, 1933), pp. 346–7.

[2] *Epistolae praepositorum generalium ad patres et fratres Societatis Iesu* (Roeselare, 1909), i. 280.

[3] *Ratio atque Institutio Studiorum Societatis Iesu* (Rome, 1606), p. 7.

[4] *Institutum Societatis Iesu* (Rome, 1870), ii. 16 (Regulae concionatorum). Same wording in the rules of 1606.

[5] A.P. Farrell, *The Jesuit Code of Liberal Education* (Bruce, 1938), p. 10. I. Iparraguirre S.J. *Obras completas de San Ignacio de Loyola* (Madrid, 1963), pp. 763, 772–3. Also *Monumenta Paedagogica Societatis Iesu*, i [1540–56], ed. L. Lukács (Rome, 1965), 310.

Augustinian order lays down very similar requirements for the practical training of preachers in its Constitutions of 1581 and 1625.[1]

The Discalced Carmelites, drawing up the Constitutions of Alcalá in 1599, had voted unanimously 'que no se dé licencia de aquí en adelante a ningún religioso para predicar si no huviere oído Artes y Teología tres años o por lo menos dos, o sea licenciado en Derecho Canónico; so pena que quede suspenso sin usar de la predicación'.[2] Here again it is only a bare minimum of theological competence that is required: enough scholastic and positive theology to guard against elementary doctrinal error—'no para disputar cuestiones en el púlpito, *sed ad intelligendam scripturam, et ad defendendam doctrinam quam praedicat*'[3] —rather than any refinements calculated to make the preacher more persuasive, let alone the monster of erudition that many theorists would like him to be. The Alcalá theology course consisted almost exclusively of study of the Bible and the *Libri Sententiarum* of Peter Lombard. Huarte de San Juan, for his part, firmly discourages the ambitions of preachers to become fully fledged 'speculative' theologians, since according to his theory of the humours the two activities are mutually exclusive: . . .la teología escolástica pertenece al entendimiento. Ahora decimos y queremos probar que el predicar—que es su prática—es obra de la imaginativa, de la misma manera no se puede compadecer que uno sea gran teólogo escolástico y famoso predicador [cap. x of 1575 edn.][4] Later, referring to the Aristotelian distinction between philosophy and oratory, he warns that:

Esta misma diferencia hay entre el teólogo escolástico y el positivo: que el uno sabe la razón de lo que toca a su facultad, y el otro las proposiciones averiguadas y no más. Y siendo esto así, es cosa muy peligrosa que tenga el predicador oficio y autoridad de enseñar al pueblo cristiano la verdad, y el auditorio obligación de creerlo, y que le falte la potencia con que se saben de raíz las verdades. (pp. 236–7).

No wonder so many of the best-known preachers were at pains to produce testimonials to their theological competence in terms of the university chairs they had held. The theological perspective of the sermons of the Golden Age will be discussed in the final chapter of this book.

The distinction drawn by Ximénez Patón between preacher and theologian is of a different order entirely:

El Teólogo sólo profesa Teología, mas el Predicador no será perfecto si

---

[1] H. Andrés Puente, *La reforma tridentina en la orden agustiniana* (Valladolid, 1965), pp. 43 and 72 ff.

[2] *Constitutiones carmelitarum discalceatarum 1567–1600*, ed. Fortunatus a Iesu (Rome, 1968), p. 368.

[3] Estella, *Modo de predicar*, ii. 13.

[4] *Examen de Ingenios para las Ciencias* [1575 and 1594], ed. Rodrigo Sanz (2 vols., Madrid, 1930), ii. 227.

después de ser sabio en la Teología no tiene noticia de las Matemáticas, y es en Retórica de buen lenguaje y acción. Canones y leyes sabe, de la Música entiende, de la Historia no ignora, de Medecina tiene principios, en Cosmografía y Geografía es muy perspectivo, y con esto se halla en él gran fe, caridad, prudencia, bondad y santidad.[1]

In fact, the preacher is envisaged as being closest to the poet, or even to Don Quijote's ideal of the *caballero andante*, except in 'la acción corporal'.[2]

Whereas a large part of the preacher's charism comes from his spiritual perfection and prayer, '*Ministerium verbi* . . . propio de los profesos, y por esto han de ser muy adelante en el espíritu y letras, y caminar muy adelante en la perfección'[3] it is also assumed, increasingly in the seventeenth century, that the preacher needs to become a compendium of universal, and at times esoteric, knowledge. Juan Rodríguez de León, in the first book of *El Predicador de las Gentes, San Pablo* (Madrid, 1638) describes no fewer than thirty-five branches of science, human and divine, which he feels that the preacher should have at his fingertips in the form of an *academia predicable*. These include Meteoroscopia, Dioptrica, Scenofactoria, or 'Arte de formar Tabernáculos', and 'Pesca'. Not altogether surprisingly we do not find any precise indications as to how this intellectual furniture is to be acquired in the Rule or Constitution of any religious order, although the Jesuit Master General Aquaviva, in a letter of 28 May 1613 headed *De formandis contionatoribus*, warns against 'incautus delectus in studii materia', especially when it leads to neglect of Scripture and the Fathers.[4] Voluminous collections of commonplaces and 'potted' erudition were indispensable items in every preacher's library and this miscellany literature comprised such standard works as the *Exempla virtutum et vitiorum* (Lyons, 1554), the *Concordata* of Nicholas of Lira, the *Catena aurea* of St. Thomas Aquinas, the *Index conceptuum ad praedicatorum usum* of El Tostado, and the *Biblia pauperum* of Nicholas de Hannapes.[5]

Each of the preaching orders—Dominicans, Franciscans, and Jesuits —attaches importance to the training of its ministers of the Word but, except in the case of the Jesuits, who produce standard treatises on

[1]   *Eloquencia española en arte* (Toledo, 1604), fo. 3[V].
[2]   *Don Quijote de la Mancha*, ed. M. de Riquer (Barcelona, 1968), pp. 664–5. The reference is to Pt. II, Ch. 18.
[3]   P. Jerónimo Nadal, S.J., *Pláticas espirituales en Coimbra* [*1561*], ed. M. Nicolau (Granada, 1945), p. 157. See also Terrones del Caño, *Instrucción de predicadores*, p. 25 and Ch. IV below.
[4]   Op. cit. i. 340–5.
[5]   Recommended by Diego de Estella, Suárez de Figueroa, and Juan Pérez de Montalbán in their preaching manuals.

sacred rhetoric for their preachers,[1] there is no very clear differentiation
or distinctive 'style' attributable to the order's education methods. The
Franciscan Rule enjoins upon its preachers 'llaneza de estilo', but this
is the only clear indication we have of a 'school' of preaching.[2] What
is more likely is that similarities develop within individual communities,
fostered by the common life and the sense of a special place in the
whole life of the Church. Where there is a strict hierarchy (of preachers)
within an even more complex hierarchical society (the Church), certain
patterns of emulation and conformism are bound to occur. Besides,
beginners are constantly being urged to listen to good preachers, as
well as to accept criticism of their own sermons by those appointed
to judge them.[3]

A preacher's role within the community is not supposed to be so
markedly differentiated that it conflicts with his obligations as a
friar; according to the constitutions of the Carmelites '. . .él que la
mayor parte del año faltare en vida común y regular por sólo acudir
al ministerio de la predicación, el provincial o visitador le suspenda de
oficio,'[4] and this is also the case of the Jesuits: 'Praecipue vero circa
concionatores invigilet, vt si quis ex iis ad suas se regulas forte non
accomodauerit, a concionandi munere amoueatur et in aliis Societatis
nostrae ministeriis occupetur.'[5] Yet within the Dominican order, from
its foundation, there has been a hierarchy of preachers and distinction
of roles. First, the deacon, permitted to preach inside the community;
next, the *praedicator communis*, who preaches to the laity within the
area served by the house, and, finally, the largely honorific grade of
praedicator generalis, reached with age and experience and carrying
with it certain consultative responsibilities.[6] In both the Franciscan
and Dominican orders, during our period, no friar was allowed to
preach publicly before the age of twenty-five, which was the minimum
age for ordination to the priesthood. The Council of Trent (Session
xxv, caps. 15 and 19) had declared invalid monastic vows taken before
the age of sixteen, and this was raised to nineteen for some orders
by Pius V. Ximénez Patón is adamant that these age requirements be
observed, yet implies that there were exceptions: 'Por esto no deben

---

[1] Aquaviva recommends Carolus Regius, Mazarinus, and Cipriano Sóares, all
members of the Society (see List of Works Consulted).

[2] Quoted by Estella, *Modo de predicar*, ii. 13 and Murillo, *Discursos predicables [Quaresma]*, i, Prólogo, sig. ¶ 8.

[3] Regulae concionatorum in *Institutem Societatis Iesu*, ii. 16. Also Ximénez
Patón, *El perfecto predicador*, cap. xvi.

[4] *Constitutiones carmelitarum discalceatorum* for Madrid, 1597. (Rome,
1968), p. 614.

[5] *Regulae provincialis* (Lyons, 1606), p. 45.

[6] G.R. Galbraith, *The Constitution of the Dominican Order 1216–1360*
(Manchester, 1925), pp. 162–74.

predicar en edad no perfecta, aun más de la que se pide para Sacerdotes. . .
Así que hacen mal los que asayan [sic] a sacar en público niños a
predicar, negocio que más parece cómico que predicable.'[1] No other
records of child-preachers have been found so far. Might there not be
some connection with the burlesque sermons of the *obispillo*?[2] In 1512
Dean Colet provided that every Childermas (27 December) the St.
Paul's scholars should 'come to Paul's churche and hear the Chylde-
Byshop's sermon'. This custom was banned in the reign of Henry VIII
but temporarily restored under Mary.[3] Later, in *Fray Gerundio de
Campazas* (1757), a reference to 'predicadores sabatinos' is annotated
thus:

Los que, por su poca edad o escasas facultades, sólo en casos extraordinarios podían utilizarse para una festividad o día de gran concurso: pero en cambio servían perfectamente para los sábados u otros
días en que la concurrencia era muy limitada.[4]

Most preachers could count on a preaching career of about thirty
years, or 'hasta perder los dientes'.[5] However, unless they were truly
outstanding in the pulpit, or nominated *Predicador del Rey* (an appoint-
ment which generally only lasted for a year or two),[6] many of the
most able men in religious life would find their energies diverted into
administrative tasks as Prior or Provincial, while others would become
full-time academic theologians. In fact, the sermons that they publish
(in the form of *sermonarios* or complete sermon cycles) during the
first three decades of the seventeenth century have often been preached
ten, sometimes twenty, years earlier.

[1]   *El perfecto predicador*, fo. 85.
[2]   N. Shergold, *A History of the Spanish Stage* (Oxford, 1967), pp. 20–3.
R.B. Donovan, *The Liturgical Drama in Medieval Spain* (Toronto, 1958), pp.
65–6, 190–2.
[3]   E. Duncan, *The Story of the Carol* (London, 1911), pp. 172–7.
[4]   Clásicos Castellanos, i. 88 n.
[5]   Pedro de Valderrama, in F. Pacheco, *Libro. . .de verdaderos retratos*, fo. 20.
[6]   They were appointed by *Real Cédula*, with or without remuneration ('gajes'),
and had to seek permission to preach away from Court during their term of office:
c.f. Andrés Soria Ortega, *El Maestro Fray Manuel de Guerra y Ribera y la oratoria
sagrada de su tiempo* [Anejos del *Boletín de la Universidad de* Granada, iii](Granada,
1950), pp. 38–9 and 319–20.

II

THE SERMON IN PRINT:
TRANSMISSION, READERSHIP,
AND RHETORICAL STRUCTURE

Not all sermons preached in the Golden Age appeared in print, and not all the printed ones have survived, but it is nevertheless possible to divide them initially into two main categories: the *sueltos* and the *sermonarios*. The former are intended as a record of what was actually preached on a particular occasion and are usually published very shortly afterwards, together with the date and place of preaching as part of the title.[1] They may, on the other hand, be incorporated into, rather than simply bound together with, the *relación* of the ceremonies which composed that occasion—be it state funeral or canonization of a patron saint.[2] In seventeenth-century Spain this type of sermon tends to be either a funeral oration or the panegyric of a saint, and I have not, so far, been able to find traces of anything that approximates to the Paul's Cross sermons,[3] or to the political preaching of John Preston.[4] In the reign of Charles V there are several reports of 'political' preaching on behalf of the *Comuneros*, as well as against them, but it appears that no printed texts survive.[5] This is not to say that Spanish sermons of this period do not contain polemical passages or that preachers were politically naïve or neutral,[6] but rather to draw attention to the fact that no overtly political or even topical sermons have survived in the form of *sueltos* (if we except sermons at *autos-de-fe* or on controversial topics like the Immaculate Conception).[7]

[1] Preparation for publication would, of course, often imply textual modification.

[2] See *Relación de las exequias que Zaragossa ha celebrado por el rey don Philipe* (Saragossa, 1599) and *Relación de la fiesta de la beatificación de San Ignacio de Loyola* (Seville, 1610).

[3] M. Maclure, *The Paul's Cross Sermons, 1534–1642* (Toronto, 1958).

[4] C. Hill, *Puritanism and Revolution* (1st edn., London, 1958; Panther, 1968), pp. 234–66.

[5] Joseph Pérez, 'Moines frondeurs et sermons subversifs en Castille pendant le premier séjour de Charles-Quint en Espagne', *BH* lxvii (1965), 5–24, and earlier article *BH* lxv (1963), 278–9.

[6] C. Pérez Bustamante, *Felipe III: semblanza de un monarca y perfiles de una privanza* (Madrid, 1950), p. 106 refers to intrigues among royal preachers and confessors in this reign, including P. Jerónimo de Florencia.

[7] Edward Glaser, '*Convertentur ad vesperam*: on a rare Spanish translation of an Inquisitorial sermon by Frei João de Ceita' in *Collected studies in honour of Américo Castro's 80th year*, ed. M.P. Hornik (Oxford, 1965), pp. 137–74. See Ch. V below.

This may be because they were suppressed by censorship, or simply because such flimsy productions have not weathered the passage of time as successfully as the more solidly bound *sermonarios*. The *sueltos* which have survived have often been bound together as anthologies, or simply collected together at a later date.[1]

As for the *sermonarios*, these represent a preacher's personal selection of his sermons, often spanning the whole of his preaching career, and although the individual sermons they contain sometimes bear a date and place of preaching,[2] they are intended as models for apprentice preachers, or as compendia of *materia predicable*, rather than a record of what was said on a specific occasion. For instance, Fray Luis de Rebolledo, in his *Primera parte de cien oraciones fúnebres* (Madrid, 1600) presents a set of 'blueprints' for sermons appropriate to the obsequies of a wide variety of people—including 'un Mercader que perdió la hacienda y se ahogó en la mar, dejando muchos hijos' (oración viii)— together with a set of variations on the theme of *memento mori*, which another preacher would be able to adapt and personalize as the situation demanded. Fray Francisco de Rojas, in his *Teatro funeral de la Iglesia* (Madrid, 1637) alongside Pope, Cardinal, and Archbishop, has 'una persona que gastó su vida escribiendo libros'. Rebolledo's sermons were all, he assures us, actually preached at some stage, and it would be unwise to see the contents of the *sermonarios* as exclusively paradigmatic and totally removed from the realities of pulpit delivery.

The *sermonarios* are customarily arranged according to the liturgical year and the lectionary. Miguel Herrero García has already drawn attention to the two great cycles which, revolving concurrently and with the regularity of some gigantic clock-mechanism, comprise the preaching year.[3] The *Temporal* cycle is composed of the seasons of the Church's year—Advent, Christmas, Lent, Easter, Pentecost—strung together Sunday by Sunday. The *Santoral* cycle consists of Saints'— days and the festivals of Christ and His Mother: the Ascension, Corpus Christi, the Assumption, and the Immaculate Conception. Although the *Temporal* and *Santoral* cycles form an interlocking pattern which is the whole liturgical year, when sermons appear in print there is a clear separation between sermons *de temporibus* and sermons *de sanctis*, which appear in different volumes. *Extravagantes* are sermons

---

[1] e.g. *Sermones en la beatificación de la B.M. Teresa de Jesús* (Madrid, 1615). Fray Basilio Ponce de León, *Sermones varios* (Salamanca, 1620–5).

[2] For example, every sermon in Fray Basilio Ponce de León's *Primera parte de discursos para todos los Evangelios de la Quaresma* (Madrid, 1605). Also, Avendaño's Lent and Advent collections name specific churches where sermons were preached.

[3] *Sermonario clásico*, xxiii–xxiv.

on special occasions, or 'extraordinary sermons'.[1]

In some cases the number of sermons in a particular volume will depend on the locality in which the sermons were originally preached, since regional differences affected the preaching of Lent courses in Spain. In some parts, including Catalonia and Valencia (Kingdom of Aragon), a sermon was expected for every day of Lent, whereas in Castille and Andalusia the custom was for the preacher to perform on only three days of the week besides Sunday: i.e. Monday, Wednesday, and Friday.[2] Antonio Gavin, writing about the very end of the seventeenth century and principally about Aragon, says:

There is in every City, in every Parish, in every Town and Village, a Lent Preacher; and there is but one Difference among them, *viz.* that some Preachers do preach every Day in Lent, some three Sermons a Week; some two, *viz.* on Wednesdays and Sundays, and some only on Sundays and the Holy Days that happen to fall in Lent.[3]

A distinction should be drawn between the longer sermons, preached on Sunday afternoons and in Lent, and the short homilies (5 to 10 minutes) delivered at the Mass, either before or after the Creed. It is almost certainly the former which are referred to here, and we might term them 'occasional sermons'.

Both the *suelto* sermons and those published in *sermonarios* must be consulted whenever it is a question of establishing a norm for 'The Sermon' at this period, allowing for different degrees of elaboration in the course of publication. It would be as well, at this point, to investigate the usual methods of transmission of sermons to print—methods which are closely linked to styles of pulpit delivery.

When the preacher himself prepared his works for publication he would only have before him the complete text of a sermon, *as he had preached it*, if he had written it out in full, and either read it from the pulpit or delivered it, word for word, from memory. Reading sermons was not viewed at all favourably by either theorists or congregations, and Huarte de San Juan has a story of a 'famoso' preacher at the funeral of Antonio de Nebrija at Alcalá in 1522 who 'no hubo lugar de tomarlo [el sermón] de memoria: y así se fue al púlpito, con el papel en la mano. . . .Pareció tan mal al auditorio esta manera de predicar por escrito y con el papel en la mano que todo fue sonreír

---

[1] See collections by Cristóbal de Fonseca and Tomás Ramón. In the fifteenth century the term is *sermo casualis*.

[2] D. Vega, *Discursos predicables sobre los Evangelios de la Quaresma*, i, Prólogo al Lector, and Fray Angel Manrique, *Meditaciones para los días de la Quaresma* (Salamanca, 1612), i, Prólogo, sig. ¶ ¶ 6. The latter explains that the first volume is sufficient for Castilian preachers, but the Aragonese will need both. See also *Autos Capitulares* of Seville (1580–1), fo. 26ᵛ.

[3] *A Master-key to Popery* (Dublin, 1724), p. 12. The author claims to be a renegade Spanish priest from Saragossa.

y murmurar.'[1] Reciting the whole sermon parrot-fashion had its own drawbacks, as Aquaviva points out, following closely the words of St. Augustine (*De doctrina christiana*, IV. x. 25):

Non videtur laudanda eorum diligentia, qui contionem perscribunt integram, atque ad verbum mandant memoriae. Nam praeterquam quod, ut populo probe intellegat ac percipiat quod dicitur, *versandum est*, auctore S. Augustino, *quod agitur multimoda varietate dicendi; quod in potestate non habent, qui praeparata et ad verbum memoriter retenta pronuntiant*, certum est dici efficaciter eo modo, ac penitus inseri vix quicquam posse...Adde quod oratio artificiose contexta et elaborata se ipsam prodit; semperque veretur contionator ne, si vel una periodus aut etiam particula memoria excidat, totus ruat orationis contextus.[2]

The last point is also made by Huarte, who ridicules '.. .los que traen aprendido el sermón, palabra por palabra, que faltando de allí, quedan luego perdidos, sin tener quién les provea de materia, para pasar adelante'.[3] Aquaviva suggests that the sermon should be delivered from notes, after it had been broken down into *loci communes*, and this, or the memorizing of a sermon scheme, under various headings and according to different mnemonic techniques, was perhaps the most usual method of sermon delivery in the Golden Age.[4] It allows for the writing out of the sermon in full before preaching, but as a preliminary stage only, since the preacher would then extemporize on his notes. The writing-up process, preparatory to publication, was not, therefore, always faithful to what had actually been said. Referring to his funeral sermons, Fray Luis de Rebolledo says: 'con el tamaño que las dije las escribo; y aun al principio fue en borradores y cubiertas de cartas a pedazos, y cuando quise sacarlas en limpio, fue con pérdida de algunas.'[5] Fray Jerónimo Bautista de Lanuza feels obliged to explain to his patron, Prince Filiberto, why he may not recognize the sermons he had heard preached in Barcelona, 'porque como cuando V.A. fue servido mandarme los escribir, fue luego acabada la Quaresma y yo por mis muchas ocupaciones, no los escribía cuando los predicaba, hube de ponerme después a formarlos de nuevo, y disponiendo los discursos como mejor me acordaba'.[6]

If the preacher did not always have an accurate record of his own sermons there were sometimes others who did, and he would often

[1] *Examen de Ingenios para las Ciencias*, ii. 231.
[2] *Epistolae praepositorum generalium*, i. 356−7.
[3] Op. cit., 242.
[4] Terrones, *Instrucción*, pp. 158−61. Also Félix G. Olmedo's introduction to *Fray Dionisio Vázquez: Sermones* (Clásicos Castellanos, 1943), p. xi.
[5] *Cien oraciones fúnebres* (Madrid, 1600), sig. ¶ 5.
[6] *Homilías sobre los Evangelios ... de la Quaresma* (Barbastro, 1621), i, Dedicatoria, sig. a4−a4[V]. Sermons preached in 1615.

THE SERMON IN PRINT   33

have cause to complain that these records, produced by 'escribientes
con más mentiras que letras', had been used to publish pirated versions.[1]
Fray Pedro de Valderrama, too, speaks sourly of:
tantos escribientes que falsean y adulteran los originales de sus dueños
. . .que venden en público lo que en secreto han hurtado, sin temor que
les quiten las orejas, y. . .haciendo mil traslados, y en ellos mil traslaciones unas falsas, otras más que arábigas, y todos ininteligibles.[2]
Similarly, Fray Diego de Arce comments on: 'la mucha ignorancia de
los escribientes corrompiéndolos de mil maneras. Que a unos los acor-
taban: otros dejaban renglones en blanco: otros por un nombre ponen
uno muy diferente.'[3] It seems, however, that he continued to rely on
such 'scribes', since at the end of his sermon *De la Cruz y el Ladrón*
(Murcia, 1607) Arce writes: 'Olvidóse el escribiente de poner en su
original las palabras que se [sic] siguen' ('Al Lector', fo. 69ᵛ). In this
case the scribe seems to have been legitimately employed, if inaccurate
in his reporting, whereas more often the preachers employ the topic,
used by other men of letters in their prologues, that they have been
forced into print because so many corrupt and clandestine copies of
their works are in circulation already. Fray Diego Murillo decides to
bring out an authoritative edition of his sermons: '. . .porque tengo
aviso de que le han impreso sin mi licencia algo trocado, me será forzoso
hacer nueva impresión añadida y correcta, para que conste cuál es el
original verdadero'.[4] We are reminded, too, of another pulpit/theatre
parallel when we think of the mode of transmission of the texts of
certain Golden Age *comedias* and the activities of the *Memorilla* or
Gran Memoria, of whom Luis Remírez de Avellano was a well-known
example.[5] Prodigious feats of memory were not uncommon among
sermon-goers, but it is perhaps less usual for the sermon memorized to
be transformed into verse and regurgitated in printed form. This was
the treatment given by don Francisco de Tamayo y Porres to a sermon
preached in Barcelona in 1627 by Fray Antonio Morato: 'pues de oírle
en espacio de ocho horas. . .lo mudé de la prosa elegante que tenía a
verso inculto y grosero'.[6] In seventeenth-century England children

[1] Rebolledo, *Cien oraciones fúnebres*, sig. ¶5ᵛ. Mateo Alemán, *Guzmán de
Alfarache* (Madrid, 1599 and Lisbon, 1604), II.iii.5 (ed. S. Gili y Gaya, Clásicos
Castellanos, 1927–36, v.60): 'Yo conocí en Sevilla un hombre . . . el cual trataba
de sólo trasladar sermones y le pagaban a medio real por pliego'.
[2] *Exercicios espirituales para la Quaresma* (Seville, 1603), i, sig. ¶¶4.
[3] *Miscelánea primera*, sig. A2ᵛ–A3.
[4] *Discursos predicables [Adviento]*, sig. 8ᵛ.
[5] Suárez de Figueroa, *Plaza universal de todas ciencias y artes*, pp. 254–5.
H.A. Rennert, *The Spanish Stage in the time of Lope de Vega* (New York, 1963),
pp. 175–6.
[6] *Sermón en la festividad de San Pedro* (Barcelona, 1627), bound with Fray
Cristóbal de Avendaño's *Sermones . . . de santos* (Barcelona, 1630), in Barcelona
University.

were encouraged to memorize sermons, sometimes word by word and
sometimes only in outline, and reproduce them in the presence of their
elders as an exercise in both piety and prose style.[1]

Reports of sermons openly being taken down in note form are quite
frequent in several parts of Europe in the sixteenth and early seventeenth centuries, although comparisons between them would be ill
advised, since they occur in very different religious climates. For
example, we have a report of 'estudiantes, Eclesiásticos y gente docta'
assiduously copying down, 'mientras predicaba', the sermons of the
learned Dominican scripturalist Juan de Espinosa;[2] whereas in Geneva,
from 1549, a certain Denis Raguenier took down, word for word, the
extempore sermons of Jean Calvin, using a kind of shorthand.[3] For
this invaluable service the Compagnie des estrangers paid Raguenier
and other scribes a stipend, and the sermons, when transcribed from
shorthand and edited under supervision by the preacher, were deposited
with the deacons for anyone to read.[4] It is also reported that the
French Oratorian Jean François Senault (1601-72) had at least twenty
scribes at the foot of the pulpit while he preached, and this was not
uncommon in both France and England during the seventeenth century.[5]
I have not been able to ascertain whether this practice was widely
followed in Spain, after the era of San Vicente Ferrer, although it is
assumed that many of the sermons of San Juan de Avila, 'Apóstol de
la Andalucía', were preserved in this way by his disciples.[6]

Among the preachers selected for this study, there is none who
appears to have commanded such a following that his sermons were
painstakingly and zealously recorded as they were preached. The
preacher generally had to be his own publisher and publicist and
bring out editions of his sermons at his own expense, unless he could
find a wealthy patron or bookseller willing to sponsor him,[7] or unless

[1] W. Fraser Mitchell, *English Pulpit Oratory from Andrewes to Tillotson*
(London, S.P.C.K., 1932), pp. 30–8.
[2] F. Pacheco, *Libro de verdaderos retratos* (no fos.), Espinosa died in 1598.
[3] B. Gagnebin, *L'Incroyable Histoire des sermons de Calvin* (Geneva, 1956),
pp. 5–11.
[4] T.H.L. Parker, *Supplementa Calviniana* (London, 1962), p. 8.
[5] M. Michelot, *Les Systèmes sténographiques* (Paris, 1959), p. 36. E. Griselle,
Bourdaloue, i (Paris, 1901), 17-20. Shorthand (*tachygraphia*) was used for taking
down sermons from the reign of James I in England, see Robert F. Young,
Comenius in England (London, 1932), p. 65.
[6] Julio Simancas, in his edition of Juan de Avila's sermons (Madrid, 1957),
says: 'Estos sermones . . . fueron recogidos al vuelo por sus discípulos a la hora de
ser predicados, y, después, retocados por el mismo Maestro, casi siempre. Algunos
son prácticamente el guión de la predicación'. To confirm or refute this statement
would involve examination of manuscript sermons, which I have not undertaken.
[7] Fray Agustín Núñez Delgadillo appeals to 'los Mercaderes de Libros y
Impressores' to print his sermons for him, 'porque soy Frayle pobre', in *De la*

his order agreed to subsidize his works and had a printing-press on the
premises, as in the case of Fray Pedro de Valderrama at the Seville
convent (operated by Franciso Pérez) and of Fray Tomás Truxillo at
Barcelona (operated by Sebastián Cormellas in the convent of Sta
Catalina).[1]

Even when we turn to the Trinitarian Fray Hortensio Félix Paravicino,
who perhaps attained the greatest celebrity of any preacher in his lifetime, it appears that those sermons which he did not prepare for
publication himself were edited posthumously from 'borradores' found
in his cell.[2] This implies that he wrote out his sermons in full before
delivering them, and the same can be said of Fray Pedro de Valderrama,
whose collection *Teatro de las Religiones* was published by the Prior
of the Seville house after his death (1612).[3] A well-recorded instance of
a sermon-script being 'stolen' is that admitted to by Lupercio Leonardo
de Argensola in his preface to the funeral sermon preached by Dr.
Terrones del Caño on the death of Philip II (19 October 1598). He
claims to have transcribed the text from the preacher's own copy,
'habiendo llegado a mis manos', but without his knowledge or permission ('póngome a peligro de que su Autor se enoje. . .'). It is quite
clear that the transcription is from a copy—'que él no pudiera conservar
en la memoria; está sacado del original que el Autor tenía para sí'.[4]

Although it had long been customary for preachers, especially those
living in a religious community, to make use of one another's sermons
in manuscript form, often renumbering the points and reallocating the
material they found there,[5] the possession and circulation of such
sermons was officially banned by the Inquisition in 1559:
[se prohiben]. . .todos y qualesquier Sermones, Cartas, Tratados,

---

Victoria de los Justos, sig. ¶4. In 1602 the Augustinians of San Felipe el Real
gave Fray Cristóbal de Fonseca 300 *ducados* to print the second part of the
Vida de Christo. See MS. 9.5395, fo. 216 in Real Academia de Historia, Madrid.
    [1] Cf. *Conciones quadragesimales quadruplices* (Barcelona, 1591).
    [2] *Oraciones Evangélicas de Adviento y Quaresma* (Madrid, 1636) and *Oraciones
Evangélicas en las Festividades de Christo* (Madrid, 1638) are both edited by Fray
Fernando Remírez and *Oraciones Evangélicas y Panegíricos Funerales* (Madrid,
1641) by Fray Cristóbal Núñez. Paravicino died in 1633.
    [3] Fray Luis de Oliva's sermon on the Visitation (1616) was 'trasladado
fielmente de . . . un borrador . . . escrito de su letra y firmado de su mano' and
published in Herrera, *Descripción de la Capilla de N^a S^{ra} del Sagrario* (Madrid,
1617), fos. 81 ff.
    [4] A *suelto* in my possession. Printed by order of Barrionuevo de Peralta, no
date or colophon, fos. 1 and 1^V (Madrid, 1599?).
    [5] Annotations found on Lent sermons in Trinity College, Dublin (MS. A.5.25).
These are undated but probably early seventeenth century. In Spanish, they
have numbers in the margin in a different hand and *vidi* at the top of some
sermons. Preachers would naturally keep copies of their own sermons and use
them several times, e.g. Jerónimo Gracián, *Obras*, iii. 381.

Oraciones, o otra qualquier escritura escrita a mano, que hable o trate
de sagrada escriptura, o de los Sacramentos de la Santa Madre Iglesia, y
religión Christiana, por ser artificio del que los herejes usan para comuni-
carse sus errores.[1]

This may well be connected with the practice of the followers of the
crypto-Protestant preacher Dr. Constantino Ponce de la Fuente, who
kept his sermons and Bible commentaries in manuscript form and, when
persecuted by the Inquisition, took them for safe keeping to sympathizers
in Germany.[2] This prohibition is unlikely to have been successfully
enforced, to judge by the numbers of manuscript sermons still in existence
and by the necessity for a further edict, issued by the Holy Office in 1577,
requiring that all those who had in their possession manuscript sermons
by others were to give them up to the Tribunal of the Inquisition.[3] These
two pronouncements, while not effectively eliminating the circulation of
manuscript sermons, may have prepared the way for the flood of
printed sermon collections (*sermonarios*) which appeared in Spain
between about 1580 and the end of the eighteenth century.

These *sermonarios* seem, at first sight, to be principally designed for
the use of preachers. Throughout the Middle Ages preachers had
relied on the hackneyed Latin collection known familiarly as *Dormi
secure*, and this was still being printed for lazy or uneducated parish
priests throughout the fifteenth and early sixteenth centuries.[4] The
Biblioteca de Ramírez de Prado contained a copy of *Sermones Dormi
secure Dominicales et de Sanctis* (Lyons, 1495) alongside 'modern'
preachers and theorists like Panigarola.[5] Miguel Herrero García, in his
Sermonario clásico, quotes a rather dismissive comment made about
such books by Fray Diego López de Andrade in his dedicatory epistle
to the *Tratados sobre los Evangelios de Quaresma* (Madrid, 1615),
but one which suggests that they were no longer in general use because
congregations were now more demanding and difficult to please.[6] On

---

[1] *Index librorum qui prohibentur* (Valladolid, 1559), p. 50.
[2] M. Menéndez y Pelayo, *Historia de los heterodoxos españoles* (8 vols.,
Buenos Aires, 1945), v. 95. See also Bataillon, *Erasmo y España*, pp. 527–40.
[3] P. Félix G. Olmedo's prologue to Terrones, *Instrucción*, p. cxi.
[4] *Sermones dominicales per totum annum . . . qui Dormi secure: Vel Dormi
sine cura ideo sunt inscripti, quo celeri studio: et absque magna difficultate a
viris mediocriter doctis intellegi possunt: et populo predicari.* Attributed to John
of Werden (*c.* 1330). See Owst, *Preaching in Medieval England*, pp. 237–8. The
British Museum catalogue lists editions of the latter collection dating from between
c. 1475 (Nuremberg) and 1530 (Paris).
[5] J. de Entrambasaguas, *La biblioteca de Ramírez de Prado* (2 vols., Madrid,
1943), i. 34.
[6] Ensayo, p. liii: 'éste sí que era siglo bien contentadizo de sermones . . . y no
ahora, que aun sin dormir ni sosegar a derechas y estudiando por tantos y tan
diferentes libros, apenas se halla un solo predicador de quien diga el mundo que le
da gusto cumplido'.

the other hand, there continued to be large numbers of compilations of
loci communes (in Latin) for the use of preachers, but which had no
claims to be actual sermons.[1]

The publication of *materia predicable* in the form of complete
sermons in the vernacular, specifically addressed to 'predicadores mozos'
and 'predicadores principiantes', appears to have been a new development in the 1590s.[2] Fray Diego Murillo offers his Advent collection,
first published in 1603, to the 'predicadores tenidos por menos doctos'
who

se aplican a predicar en los pueblos pequeños, porque su pobreza les
humilla los pensamientos: y por ventura no lo harían, si se viessen con
caudal para predicar en las populosas ciudades. ¿Qué harían pues los
pobrecillos que viven en las aldeas, si Dios no proveyese a su Iglesia de
Predicadores que se acomodasen a predicarles?[3]

However, this type of publication provoked much controversy, the
first objection being one of 'spoon-feeding' the preacher by providing
not only copious indices and *Tablas de conceptos predicables* but
ready-made sermons. Ideally each preacher should compile his own
florilegium from his reading of scripture, commentaries and the Fathers:
'. . .ha de tener un cartapacio alfabético, y leer los Doctores con la
pluma en la mano, sacando lo bueno de ellos. . .y otro códice de los
Evangelios del año, donde puedes apuntar lo que hallares, hurtando de
los libros y aplicando sus lugares a tu propósito.'[4] In fact, as Fray
Agustín Núñez Delgadillo tells us: 'hay algunos que no miran los Padres
de la Iglesia, ni los expositores graves de la Sagrada Escritura, sino
libros predicables en romance or latín, donde esté todo dispuesto y
trabajado'.[5] He is, as it happens, seeking to exonerate himself from the
charge of having produced just such a book, on the grounds that
his *Minas* are 'por labrar' and still provide the reader/preacher with
an opportunity to exercise his ingenuity and originality—unlike the
majority of *sermonarios* which, according to Suárez de Figueroa,
'causan notable daño'. Suárez expands this point:

Quitan la invención propia, la elegancia del lenguaje, la agudeza de los
pensamientos y concetos levantados. Son ocasión de que estudien los

---

[1] i.e. Francisco de Labata, S.J., *Apparatus concionatorum* (3 vols., Lugduni,
1615–21). Others are entitled *sylvae* or *thesauri*.

[2] [1601] 'En esta Corte y fuera della se ha comenzado a usar de pocos años a
esta parte de escribir y trasladar sermones de los más famosos predicadores de
estos Reinos para tratar en ellos comprando y vendiendo', in Urbano González de
la Calle, 'Documentos inéditos', 272.

[3] *Discursos predicables para los quatro domingos de Adviento*, sig. *7^V.

[4] Estella, *Modo de predicar*, ii. 19. Also Terrones, *Instrucción*, p. 33.

[5] *Minas Celestiales* (Madrid, 1629), Al Lector. In *De la Victoria de los Justos*
he has produced 'lugares comunes para predicadores, mas disimulados y útiles
para todo género de personas' (Prólogo al Lector, sig. ¶3).

principiantes, asidos a sus romancistas. Hacen dar a menudo en cosas
comunes y trilladas, que todas lo son para andar en tantas manos y
en lengua de quien no los entendiera en latín.[1]
The discussion seems to have shifted from whether sermons should be
printed at all to whether they should be printed in the vernacular. This
debate is fully reported in Pedro Urbano González de la Calle's 'Documentos inéditos acerca del uso de la lengua vulgar en los libros espirituales'.[2] The 1596 *Index* of Clement VIII appears to sanction some
sermons in the vernacular: '[Regula vi] Qui verò de ratione bene vivendi,
contemplandi, confitendi, ac similibus argumentis vulgari sermone
conscripti sunt, si sanam doctrinam contineant, non est cur prohibeantur,
sicut nec sermones populares, vulgari lingua habiti.'[3] The Sandoval
Index of 1612 has no ban on sermons either, although it reiterates the
proscription on the Bible 'con todas sus partes impresa, o de mano, en
cualquier lengua vulgar'.[4] However, the Jesuit General Aquaviva, in a
letter of 5 April 1604 to the Provincial of Castille, states firmly that:
'Ya tengo escrito a V.R. que en ninguna manera conviene que los nuestros
impriman sermones en romance. Ahora añado que no se revean, sino
después que se hayan hecho en latín.'[5] I have found no similar statements on behalf of other orders.

Most preachers who print sermons in Spanish during the first quarter
of the seventeenth century preface them with a statement of the
reasons which have prompted them to do so. These may be summarized
as follows:

(a)   *más general provecho*: sermons to be read by the laity.
(b)   the equivalent of a *Défense et Illustration* of the Spanish language.
(c)   a topic which corresponds to 'Why should the Devil have all the
      best tunes?', whereby sermons in the vernacular are supposed to
      provide an antidote (*contrayerua*) to the insidious poison of
      secular fiction.[6]

Fray Basilio Ponce de León takes up the last two points: 'Que no se
hizo el buen romance y la agudeza solamente para la copla y el billete,
sino mucho más para servir a la divina Escritura.'[7]
Many of these arguments are particularly interesting because they

[1] *El Passagero* (Madrid, 1914), p. 194.
[2] See above, p. 7.
[3] *Index Librorum Prohibitorum cum regulis confectis per patres a Tridentina
Synodo delectos* (Rome, 1596), praefatio, p. 15.
[4] *Index librorum prohibitorum... D. Bernardi de Sandoval et Roxas*, Madrid,
1612, regla iv, pp. 3–4.
[5] A. Astraín, *Historia de la Compañía de Jesús en la asistencia de España*
(7 vols., Madrid, 1902–25), iv. 15 n. 1.
[6] Fray Diego Murillo, *Discursos predicables [Quaresma]* (Saragossa, 1605), i,
Al Lector, sig. ¶ 7.
[7] *Discursos para diferentes Evangelios* (Salamanca, 1608), i. 174b.

acknowledge that sermons printed in the vernacular are going to be widely read by the laity, and not just by preachers in search of fresh inspiration, although Fray Juan Galvarro suggests, rather cynically, that the initial demand came from the clergy:

Escribí en latín las homilías del Adviento, ni tan claro que fuese bárbaro, ni tan elegante, que fuese oscuro. Contentó a los sabios el idioma, y no les desagradó el discurso. Al común de los predicadores no, por ser en latín. Huyen del trabajo y quieren facilidad y brevedad en el ejercicio de su oficio.[1]

However, the preacher who intended to make wholesale use of the contents of the printed *sermonarios* in his own sermons would not relish the possibility of members of his congregation having access to the same sources, as Fray Pedro de Valderrama comments: '. . .que es lástima que el otro desde su silla, y la monja desde su coro, estén diciendo el punto que está por venir: porque ya sabían el que había dicho el predicador; estos inconvenientes tienen los sermones que en nuestra lengua fueron con traza . . .'[2] The *gracioso* Batín in Lope's *El castigo sin venganza* gives way to the same imaginings:

Si estoy en la iglesia oyendo
algún sermón imagino
que le digo que está impreso.[3]

Fray Diego Murillo summarily dismisses this objection, 'para los que entienden algo de predicar, bien cierto es que no les parecerá muy grande: porque como gente diestra en este ejercicio, saben de una misma sustancia hacer diferentes guisados. . .sólo con trasponer las materias a diferentes lugares'.[4] He feels, moreover, that the laity should be encouraged to read sermons: 'que cada qual tenga en su casa un predicador que le enseñe el camino del cielo'.[5] Fray Miguel Angel Almenara is of the same mind:

. . .que por ventura les será de más provecho un sermón dellos leído con consideración en su oratorio, que muchos oídos de paso y divertidos en las Iglesias, y también para desterrar con estos libros de entre los Christianos, los profanos y fabulosos, que con los amores deshonestos de que tratan, suelen emponzoñar las almas de los que los leen con

---

[1] *Glosa moral sobre los Evangelios de Quaresma* (Sanlúcar de Barrameda, 1622), Al Lector.

[2] *Exercicios espirituales [Quaresma]* (Madrid, 1604), ii, sig. ¶ 7ᵛ. The same point about 'seglares' and 'mujeres curiosas' who echo and sometimes anticipate the preacher, having read the printed sermons he is using, is made by Jerónimo de Lanuza. He uses this as a justification for sermons being longer in their published form than in the pulpit, *Homilías* (Barbastro, 1621), i. sig. e4ᵛ.

[3] Ed. C.A. Jones (Oxford, 1966), p. 56, vv. 945–7.

[4] *Discursos predicables [Quaresma]*, i. sig. ¶ 7.

[5] Ibid., sig. ¶ 7ᵛ.

gusto, para pasar el tiempo.[6]

By the 1630s it is taken for granted that sermons will be quite widely used as books of private devotion, and preachers preparing their sermons for publication often adapt them to this use: 'hoy usan grandes señoras y ministros, occupados estas pláticas en sus oratorios y es forzoso que se conforme la doctrina con sus estados y ocupaciones'.[2] This idea lies behind Fray Luis de Granada's *Guía de pecadores* (1556–7) which may possibly be based on actual sermons: he calls it 'este familiar predicador en casa para todas las veces que le quisiesen oír'.[3] It is also expressed by the Jesuit P. Jerónimo de Florencia, when he informs his patrons, the Infantes don Carlos and don Fernando, that he has been specifically commanded by their late father, Philip III, to print his *Marial* collection in the vernacular, in order that 'la gente ordinaria, ignorante de la lengua latina e incapaz de la lectura de los santos' may profit by the important doctrine it contains.[4]

He joins to this pragmatic justification ('para más común provecho') an ardent defence of 'la lengua materna con que nos criamos':

y más cuando ella es tan elegante, tan abundante, tan graciosa como es la Española; a quien hace mucho agravio quien piensa que no caben en ella los altos conceptos, y los grandiosos discursos que están en los Santos; caben por cierto, y en muchas ocasiones les da un donaire y gracia que ni la lengua Latina ni la Griega se la puede dar.[5]

In very similar vein another famous preacher of the previous generation, Fray Hernando de Santiago, had prefaced one of his *sermonarios* with the following assertion:

...y pues ya nuestra lengua no está tan grosera como antiguamente... antes está tan adornada de tropos y figuras, que no sólo declara con propiedad los más delgados conceptos, pero encarece lo bueno y vitupera lo malo dentro de los límites de la verdad con mayor rigor que otra.[6]

A growing confidence in Spanish as a sharp linguistic instrument, capable of dealing with even the most subtle points of speculative theology, becomes apparent at the beginning of the seventeenth century

[1] *Pensamientos literales y morales*, sig. ¶¶6[V]. Also Fray Basilio Ponce de León, *Discursos para diferentes Evangelios* (Salamanca, 1608), i. Al Lector, sig. ¶4[V]. 'Predicar por escrito ... pues en el libro puede leerse despacio, a todas horas ... y releer lo que prendiere y tocare en el alma'.
[2] J. Rodríguez de León, *El Predicador de las Gentes, San Pablo* (Madrid, 1635), II. xi. 138–9.
[3] Ed. M. Martínez Burgos (Madrid, 1929), p. 31.
[4] *Marial* (2 vols., Alcalá, 1625), Dedicatoria, sig. ¶4[V].
[5] Ibid. See also D. Vega, *Parayso*, ii, Al Lector, sig. b8[V]: 'nuestra lengua Castellana ... puede competir con la Latina, y aun en parte la vence, pues hay en ella mil phrasis y maneras elegantes de hablar, que de ninguna suerte las puede explicar el Latín'.
[6] *Consideraciones sobre todos los Evangelios de ... Quaresma* (Madrid, 1606). Also in prologues by Ponce de León, Valderrama, Murillo, and Paravicino.

and when we come to consider the status of the vernacular sermon at
this period and the part it played in such a re-evaluation we may note
with interest that perhaps the earliest printed preaching manual to
appear in Spanish—Bartolomé Ximénez Patón's *El perfecto predicador*
(Baeza, 1612)[1] —is published and bound together with an *Apología
orada en público concurso en prueba de que conviene que se escriban
éstos, y otros libros de qualquier facultad en nuestra lengua vulgar
Española* by El Licenciado don Fernando de Vallesteros y Saavedra.

All the above-mentioned topics concur in taking the printed sermon
as a fact in itself and not just the shadow cast by a preaching 'event'. It
seems that preachers expect a good deal from their published sermons
and see them as an important part of their Evangelical ministry. In
many cases what they wish to communicate necessarily takes the form
of a sermon rather than that of a devotional treatise, although it has
been suggested that 'bien a menudo los tratados ascéticos o místicos
han sido presentados o "ensayados" en forma de conferencias espirituales,
de sermones o de homilías'.[2] Fray Diego Murillo gives several reasons
for choosing the sermon form:
. . .para reparar el daño que hacen los libros profanos, me ha parecido
el más acomodado estilo entre todos, él de los sermones: porque la
variedad de materias que en ellos se trata (de más de aprovechar para
despertar el gusto) es más acomodada para el provecho universal de los
fieles, por ser más ocasionada para tratar de todas las cosas. Ofrece el
mismo Evangelio mil ocasiones, en que no hay estado, ni vicio ni
virtud de que no pueda libremente tratarse: descendiendo en particular
a la circunstancias más singulares, porque esto es propio de los sermones.[3]
He suggests that the sermon's chief appeal for hearers, or readers,
accustomed to secular literature lies in the fact that it is a type of
miscellany, whereas for the preacher it is a free form, embracing easily
the general and the particular.[4] In addition to the universality of the
sermon and its apparent comprehensiveness of subject matter, Murillo
concludes: 'Demás desto, el estilo de los sermones da lugar al que
escribe, para hablar con mayor energía: enseñando, rogando, reprehendiendo, exclamando, y usando de otros afectos que son familiares
a la predicación: y dan ocasión a que tenga más eficacia lo que se
escribe.' The sermon form implies a tone of voice as well as a structure.
How do we recognize a sermon?

---

[1] Seen (in manuscript?) by Lope de Vega in Toledo as early as 1607, cf.
Epistolario, iii, carta iv. p. 7. '. . . si su dotrina se pusiesse en práctica . . . veríamos
reformada la predicación'.
[2] Ricard, *Estudios de la literatura religiosa española*, p. 203.
[3] *Discursos predicables [Quaresma]*, i. sig. ¶ 7[V].
[4] See below, pp. 87–8.

(a) Terminology

Murillo's sermons are all entitled *discursos predicables*, which seems the commonest term at this period. *Sermón* is used almost invariably of a *suelto*, but not very often in the title of a *sermonario*. *Plática* appears to be reserved for sermons to priests or religious, and spiritual conferences at retreats.[1] *Oración evangélica* is another unambiguous term, but *consideración, meditación, tratado*, or even *exercicio espiritual* appear to be used both to describe compositions of a very similar kind, as well as to distinguish completely different concepts. For example, although both Fray Alonso de Cabrera and Fray Hernando de Santiago publish their sermons as *Consideraciones*,[2] it has been noted that this title is frequently chosen by members of the Society of Jesus when publishing sets of liturgical meditations, modelled on the Ignatian exercises, and therefore it is not applied exclusively to sermons.[3] Moreover, Fray Basilio Ponce de León explains how he prepares his sermons for publication, having 'quitado los sermones y reducídolos a Consideraciones sobre el texto del Evangelio como me pareció conveniente',[4] and he is not alone in using *consideración* to designate an internal division of a sermon, although other preachers use *discurso* or simply number points.

A preacher preparing his sermons for the press was quite likely to lengthen them and we may assume that the longer Latin quotations which we find in many *sermonarios* at this time were interpolated after the original preaching. Fray Diego de Arce admits: 'Muchos destos sermones no se imprimen como se predicaron, sino como se escribieron . . .y así son más largos en las salutaciones y en los cuerpos dellos de lo que conviene para recitarlos.'[5] However, 'se escribieron' might also imply that the sermon was written out in full *before* delivery and points selected on each successive preaching occasion. The standard length of a sermon at the beginning of the seventeenth century was that required for an hour's preaching, or at most an hour and a half, and is most easily measured in the *sueltos*. Sermons were shorter and fewer in

---

[1] Jerónimo Nadal, *Pláticas espirituales en Coimbra* is an example, as is San Juan de Avila, *Dos pláticas hechas a sacerdotes* (Cordoba, 1595).

[2] A. de Cabrera, *Libro de Consideraciones sobre los Evangelios, desde el Domingo de Septuagésima, y todos los domingos y ferias de la Quaresma* (2 vols., Barcelona, 1602) and H. de Santiago, *Consideraciones sobre todos los Evangelios de los Domingos y Ferias de la Quaresma*.

[3] M. Nicolau, 'Espiritualidad de la Compañía de Jesús en la España del siglo xvi', in *Corrientes espirituales en la España del siglo xvi: trabajos del ii Congreso de Espiritualidad de 1956* (Barcelona, 1963), pp. 345–6.

[4] *Discursos para diferentes Evangelios*, ii, Al Lector, sig. ¶ 2^V.

[5] *Miscelánea Primera*, sig. A5^V. Lanuza's sermons were also lengthened.

the summer months ('de Pascua de Flores adelante') because, as Fray
Luis de Rebolledo puts it: 'es el tiempo de más ordinarias muertes, y
extraordinario calor, especialmente para gente enlutada y que se halla
en congregación y concurso con hachas encendidas'.[1]

The word *tratado*, while it is used by two Portuguese preachers,
Fray Diego López de Andrade and Fray Antonio Feo, in the titles of
their sermon collections in Spanish, often refers to something longer
than a sermon, although its use is confusing. For instance, Fray Pedro
Malón de Chaide, at the beginning of his *Libro de la Conversión de la
Magdalena* (first published in 1588) uses the two terms as though they
were interchangeable:

Antes que comiença a tratar la historia de la bienaventurada María
Magdalena, quiero pedir licencia para no guardar en este *tratado o
sermón* el estilo acostumbrado de predicar, que es ir declarando cada
palabra del Evangelio y mostrando sus misterios particulares...Y así,
pretendo despedirme en este mi *sermón* de las leyes y preceptos que
dan los más acertados predicadores. Y gozar de la libertad de mi gusto
en el proceder.[2]

This passage does, in fact, distinguish between *sermón* and *tratado*, even
though in practice Malón bases his work on the appropriate Gospel text
for the feast of St. Mary Magdalene and begins in preacherly style with
the customary introduction and invocation of Grace known as the
salutación. It is quite possible to imagine certain sections having been
preached, in very much their present form, yet the book may more
properly be called the first *novela de santos*. Fray Diego Murillo follows
a similar procedure in *Vida y Excelencias de la Madre de Dios* (Saragossa,
1610) and explains why: 'porque esta manera de escribir es más acomodada para la historia, y da lugar a las consideraciones morales, que se
mezclan con ella, y a otras cosas que pertenecen a la amplificación de
esa misma historia'.[3] Whereas a sermon must weave several contrasting
but complementary texts together, subordinating the parts to the
whole, the more leisurely *tratado* lays equal emphasis on each of the
parts, 'según la diversidad de las materias', and is free to explore each
line of thought as far as it leads. The *tratado* has no *salutación* or prayer
and tends to include far more profane and popular references, poetry, and
exempla. Thus it emerges that a sermon is the more concentrated way of
expounding a Gospel text, and it may be recognized as a sermon in that it
proposes and illustrates a certain thematic or propositional unity.

---

[1] *Cien oraciones fúnebres*, Epístola a los predicadores principiantes. See also
Terrones, *Instrucción*, p. 123. The same public health requirements closed the
corrales at the height of summer: Rennert, *The Spanish Stage in the Time of
Lope de Vega*, p. 51.
[2] Ed. Félix García (Madrid, 1946), i. 49–50 (my italics).
[3] Al Lector, i. sig. ††3^V.

'Quien expone el Evangelio cláusula por cláusula, sin reducirlo a unidad, hace o paráfrasis, o comento, mas no oración o sermón.'[1] For example, a *homilía*, 'en que se va apostillando el Evangelio diciendo una consideración sobre una cláusula y otra sobre la siguiente',[2] may be classified as a sermon as long as it has a unified *argumento* or application, for example Christ's healing ministry or a specific Christian virtue.

The absence of any kind of structure or subordination to a chief proposition leads Fray Pedro de Valderrama to admit that his *exercicios espirituales* are not 'sermones hechos, ni con tal intento se escribieron, sino *tratados* y ejercicios, donde cada uno puede ejercitar su ingenio'.[3] He continues: 'Y así verán que no tienen salutaciones, ni introducciones formadas, sólo es un juntar de material, para que labre cada uno las casa, y le dé forma y traza conforme al sitio donde la ha de edificar.'

(b) Rhetorical structure

Neither length nor nomenclature, therefore, is infallible proof of the presence of a sermon. What distinguishes this genre is a particular form, or *dispositio*, which remains fairly constant throughout the history of preaching and lends itself to parody by virtue of being quite easy to recognize. There is always a single main text (*thema*), and always a division of the text, traditionally a tripartite one in honour of the Trinity: 'y es de tener aviso, que no se divida el sermón en más de tres partes, porque no engendre fastidio, ni menos que tres porque no parezca confusión con solos dos brazos abrazar gran multitud'.[4] There may, of course, be several divisions and subdivisons, and critics of the scholastic sermon quote gleefully actual or imagined cases of division by words,[5] or even by letters. The spelling-out, letter by letter, of any key word or proper name in the text, in Cabalistic or pseudo-Cabalistic fashion, is a method of division ridiculed by Erasmus in his *Praise of Folly* (1511) where he speaks of a Scotist preacher who set out to explain the mystery of the name of Jesus in this way, as part of the exordium of his sermon.[6] It is, none

---

[1] Suárez de Figueroa, *El Passagero*, p. 190.

[2] Terrones, *Instruciión*, p. 49.

[3] *Exercicios espirituales para . . . la Quaresma*, ii (Madrid, 1604), sig. ¶ 7 (my italics). They are much longer than his 'real' sermons—the *sueltos* and those sermons published posthumously in the *Teatro de Religiones*. By the same reckoning his *Exercicios espirituales . . . de los santos* are sermons, since they are much shorter and have *salutaciones*. In the 1608 edition each one is entitled *sermón*.

[4] 'Carta de Fr. Francisco Ortiz sobre la predicación' (c. 1530), in J. Meseguer Fernández, 'Fr. Francisco Ortiz, en Torrelaguna', *A 1–A* viii (1948), 523.

[5] Revd. Lancelot Andrewes was renowned for 'crumbling a text'; see T.S. Eliot, *For Lancelot Andrewes: Essays on Style and Order* (London, 1928).

[6] *Praise of Folly*, trans. B. Radice (Harmondsworth, 1971), pp. 169–70. This method is better adapted to the introduction rather than to the body of the

the less a method which found favour, even among humanists, well into
the sixteenth century, but Fray Diego de Arce, in a retraction of
'dubious' doctrine allegedly found in earlier sermons, draws attention
to the dangers of using such 'ficciones' as the threefold interpretation
of the initials A.C.F.R.I.C. and S.T.L.I.A., attributed to King Solomon
by the apocryphal scholar Aristeas, and which he claims to have found
in an old manuscript in the convent library.[1] Ximénez Patón also calls
this method 'poco usado' and disapproves of it, 'porque tiene más
dificultad que claridad'.[2] As late as 1630, Fray Agustín Núñez Delgadillo
was denounced to the Inquisition on account of certain mnemonic
devices 'con un olor de judaísmo' to be found in his *Puerta de la Luz,
para conocer y tener presentes en todas acciones, palabras y pensamientos a Dios nuestro señor, a Jesuchristo nuestro Salvador, su sagrada
pasión &c* (Saragossa, Pedro Verges, 1630). The *censor* Joan de Pineda
singles out for special ridicule and condemnation a passage where
Núñez Delgadillo discourses thus: 'Si comes una *Perdiz*, mira sus letras,
y hallarás en la P la Prisión, en la E el Escarnio de la Pasión; en la R, el
Rigor con que lo trataron; en la D, el Desamparo que padeció; en la C,
la Cruz (usando C por Z). Con estos picantes, come la perdiz.'[3] This
method may owe something to Núñez Delgadillo's interest in the
Lulian Art (his *Breve y fácil declaración del artificio luliano*, Alcalá,
1622, also failed to meet with Inquisitorial approval), which at the
Renaissance was assimilated by Italian neo-Platonists into the Hermetic-
Cabalist tradition. Frances Yates reminds us that, before Lull, the
practice of meditating on combinations of letters was an exclusively
Jewish phenomenon, developed particularly in the Spanish Cabala.[4]

Within the basic sermon framework—text and division, supported by
'proofs' and 'applications'—there is room for a good deal of diversity.
The Jesuit Carolus Regius (Carlo Reggio, d. 1612) comments: 'Multi-
plex enim natura rerum, variusque modus quo ordinari possunt...
dispositio Oratoria nullis praeceptis comprehendi facile possit'.[5] Most
theorists in the sixteenth and seventeenth centuries allow for this

---

sermon, and is known as 'explication by hidden terminology'; see Smyth, *The
Art of Preaching*, pp. 51–3.
[1] *Miscelánea Primera*, sig. A6ᵛ to B2: 'Prediqué luego estas dos cosas en los
primeros sermones, no sin encarecimiento de su singularidad (tan persuadido
estaba de su verdad), ni sin mucho gusto del auditorio...'
[2] *El perfecto predicador*, cap. xiv: 'De algunos modos que hay en la disposición
de los sermones'.
[3] The inquisitorial process is recorded in *legajo* 4444, ex. 45 of the Archivo
Histórico Nacional, Madrid. The book itself has not been found by me in Spain,
unfortunately.
[4] *The Art of Memory* (London, 1966; Harmondsworth, 1969), pp. 189–90.
[5] *Orator Christianus*, p. 388.

variety by subdividing sermons into different types, which are sometimes models and sometimes methods. There are five types of sermon,
according to Luis de Granada,[1] and twelve, according to Suárez de
Figueroa,[2] while other writers choose numbers in between. By com-
paring these types and examining actual sermons it is possible to
arrive at the three or four sermon structures most current in the
Spanish Golden Age.

The simplest and most common distinction is that between the
sermón de un (solo) tema and the *homilía*.

(i) *sermón de un (solo) tema*

In essence it is the classical rhetorical oration schematized by Aristotle
and consisting of four parts:

Propositio
Narratio
Confirmatio
Peroratio

Terrones describes it as being 'en cuatro partes como una oración
retórica': *exordio, narración, confirmación,* and *epílogo.*[3] However,
he proceeds to subdivide the *exordio* into a further two parts: *salutación*
and *introducción.* The former is a *divini auxilii imploratio*, sandwiched
between the two announcements of the *thema* (the second for the
benefit of late comers), and it culminates in the reciting of the *Ave
Maria.*[4] The *introducción*, on the other hand, may either be a kind of
subsidiary text (*prothema*), or it may be closer to a *praecognitio textus*
and typographically indicated by the heading *declaración de la letra.*[5]
In the latter case it follows the prayer and usurps some of the functions
of the *narración* which include division into points.

Terrones del Caño's description of the *narración* is as follows:
Tras este exordio se ha de comenzar por un dicho de un santo o una

[1] *Retórica Eclesiástica* in *BAE Obras de V.P.M. Fray Luis de Granada* (Madrid,
1863), iii. 553–9. He takes the classical distinction between *judicial, deliberativo,
demonstrativo,* and *didascálico,* drops the first and adds a type of *homilía* and a
'mixed' type, which correspond to current usage.

[2] *El Passagero*, alivio iv.

[3] *Instrucción*, p. 99. Fray Luis de Granada names six: *exordio, narración,
proposición (partición), confirmación, confutación,* and *peroración,* in *Retórica
Eclesiástica*, p. 551.

[4] In the Middle Ages the preacher's prayer was the *Veni Sancte Spiritus*, cf.
Th.–M. Charland, O.P., *Artes praedicandi: contribution à l'histoire de la rhétorique
au Moyen Age* (Paris and Ottawa, 1936), pp. 125–6.

[5] Fray Diego Murillo uses two alternative names, *introducción* and *prothema*,
for what corresponds to a *declaración de la letra* in two separate collections:
Discursos predicables [Adviento] and *Vida y excelencias de la Madre de Dios*
(Saragossa, 1610). The latter in fact is cast in *tratado* rather than sermon form,
although it contains a few ready-made sermons also.

proposición natural o moral cuerda, o una autoridad de Escritura, y sacar della alguún discursito breve, con que se proponga la materia que se ha de tratar; y si es necessario, se divida en los miembros en que se piensa tocar. Y ésta es ya la segunda parte destos sermones, que llamamos *narración*.[1]

Ximénez Patón's definition, however, is more confusing and seems to treat *narración* and *introducción* as interchangeable. He is, moreover, talking about current usage, whereas Terrones is giving precepts.

En nuestras oraciones, que son los sermones, narración es el Tema y letra que dicen del Evangelio: ésta ordinariamente la ponen algunos en su lugar, que es después del exordio; otros hacen antes de comenzar el exordio, después de la salutación, lo cual no es muy conforme al estilo oratorio que se debe guardar; otros, y pecan menos, la ponen con la salutación.[2]

Terminology becomes even more misleading when we note that in medieval sermons the word *narratio* designates an analogy or *exemplum*.

As for the *confirmación*, this usually consists of four or five points which may be headed *consideración, pensamiento, punto, discurso* (most commonly), or simply *confirmación* (in the margin). When there are more than five points, each covering three or four pages, we may assume that they are printed as alternatives from which the apprentice preacher can choose his own sermon material. These points are 'proofs' of the proposition advanced, and as such owe a good deal to Rhetoric's sister art Dialectic. Particularly appropriate methods of argument for use in sermons, according to Ximénez Patón, are 'por distinciones'[3] and 'multiplicación de efectos o causas'.[4] This aspect of preaching is expounded under the heading *didascálico* by Fray Luis de Granada, and involves Aristotelian topical theory.[5] *Confutación*, or proof by contraries, sometimes follows as part of the same section.

Finally, the fourth part of the *sermón de un tema* is the *peroración* or *epílogo*. This takes the form of a recapitulation of what has gone before and a final exhortation to the congregation. If we are to believe Fray Cristóbal de Avendaño, by the late 1620s the epilogue was being abused and ran the risk of degenerating into tedious repetition instead of

---

[1] *Instrucción*, p. 100.

[2] *Eloquencia española en arte*, fo. 114.

[3] A technique used in preaching since medieval times. It involves considering a thing (e.g. Duty) under distinct aspects (e.g. to God, to the State, to one's parents, to oneself). It may have originated in pre-scholastic juridical theory; see R.R. Bolgar, *The Classical Heritage* (Cambridge, 1954; New York, 1964), p. 146.

[4] Sermon scheme II below illustrates argument through multiplication of causes and effects.

[5] *Retórica Eclesiástica*, ed. cit. IV. vi. 567, and in more detail in II. viii. 514–6. A useful classification of topics is given by M.J. Woods in his article 'Gracián, Peregrini, and the Theory of Topics', *MLR* lxiii (1968), 854–5.

a pointed reminder:

Los epílogos los comparo yo a los mantos de seda: en sus principios
fueron de mucha estima; empezáronlos a usar las señoras excelentísimas,
luego bajaron a las señorías, bajaron más a las mujeres de los Caballeros
particulares, ya el día de hoy andan tan arrastrados, y han dado en tan
gran vituperio, que cualquier mujer de oficial mecánico quiere traer
manto de seda; por lo cual las damas de la Reina, que son las primeras
Señoras de Castilla, los aborrecen y andan en cuerpo.
    Así son los epílogos; los primeros que los usaron fueron el
Reverendo Padre Maestro Duarte de mi Religión, y el Reverando Padre
Maestro Santiago 'Pico de Oro', de la Orden de Nuestra Señora de la
Merced, ambos elegantísimos en púlpito . . . procuraron imitarlos los
grandes predicadores, luego los medianos, atreviéronse también los
inferiores, ya en el día de hoy han dado tanta baja los epílogos, que se
han quedado en los predicadores bromas.[1]

It may be interesting to illustrate these theories about the *sermón
de un tema* with outlines of a couple of sermons of this type, which
show considerable variation.

EXAMPLE I

*Sermón que predicó. . .el Doctor Aguilar de Terrones. . .en las honras. . .
del Rey D. Felipe Segundo. . .a 19 del mes de Octubre 1598.*

Margin		*Internal divisions of sermon*
Thema		***Regem cui omnia vivunt, venite adoremus***
		Office for the Dead. Repeated in Spanish.
	(a)	*Salutation*—application to Earthly and Heavenly
		King—*Ave Maria*.
	(b)	*Introduction*: purpose of sermon.
		(i) A *tratado* on Kingship.
		(ii) A description of the heroic achievements
		of Philip II.
	(c)	*Confutation* (i) Philip himself is a *tratado vivo*.
		(ii) *ante mortem ne laudes hominem*
		quemquam (Ecclesiasticus).
	(d)	*captatio benevolentiae*: modesty topics and
		precedents for this type of endeavour.
Proposición		*Division*
fo. 5		(i) Personal virtues of Philip.
		(ii) Kingly virtues (more appropriate).

[1] *Otro tomo de Santos* (Valladolid, 1629), Prólogo, sig. ¶ 7. Terrones also
insists that the *epílogo* should not be slavish repetition but should consist of
enumeración (précis) and *amplificación* ('con palabras más fuertes, más signifi-
cativas y aun hiperbólicas, más apriesa, con voz más alta, mayor conato y afecto'):
Instrucción, pp. 102–3.

A. *Regem*

Ezekiel's vision of four-faced beast (Ezekiel 1: 10).

Confirmación I
fo. 7

Aguila Imperial—keen-witted, far-sighted, wise. Examples from life.

Confirmación II
fo. 8[V]

Hombre—devout in his duty to God and benevolent in his duty to his neighbour. Trent, Lepanto, missions.

Confirmación III
fo. 12

León—energetic (i) in war (ii) in peace. Just and merciful (with *Carnero*). Also *Basilisco*: preacher's anecdote.[1]

Confirmación IV
fo. 15[V]

Buey—(i) prudent (ii) hard-working. Examples of monarch's sufferings in life and acceptance of death.

Confirmación V
fo. 20[V]

Ramillete of virtues.

Confutación I
fo. 21

Answers the bold objections of Philip's critics by drawing attention to the responsibility of his advisers in his decisions.

Confutación II
fo. 21[V]

Answers those who claim that death is the end by proving (by *consecuencia*) that Philip's soul and virtues live on (i) in Heaven
(ii) in his heirs.

Comparación with the phoenix, reborn from the 'grid-iron' (*parrilla*) of San Lorenzo de El Escorial.

B. *cui omnia vivunt*

Epílogo
fo. 25[V]

Let us rejoice in the new king who preserves the virtues of the old.
Prayers for the new king—prayers to old (and

---

[1] This appears to be a personal recollection from Terrones: 'Cinco años había hechos que le predicaba cierto predicador, y un segundo Domingo de Quaresma en Aranjuez acabada su salutación, queriendo comenzar su sermón le miró de hito en hito, y se turbó de manera, que del todo se olvidó el sermón: lo que entonces creístes que fue vaguido de cabeza, la verdad es que fue temblor de corazón de ver tan extremada severidad, y fue forzoso hundirse en el púlpito, y cobrar aliento con que volvió en su memoria y predicó, que de espanto no había podido' (fo. 14). This affords us another instance of a sermon memorized before delivery.

King of Heaven).

'The King is a god in human form' (Plato).

C. *venite adoremus*

Whole *thema* reiterated one more time.

In this *sermón de un tema*, which is at the same time a *panegyric* of a simple kind, much used in funeral orations by Jerónimo de Florencia,[1] the exordium (consisting of *salutación, introducción,* and *captatio benevolentiae*) is composed in such a way as to form a mini-sermon with its own division, confirmations, and confutations. Apart from the rhetorical divisions of the sermon, indicated in the margin, the sermon falls into three main sections, corresponding to a threefold division of the text, which both opens and closes the sermon. The last division (*venite adoremus*) is a very explicit peroration which does not need the same amplification as the first (*Regem*). The theme of Heavenly and Earthly Kingship unifies the sermon.

EXAMPLE II

Fray Cristóbal de Fonseca, 'La Conversión del Buen Ladrón', *Discursos predicables*, Madrid, 1614, fos. 411–21.

Thema: **Cum eo crucifixi sunt duo latrones, unus ad dextris, et alter ad sinistris** (Matthew 27 given: really Luke 23: 39-43).

Internal divisions of sermon – no marginal indications.

Introduction (no *Salutation*): Thief compared to
(a) Mary Magdalene
(b) St. Paul
His conversion far more miraculous than either of theirs: 'no vio milagro, ni sermón, ni ejemplo, ni gloria, ni luz, ni voz, sino a Christo, roto y deshecho en la Cruz'.

Narration (with confirmations)

Division I: what does this conversion show?
(a) *sabiduría de Dios* ('en juntar todos extremos')
        Ecclesiastes 3:1–8.
(b) *omnipotencia de Dios* (i. 'alumbrar un entendimiento ciego';
                            ii. 'tomar el ladrón por instrumento para
                            vengarse del Demonio de los Fariseos,
                            de Pilatos y del pueblo').

---

[1] Particularly the *Sermón . . . en las honras del Conde de Lemos* (Madrid, 1622).

(c) *misericordia de Dios* ('el salvar al ladrón fue el intento de morir entre ladrones').

(d) *providencia de Dios* ('puestos y escondidos sus tesoros en un ladrón').

Thema repeated

Division II:

Duda—why was one thief saved, the other damned?

(a) *Literal sense*—St. Augustine: 'de la predestinación no hay causa'. Matthew 24:40–41.

(b) *Moral sense*—'señalarnos en estos ladrones el camino más fácil y más seguro del Cielo, que es vivir un alma entre temor y esperanza'. Bad thief should be a warning to us as well.

Nos quidem digna facti recipimus, hic autem.[1]

Division III: story resumed under 4 heads.

(a) los motivos que tuvo este ladrón para convertirse:

  (i) inscription on the Cross: Christ's Kingdom begins there
  (ii) seeing Christ's sufferings
  (iii) hearing Him forgive His persecutors
  (iv) seeing the portents in the firmament
  (v) the intercession of the Blessed Virgin

(b) las venturas grandes que gozó:

  (i) such unusual circumstances—never before or since
  (ii) the joy of being at Christ's side
  (iii) dying on the Cross—receiving the keys of Heaven
  (iv) being able to stand up for Christ when He was abandoned by all others
  (v) arriving in time for Christ's coronation and betrothal

(c) la diligencia que puso de su parte para que Dios le perdonasse y le favoreciesse:

  (i) on finding the treasure he sold everything to buy it
  (ii) he did not wait until last moment, but first moment of knowing Christ
  (iii) he confessed his sins
  (iv) his petition was humble, modest but 'discretísima': *Memento mei*
  (v) his virtues of Faith, Hope, and Charity, cf. St. Gregory

---

[1] Vulgate gives verse 41 as: 'Et nos quidem iuste, nam digna factis recipimus: hic vero nihil mali gessit', which is the Good Thief's confession of faith.

(d) el premio grande que le dio y la merced que le hizo:
     Hodie mecum eris in Parayso
     (i) Heaven itself is the greatest good that God gives us. Thief
         'stole' it; did not earn it
     (ii) he was given a special, privileged place in Heaven, moreover
          (parable of labourers in vineyard)
     (iii) the gates of Heaven were reopened for the first time since
           Adam's expulsion
     (iv) the speediness with which it was done: *Hodie*
     (v) it was more than what was originally asked for: examples of
         Abraham, Jacob, Tobias, Judith, etc.

Conclusion: A new kind of victory—*victoria dulce.*

Duda—could the thief be called a martyr?
He is called one by Saints Jerome and Cyprian because he suffered
with Christ and his confession on the Cross is as though he were
crucified *for* Christ ('como si le crucificaron por Christo').

This sermon deals with a number of questions and propositions
arising from the *thema* according to the 'multiplicación de efectos y
causas'. There is no *prothema* and none of the patterning of imagery
found in the other three examples. A single situation is explored in
depth and thus this sermon scheme seems to border on the *homilía*,
but for the fact that its technique of exposition is dialectical rather
than exegetical.

(ii) *homilía*

Whereas the *sermón de un tema* keeps quite closely to the model of
the classical rhetorical oration, the *homilía* is simply an 'exposición de
la letra del Evangelio', and as such has a much freer form, as Fray Luis
de Granada points out: 'Porque en esta doctrina sólo se ha de tener por
invariable el que nada se haga invariablemente; sino que conforme sean
los Evangelios, los tiempos y los oyentes, así todo ha de variarse, según
la prudencia del orador.'[1] According to Terrones del Caño, the *dispositio*
of a *homilía* consists simply of a *salutación* ('brevísima'), an *introducción*,
and *el cuerpo del sermón*, which is a clause-by-clause exposition of the
prescribed Gospel narrative in its correct order—'y no al revés, ni tro-
cadas'.[2] On the one hand, Terrones suggests that: 'lo más práctico es
correr a lo menos, salteándola, tantas cláusulas del Evangelio que
parezca que se comenzó desde el principio y se llega hasta el fin, o
cerca, de manera que, aunque no se consideren, como dicen, *pro*

---

[1] *Retórica Eclesiástica*, p. 565.   [2] *Instrucción*, p. 113.

singulis generum, se consideren *pro generibus singulorum*' (p. 118).
On the other hand, Fray Diego Murillo comments that it is quite usual
for only the first two or three clauses of the Gospel text to be expounded
in this way: 'de ordinario los que escriben sermones sólamente declaran
las dos primeras cláusulas del Evangelio, y éstas son las que casi siempre
se predican'.[1]

Carolus Regius defines the *dispositio* of a *homilía* slightly differently,
in order to bring out the preaching message and application to the
congregation. The parts he names are:

    (a) praeparatio per modum exordii
    (b) pars didactica (circa sensum literalem)
    (c) exhortatio morum[2]

The third and last part seems to subsume a kind of *peroratio*, which is
not elsewhere listed explicitly as part of the *dispositio* of a *homilía*.
It may serve to underline that 'unity of proposition or theme' to which
we referred above.[3]

The divisions of the *cuerpo del sermón*, although they are not always
indicated typographically, are frequently headed by clauses of the
Gospel text, and they are shaped by techniques of biblical exegesis
rather than by scholastic argumentation. The literal and moral senses
are those most commonly treated, although both Avendaño and Núñez
Delgadillo occasionally favour the allegorical.

The *homilía* form is the one most frequently to be found in the
Lenten *sermonarios* of the period, whereas *sermones de santos* and
certain funeral sermons belong to another category, that of the panegyric (q.v.).[4] Only Fray Jerónimo Bautista de Lanuza (*Homilías sobre
los Evangelios. . .de la Quaresma*, Barbastro, 1621−2 and *Homilías
sobre el Evangelio que se propone en la solemnidad del santissimo
sacramento del altar*, Barcelona, 1626) and Fray Juan Bautista de
Madrigal (*Homiliario Evangélico*, Madrid, 1602) entitle their sermon
collections with the word *homilía*, to my knowledge. Of the preachers
selected for special study, Fonseca, Vega, and Ramón most frequently
publish sermons of the *homilía* type, although in the same collection
they may include a variation on it called the *paradoxon*.

(iii) *paradoxon*

This is a term used by Ximénez Patón to denote a sermon which
weaves together, or contrasts one with the other, a Gospel text and an

---

[1] *Discursos predicables [Christo]* (Saragossa, 1607), Al Lector.
[2] *Orator Christianus*, p. 394.
[3] See above, p. 44.
[4] Sermons based on *el común de los Santos* (Martyrs, Doctors, Confessors
collectively) frequently follow the *homilía* form, as do those by Fray Tomás
Ramón in *Flores nuevas* (2 vols., Barcelona, 1611−12).

'Autoridad' (which may be from the Epistle for the day, or from the
Breviary). Of this method he says that 'es el que hoy se usa más comunmente, el más practicado entre gente docta en corte, y Escuelas, y el
que tengo por mejor'.[1]

EXAMPLE III

Fray Diego Murillo, 'Miércoles de la Ceniza', *Discursos predicables
[Quaresma]*, Saragossa, 1605, pp. 56–72.

Thema: **Cum ieiunatis, nolite fieri sicut hypocritae tristes**, Matthew
6:16.

Introducción: 3 testimonies from Scripture:

E X O R D I U M

    (i) *ley natural* (Genesis 3:19) *Padre*.
    (ii) *ley escrita* (Joel 2:12–13) *Hijo*.
    (iii) *ley de gracia* (Matthew 6:16) *Espíritu Santo*.

Salutation–Mary's 'estrecho parentesco' with the Trinity:
Ave Maria.

Prothema I

    Memento homo, &c (Genesis 3: 19)

    Empedocles on nature of man–'compuesto de leña y fuego'.

    (a) like a tree–'inconstancia y mudanza'–seasons
    (b) like a tree–union of matter and spirit–'leña vivificada'
    (c) Dependent on God for creation and preservation.
    (d) Man's life a burning, consuming flame fanned by God's
        breath (Spirit)–'el mismo vivir es ir muriendo'–Seneca.
    (e) His final end is ashes-Wisdom 2:2-3.
    (f) Man's forgetfulness, proved by etymology (*Enos*–hombre/
        olvido: *Adam*–terreno: *homo–humus*–hombre).

    Memento homo, &c

    What are the usual sources of man's pride?
    (a) Antecedents–Hebrews are proud of descent from Abraham.
    (b) World's opinion of present achievements–Cicero.
    (c) Confidence in a better future–no examples.

    Are they justified? No, because:
    (a) Adam, created from dust, is subject to the Cross of the
        world.

---

[1] *El perfecto predicador*, fo. 101.

Quia pulvis es
(b) Body without soul is 'una imagen hecha de barro'.
    Abraham, Job, and David, when speaking to God,
    confess this.
Et in puluerem reuerteris
(c) Everything returns to its source—Job 1:21; Ecclesiastes 5–7.
Conclusion of first part: Church teaches us humility.

Prothema II

    Conuertimini ad me, &c (Joel 2:12–13)
    (a) The reason why man will return to dust is sin (St. Thomas
        ST Ia–IIae, q. 73): Adam turned his back on God.
    (b) Church's remedy—turn face and heart back to God.
        Scindite corda vestra: 'Dios es amigo del corazón partido,
        pero no repartido' (Judgement of Solomon).

    In ieiunio, & flectu & planctu

    (a) Fasting a fitting remedy for gluttony.
    (b) Ashes and tears together become a 'lejía maravillosa para
        lavar las manchas'. Psalm 50 [51 in AV].
    (c) Ashes and holy water represent the body and tears of
        repentance.

Thema: **Cum ieiunatis nolite fieri, &c.** (Matthew 6:16)

    Recapitulation:

    (a) The Gospel teaches us to do good works.
    (b) To avoid hypocrisy—nothing so dangerous to dust as wind
        (*vanagloria*).
    (c) To set outselves in a high place, out of the wind. Christ/
        Monte (Isaiah 30:29).
    (d) To put our eyes in our Head (Christ) and not walk in dark-
        ness like the fool (Ecclesiastes 2:14).

    Exhortation: 'antes de salir de la Iglesia, ofrezcamos a Dios
    todos los ayunos y buenas obras desta Quaresma'. *Quam mihi &*
    vobis &c.

PERORATION

In this sermon three scriptural texts (a *thema* and two *prothemata*)
are taken as a continuous passage, providing an examination of man's
sin, its causes, consequences, and remedies. The *Introducción* provides
an analogy with the presentation of the theological history of mankind
in the *autos sacramentales*, particularly as regards its division into three
stages or epochs. Each proposition that arises from each of the three

'texts' is confirmed by subsidiary scriptural and philosophical 'authorities'. The use of proof by etymologies should also be noted: it occurs a second time on page 64, when the name *Adam* is broken up into its four letters, each the initial of a star (*Anathole, Disis, Arcto, Mesembria*). These stars in the firmament take the shape of a cross, as St. Cyprian notes in his treatise on Mounts Sina and Sion.[1]

(iv) *panegyrico*

This term is used in the 1630s, by Paravicino and others, both for a *sermón de un santo*, preached on his feast-day, and also for a funeral oration, embellished with scriptural references. It may be either a *sermón de un tema*, or a *paradoxon*, never a *homilía*.

EXAMPLE IV

Fray Pedro de Valderrama, '3° sermón de alabanzas. . .de San Nicolás de Toletino', *Teatro de las Religiones*, Seville, 1612, pp. 169–77.

Thema: **Erit tanquam lignum quod planctatum est, secus decursus aquarum, quot fructum suum dabit in tempore suo, et folium eius non defluet, sed omnia quaecunque faciet prosperabuntur,** Psalm 1:3.

Introduction	'En estos huertos cerrados de la Religiones. . . hay tanta variedad de árboles preciosos'—among them 'árboles del Sol', from which the temple of Apollo at Delphi was made.
Prothema 1	(i) *sol* en el pecho (St. Nicholas's insignia).[2] (ii) en quien resplandecieron los oráculos del *Sol de justicia*. [Malachi 4:2].
Thema	(i) *fruta* para sustento. (ii) *hojas* para medecina. (iii) *desengaño* de nuestra vida.
Salutation	For all this to be made available to us we need the intercession of Our Lady—*Ave Maria*.
Development of *thema*	*vestido/hojas*—outer garment of virtue and sanctity: (a) Man's first garments were fig-leaves: 'así

---

[1] An apocryphal work: *De duobus montibus* in *Corpus Scriptorum Ecclesiasticorum Latinorum*, III. iii. 104–19; ref. to p. 108.

[2] St. Nicholas of Tolentino is known by his star-spangled habit; see A. de Ledesma, *Conceptos espirituales* (Madrid, 1969), iii. 229, no. 103: 'pues rayos de gloria das/con tu vestido estrellado'.

por el vestido áspero y riguroso de hojas de higuera. . .la fruta que habían de llevar los pecadores había de ser penitencia'.

Prothema 2   (b) *omnis gloria eius ab intus. . .adstetit regina in vestitu deaurato circumdata varietate*, Psalm 44 [45].

    (i) *Herod* dressed in gold and sat in sun to appear divine [Acts 12:21-3].[1]

    (ii) Highpriest Aaron inspired respect in sinful Israel by gold armour [Leviticus 8].

    (iii) Alexander the Great went to war in gold and jewels to dazzle and dismay enemies.

'*San Nicolás* en lo exterior es un Cielo, y las hojas que lo adornan son un *Sol*.'

Development of   *fruta*—fruits of the Holy Spirit [Galatians 5:22
Thema   -3].

    (a) *caridad*—Nicholas's love for God and the favours shown to him / / St. Louis of France.

    (b) *paz*—reconciles both men and the elements. Bread = symbol of concord.

    (c) *paciencia*—'los diablos le persiguieron cruelmente, jugando con él a la pelota, dejándole cojo de una pierna de los golpes que le dieron'. Devils also shattered the light in his oratory, but the light of his patience, like that of Christ, shone through his 'wounds'.

    (d) *benignidad*—kind even to criminals. Saved thief from the gallows and raised 50 people from the dead.

(Return to Prothema   *sol* en pecho = fuente de vida.
1)

    (e) *castidad*—2 miracles:
        1. He found water by striking the ground with his *caña* (= flaqueza).
        2. So that he could keep his vow of abstinence from meat, even when ill, a partridge set before him by

---

[1] Reference to Herod Agrippa I who, according to Josephus, went to Caesarea in a silver robe and was hailed as a god (*Antiquities of the Jews*, XIX. viii. 2.).

his Superiors flew up from his
plate, 'vivo y vestido de pluma,
habiendo estado primero asado',
so that he should not eat 'un ave
tan sensual como es la Perdiz',
being himself 'un santo tan casto'.

Epilogue and Peroration   Let us sit beneath the shade of this mar-
vellous tree and eat of its copious fruit,
so that we shall love God (*caridad*), our
neighbour (*paz*), ourselves, and our lives
(*paciencia*), and finally, through *castidad*,
we shall see God—*gracia and gloria* [sol].

This sermon is at one and the same time a panegyric, in which
specific praise of the saint in question outweighs more universal con-
siderations arising from the scriptural text, and a *paradoxon*, in which
two (or, as in this case, three) texts are set in counterpoint. The image
of the saint as a fruitful tree, established by the *thema*, provides the
substantive framework of the sermon, but references to the sun, light,
and gold are constantly introduced through the *prothemata*. The link,
forged in the Introduction, is the identification of the Psalmist's tree
with the oracular groves of the sun-god Apollo ('árboles del sol') and
this is confirmed by the star-insignia adorning the habit of St. Nicholas
and the additional association with Christ in his manifestation as 'Sol
de Justicia'. The saint's habit then becomes the leafy covering of the
tree and thus binds together *thema* and both *prothemata*.

Fray Luis de Granada mentions another kind of 'mixed' sermon
which contains two main parts: a *declaración de la letra*, followed by
a single *argumento*, treated according to the *género suasorio o demonstrativo*.[1] He argues that this type of sermon combines the best qualities
of the *homilía*, which are variety and naturalness, and those of the
sermón de un tema, which are vehemence and persuasiveness. However, he ends his remarks on the superiority of this type of sermon over
all the others by reminding us that there must be accommodation of
style and rhetorical structure to both the subject-matter and the
audience concerned: 'pues no a todos los ingenios ni tampoco a todos
los asuntos vienen bien unas mismas cosas' (ibid.). A similar conclusion
is reached by Fray Pedro de Valderrama, but he qualifies it with a very
strict demand for appropriate ordering of the preacher's material
(*dispositio*):
Predicadores hay, que verdaderamente son acarreadores, y traen un

---

[1] *Retórica Eclesiástica*, p. 567.

sermón cargado de muchos lugares, comparaciones, humanidades, etc.
pero como va sin orden ni concierto, ni puesto a cordel, ni las cosas
en su lugar, sino amontonadas, no aprovechan ni las entienden los
oyentes, porque no son para ellos; y así salen lastimados, como quien
tropezó y cayó en medio de la calle y se vuelven sin haber entendido
nada, como si no hubieron pasado por allí. El buen predicador ha de
proceder con cuenta y asentar la doctrina a cordel, unas piedras en un
lugar, otras en otro, conforme viere que conviene al auditorio y sujetos
a quien predica.[1]

Thus we are brought back once more to the definition of a sermon as a
religious function rather than as a single rhetorical form. An appropriate
ordering of material, therefore, becomes a pragmatic rather than an
aesthetic necessity, and each sermon is shaped to its purpose.

---

[1] *Exercicios espirituales [Santos]* , i. 236. This passage occurs in a sermon
on the feast of St. Lucy, which reinforces our impression that many sermon
collections (particularly Valderrama's *Exercicios*) were printed primarily for the
use of preachers, as they so frequently contain precepts and advice to beginners
in the ministry.

III
THE PREACHER IN ACTION

Common to all the sermon schemes and rhetorical structures outlined above is a threefold movement, corresponding to the Ciceronian requirements of the orator—*ut probet, ut delectet, ut flectat*—and translating them into preacherly diction and action.[1] This threefold movement is supplied by three different parts of rhetoric: *inventio* (which furnishes arguments, proofs, and *sententiae*), *elocutio* (which suits style to subject, and 'adorns' the arguments with figures and tropes), and *actio* (which arouses fervour in the audience, driving the message home with a 'spirited' delivery). It is also reflected in the three tones,[2] which orchestrate the sermon with variations of pitch and tempo. Fray Diego de Estella observes that: 'El predicador ha de usar en sus sermones tres maneras de locuciones. La primera es enseñar: la segunda, reprender. Estas diversas maneras de locuciones tienen diversos tonos naturales. Y si el predicador no guarda consonancia, dará molestia a los oyentes.'[3] Similarly, Fray Cristóbal de Avendaño notes how the preacher chooses his tone according to the effect he intends to produce in his congregation: '. . .así los predicadores somos un órgano de varias voces: unas veces predicamos en familiar, para amonesta; ya levantamos en contralto, para aterrar; ya sonamos como trompeta para despertar; ya nos enternecemos para hacer llorar'.[4]

Thus all sermons, of whatever type, *at the moment of their delivery*

[1] Cicero, *Orator*, xxi. 69 (Loeb edn., p. 356). St. Augustine, *De doctrina christiana*, IV. xii, 27 (Migne, *PL*. xxxiv. 101): 'ut doceat, ut delectet, ut flectat'. Granada uses 'enseñar, deleitar et inclinar' in *Retórica Eclesiástica*, p. 595.

[2] Probably first used by Italian preachers; cf. F.A. Yates, *French Academies of the Sixteenth Century* (London, 1947), pp. 166–7. Still used in the Society of Jesus by novices as preaching practice as late as the 1960s. See G.M. Robinson, 'Jesuit use of "tonnes" in sermon delivery training in Spain and elsewhere' (appendix to unpublished PhD thesis). The three tones are subdivided and become twelve, illustrated by set passages.

[3] *Modo de predicar*, ii. 152. Also Terrones, *Instrucción*, p. 151: 'Al vulgo, a gritos y porrazos; al auditorio noble, con blandura de voz . . . a los reyes, casi en falsete'. See also Fray Agustín de Salucio, *Avisos para los predicadores del Santo Evangelio*, ed. A. Huerga (Barcelona, 1959), pp. 194–6.

[4] *Sermones del Adviento*, pp. 226–7. This corresponds to the oft-quoted Pauline instruction: *argue, obsecra, increpa* (2 Timothy 4:2). The *Ad Herennium*, III. xiii, 23 (Loeb edn., p. 196) specifies three tones of voice, to be selected by the orator in accordance with the rules of decorum, and these are *sermo, contentio*, and *amplificatio*. See also Cicero, *Orator*, xxi: 'Sed quot in officia oratoris tot sunt genera dicendi: subtile in probando, modicum in delectando, vehemens in flectendo' and Quintilian, *Institutio oratoria*, I. x. 24–8 (Loeb edn., i. 171–3) with emphasis on pitch.

fall roughly into three parts: first, to win the attention of the congregation by the appeal of novelty or erudition; secondly, to delight both senses and intellect with sureness of touch and suavity of diction; thirdly, to engage the emotions of the congregation, so that they are moved to embrace a new and better way of life in the future.[1] Juan de Guzmán in his *Primera parte de la Rhetorica* (Alcalá, 1589; fos. 64 seq.) had set out his scheme for the rhetorical oration or sermon as follows, each part with its intended effect on an audience:

exordio — deleyte
proposición — enseñe
confirmación — mueva
peroración — procure de alcanzar.

Avendaño, in his 'breve instrucción para Predicadores mozos, de las partes de que ha de constar un sermón',[2] also enumerates four parts (including an epilogue) which he compares to the four seasons of the year. However, since he considers that the epilogue has become so debased and repetitious as to be almost an anticlimax,[3] he concentrates on the first three seasons, leading up to Autumn, 'en que se cogen los frutos'.

The first part is clearly a kind of *prothema* and corresponds closely to Terrones' definition of the *introducción*.[4] According to Avendaño: La primera parte dél ha de ser de invierno helado; quiero decir, que empiezes con gravedad y señorío tu sermón (que ya se pasó el tiempo en que lobo empezaba aullando), introduciendo con un lugar breve de Escritura y procurando que el lugar sea paráfrasis del Evangelio—esto es una profecía que desde lejos dijo los misterios que él ahora canta, ajustándose el lugar con los misterios presentes. (sig. ¶5ᵛ)

The salient points which Terrones' and Avendaño's definitions have in common are brevity and 'far-fetchedness' ('cuanto más lejos, tanto mejor', Terrones). Avendaño continues by insisting that his apprentice preacher does not overload the first part of his sermon with too many 'authorities', although he may begin it with 'un artículo de Santo Tomás, o un reparo muy agudo de un Santo':[5] 'no has de traer muchas exposiones de Santos, como se traían en tiempo del Cid, sino pocas, y sus lugares no largos, sino cortados con la punta de una tijera, porque no tenga gran cabeza tu sermón, pues con eso todo lo demás vendrá a

[1] Murillo calls preaching a 'voz que engendre aguas para lavar las culpas; voz de trueno para causar terror; pero también ha de tener artificio, que deleite como la música de las vihuelas': *Discursos predicables [Quaresma]* , i. 784. A balance must be maintained between these functions.
[2] In the prologue to *Otro tomo de sermones de Santos*, sigs. ¶5ᵛ–¶7.
[3] See above, p. 47-8.
[4] *Instrucción*, pp. 100 and 108–9. See also above p. 46.
[5] Pagan authors are categorically excluded, 'pues sabemos que están en el infierno'. Avendaño takes an extreme line on this question; see below, p. 104.

ser enano, y por el consiguiente será monstruo'. The beginning of a
sermon must, therefore, whet the appetite by its novelty and by putting
forward 'lo especulativo' first, followed by 'lo moral'. It should not,
however, be so deliberately unusual and elaborate that it could be
compared to a theatrical *loa*, the prelude to an *auto sacramental* or
comedia.[1] The preacher, in this part of the sermon, must start modestly,
in a low-pitched voice, so that he can build up, in a controlled *cres-
cendo*, to a passionately eloquent climax in the third and final part.

In Avendaño's scheme the second phase of the sermon is Spring:
'en el cual empiezes a vestir de casto lenguaje lo que vas diciendo no
culto' (sig. ¶6). He explains that 'aquí es donde se han de ver las flores
de los conceptos', and that *conceptos* are 'el pasto del entendimiento',
to be used not as an end in themselves but as part of an assault on the
understanding and will of the hearer. They are designed to predispose
him to hear and accept 'lo moral' which is to follow. *Concepto* may be
read as a general term, referring to a whole range of 'figuras de palabras'
and 'figuras de sentencias', including proofs or 'confirmaciones'. It can
also be seen as an allusion to the particular phenomenon of the *concepto predicable*: an extravagantly witty metaphor turned to the
preacher's purpose, which we discuss below. Thus *conceptos* belong
both to the logical part of *inventio*, which seeks to convince through
argument and syllogism, and also to that other part of *inventio*, called
amplificatio, whose purpose is not only to persuade the understanding
but also to 'inducir también a la voluntad al amor, o al odio, o a cualquier afecto'.[2]

'Primavera' is, at the same time, the most clearly dogmatic part of
the sermon, in which scriptural or doctrinal points are proposed and
expounded, with the aid of *conceptos* or topics. These 'figures of
thought' are of two main kinds: the one seeks to intrigue the congregation by raising complexities inherent in the text or argument
(as Avendaño says elsewhere: 'quiero dificultar un poco'), while the
other serves to make plain ('allanar') or to illuminate ('aclarar') with
simile and example. In both cases it is not so much the information
conveyed that is at stake, as the way in which the congregation becomes
involved and closely concerned in the transmission of the information.
Fray Basilio Ponce de León sums up the preaching technique to be
used in this part of the sermon with reference to his own practice:
'Y no me contento con predicar lugares [de Escritura] sino razones
también, que, convencido el entendimiento, mucho está andado para

---

[1] Terrones, *Instrucción*; p. 109: 'no se hagan las entradas con palabras arti-
ficiosas y que lleven torrente, como los de comedia . . . que ha llegado el abuso a
términos, que en cierta provincia algunos religiosos mozos la llamaban a la introducción la loa'.
[2] Granada, *Retórica Eclesiástica*, p. 530.

que la voluntad se rinda ... Y si el libro puede enseñar y persuadir, no sé
porque se ha de mirar a lo uno sólo, y dejarse lo otro.'[1] This same part
of the sermon, according to Avendaño's scheme, is characterized by
'una acción extraordinaria de todas las demás, no descomposada, y una
voz con afecto singular a un tiempo con la misma acción, para obligar al
auditorio no bosteze, ni se canse, hasta que llegue lo moral, que si tu
eres buen Predicador con lo moral le tendrás suspenso' (sig. ¶6). It
would appear from this that the middle section of a sermon needs to be
decked out in all the most attractive robes of rhetoric to avoid forfeiting
the attention of the congregation.

The final phase of the sermon Avendaño compares to Summer, a
'Verano fogoso': '. . . aquí todo ha de ser fervor, todo moral, todo
desengaño, todo a las costumbres, unas veces hablando en familiar con
el auditorio, haciéndole muchos argumentos de razón, obligándole a
que deje el vicio, y entre por las sendas de la virtud'. The preacher may
here raise his voice 'en contra alto' and thunder at his congregation,
'ponderando el rigor de la cuenta, la eternidad sin fin, la intensión de las
penas, y lo que más es, la pena de daño, que consiste en no ver a Dios'
(sig. ¶6ᵛ). It is at this critical stage of the sermon that the preacher
'pulls out all the stops', and is careful to conclude swiftly, before there
is any decrease in volume or emotional intensity. Suárez de Figueroa
testifies, as a sermon-goer, to the efficacity of this approach: 'Certifico
no se halla cosa en que de mejor gana gaste el tiempo que en sermones,
por tener la acción y voz viva grande eficacia para regalar los oídos y
mover los corazones.'[2]

The sermon may, therefore, be considered not only as a conceptual
but also as a musical structure. The preacher must be able to perform
with the control of an actor, fitting words, tone, expression, and gesture
together appropriately, yet without seeming in the least theatrical.
Whereas certain variations of pitch and pace are essential in order to
differentiate the successive stages of the sermon, and to ensure that the
whole does not become a monotonous drone, the preacher's chief
preoccupation should be that 'vaya la voz la más al natural que pudiere
en lo que tratare'.[3] Provided that he speaks loudly enough to make himself heard at the back of the church, he should act as though he were
addressing a single individual in his congregation in a father-to-son manner,
or as if to 'dos or tres compañeros'.[4] Terrones makes the point succinctly:
'Los gritos no son oídos de los ausentes, y cansan a los presentes'.[5]

[1] *Discursos para todos los Evangelios de la Quaresma*, Prólogo al Lector,
sig. ¶4ᵛ.
[2] *El Passagero*, p. 157.
[3] Estella, *Modo de predicar*, ii. 152. Also Terrones, *Instrucción*, p. 146.
[4] Estella, *Modo de predicar*, ii. 157.
[5] *Instrucción*, p. 147.

Likewise he enjoins the preacher to moderate his mannerisms in the pulpit—'no han de ser vehementes ni descompuestas, hundiéndose en el púlpito, braceando apriessa'[1] —and to avoid what seem, to us, obvious absurdities: 'Si decimos que llegó a Christo un cojo a pedir salud cojeando, no ha de hacer el predicador meneos de cojo. Si se trae una comparación de los que se acuchillan, no se han de dar tajos, ni revés, ni abroquelarse en el púlpito' (p. 153). The preacher must not be guilty of 'acciones de representantes, sino representar grave y modestamente'. However, according to a contemporary English source, Thomas Wright in *The Passions of the Mind in General* (1604), 'in the substance of external action [i.e. delivery] for most part orators and stage players agree',[2] and for the Elizabethan actor, as for the orator, to 'saw the air' was to act badly. Moreover, both based their rhetorical gestures on an agreed system of natural and familiar motions of the head, hand, and body, such as those illustrated in John Bulwer's two treatises *Chirologia* and *Chironomia*, published together in 1644.[3] We may also note the very precise language of gesture and stance which can be 'read' in Renaissance iconography, and which adds a narrative, even dramatic, dimension to a picture.[4]

Thus a certain repertoire of gesture and mime is expected of the preacher, ranging from the wagging finger of admonition to the clasped hands and beatific expression of one anticipating ecstasy. Such gestures were parodied, but not in a wholly critical spirit, in a procession organized by the University of Seville in 1617, on the occasion of the *juramento* in favour of the Immaculate Conception.

Despertaban la risa cuatro Predicadores, representados por cuatro Religiones, cada uno en su mula, en un púlpito, aderezado con su paño de tela o brocado, hecho con ingeniosa invención. El primero era del Seráfico Padre San Francisco, y a su lado otro de la Compañía de Jesús, otro de San Benito, que representaba un Monje venerable, y a su lado otro de nuestra Señora del Carmen. Estos iban haciendo ademanes de que predicaban. . .braceaban hacia todas partes, daban palmadas, limiábanse el sudor, volvían a levantar el rostro y manos al Cielo, otras veces a la gente, que les prestaba atención viéndoles, como si los oyeran.[5]

Despite the grotesque exaggeration of this display, the preachers' antics have the desired effect, and the populace is spellbound. Quevedo, in

[1] Ibid., p. 152. Also Ximénez Patón, *El perfecto predicador*, fo. 76^V: 'Las acciones no sean gesticulosas, y que provoquen risa, ni los gritos descompuestos, ni fábulas fingidas'.
[2] Quoted by B.L. Joseph in *Elizabethan Acting* (2nd edn., Oxford, 1964), p.5.
[3] Ibid., p. 21.
[4] M. Baxandall, *Painting and Experience in Fifteenth Century Italy* (Oxford, 1972), pp. 61–6.
[5] *Relación de la fiesta que el colegio mayor de Santa María de Jesús, Universidad de la Ciudad de Sevilla, hizo* (Seville, 1617).

one of his tongue-in-cheek *premáticas* for 1600, has this plea to preachers whose mannerisms he finds annoying: 'A los predicadores pedimos que se enmienden en pedirnos atención, "vayan conmigo", dar palmadas, hablar con tonete.'[1]

Apart from being irritating for the congregation, too much gesticulation might also have unpleasant consequences for the preacher. Fray Jerónimo Gracián writes to the Carmelitas Descalzas of Consuegra in April 1603 that: 'desde mediada Quaresma que predicando con gran furia y rabia en un convento de monjas de Madrid, del bracear me quedo con dolor en el brazo derecho',[2] and Juan Bonifacio tells us of an earlier preacher (unnamed) who died ('reventó') three days after having shouted too loudly in a sermon.[3]

Some of our preachers affect to disdain any kind of theatrical behaviour in the pulpit, arguing that it panders to the lowest tastes and to cheap sensationalism. Fray Diego de la Vega speaks of the *vulgo* as 'necio y voltario, bestia de muchas cabezas y monstruo fierísimo, sin razón ni discurso. . .amigo de novedades, y de cosas que salgan de lo ordinario, y hagan ruido' and claims that it cannot distinguish the real from the counterfeit: 'Entrará el otro predicador predicando en una ciudad, con menos letras y menos partes que otros, y porque saca una calavera, una cruz, o otra novedad a este tono, arrebata el vulgo y la gente ye se la lleva tras sí.'[4] Juan Bonifacio confesses to mixed feelings about so-called *sermones de aparato*, which are sermons 'que podemos llamar extraordinarios, en que el predicador saca una cruz o una calavera, o hace alguna otra cosa extraordinaria', because distinguished precedents can be found among the Prophets for this kind of behaviour. However, in Passiontide and especially on Good Friday when the liturgy becomes particularly dramatic the preacher's theatricals should not be carried to excess.[5]

On the other hand, several preachers at this period show fewer scruples about playing on the credulousness of their congregation and staging spectacular surprises to move them to tears of compunction. Fray Pedro de Valderrama, whose 'talento de mover y sacar lágrimas' is much extolled by biographers, was responsible for a very elaborate show in Saragossa in the early 1600s. He first blacked out the church and concealed two torches, 'a modo de ciriales', behind the pulpit. Then he placed 'cantores famosos y músicos de Cornetas. . .a cuatro coros, en los ángulos de la Iglesia', to be brought into action at a given

[1] *Obras completas: Prosa*, ed. L. Astrana Marín (Madrid, 1932), p. 23.
[2] *Obras*, iii. carta lxix. 371. [3] Olmedo, *Juan Bonifacio*, p. 201.
[4] *Empleo y Exercicio Sancto*, i. 89–90.
[5] Olmedo, *Juan Bonifacio*, p. 204. The direct quotation is from Olmedo's paraphrase of *De sapiente fructuoso* (1589).

signal. These preparations made, 'con todo secreto', he was ready to preach his sermon on the Conversion of St. Mary Magdalene. Half-way through he suddenly broke off and, 'dando una voz con fuerza extra-ordinaria', said: 'Señor mío, Jesu Christo, parezca aquí vuestra divina Magestad, y vea este pueblo el estrago que con sus pecados han hecho en su Santa persona, tan digna de respecto y veneración.'[1] No sooner had he finished speaking than there suddenly appeared 'la santa imagen de Christo, puesto en Cruz, y a los lados las antorchas'. We have no record, unfortunately, of whether the 'heavenly choirs' and trumpeters intervened at this point, or what they played, but the effect on the congregation, taken by surprise, was truly dramatic. Shrieks, wails, and lamentations rent the air. The 'mujeres perdidas', who were en-couraged to hear Lenten sermons and who were standing at the foot of the pulpit, flung themselves around in an agony of remorse, tearing their hair and beating their breasts, 'como gente de veras convertida'. The biographer, full of admiration, comments that the confusion inside the church 'parecía una pintura o representación del juicio final'.

This cannot have been an isolated incident, even within Fray Pedro's own preaching career. Baltasar Gracián's 'stunt' of promising to read a letter from Hell in the pulpit (Valencia, 8 December 1644) is well known, but only recorded by his enemies,[2] and we have an example of a rather similar incident reported by P. Antonio Vieira in a sermon, as an illustration of how the preacher should *show* the truth of his message in his life. After a verbal account of the trial of Christ, in all its detail, the congregation remains unmoved, but then:

Corre-se, neste passo, uma cortina, aparece a imagem do *Ecce Homo*. Eis todos prostrados por terra, eis todos a bater nos peitos, eis as lágrimas, eis os gritos, eis os alaridos, eis as bofetadas. Que é isto? Que apareceu de novo nesta igreja? Tudo a que descobriu aquela cortina tinha já dito o pregador.[3]

Most preachers would carry a crucifix, however small, that could be produced in the pulpit, but both these reports refer to *pictures* of Christ Crucified, and pictures presented in a most dramatic manner. An extended passage by Fray Diego de la Vega seems to require a comparison to be made between two pictures, one of St. Mary Mag-dalene and the other of Christ, which might actually have been pre-sented to, rather than imagined by, the congregation.[4] Moreover,

---

[1] In F. de Luque Fajardo, *Razonamiento grave y devoto que hizo el padre M.F.P. de Valderrama*, fols. 8–9.

[2] M. Batllori and C. Peralta, *Baltasar Gracián*, pp. 92–3.

[3] *Sermão da sexagésima*, ed. J. de Almeida Lucas (Lisbon, [1964]), pp. 66–7.

[4] *Marial* (Alcalá, 1616), fo. 9. The passage contains numerous injunctions to 'Mirad': the eyes, cheeks, hair, and hands of both are contrasted in 'una des-proporción convertida en la mayor igualdad del mundo', which is the basis of a preacherly conceit (see below, pp. 78 ff.).

Fray Luis de Rebolledo refers to other 'visual aids' that a preacher might have at his disposal in almost any church: wall-paintings or stained glass. He says: 'Verdad es que por esas paredes hay infiernos pintados; pero mucho va de lo vivo a lo pintado.'[1]

On the other hand, a preacher could provoke a strong emotional response by purely rhetorical means, by *amplificatio*, which includes enumeration, hyperbole, and various kinds of comparison. The fires of Hell may be evoked in such a way as to make the listeners feel both hot and uncomfortable:

O ricos, que no tratáis sino de ser piadosos con vosotros mismos y crueles con los menesterosos, ¿quién pudiesse abrir una ventana por donde pudiessedes ver lo que pasa en el infierno, para que viessedes cómo tratan allí a los ricos que se regalan y no saben compadecerse del pobre? O si viessedes cómo cuezan sus carnes en aquellas calderas, y cómo las asan en aquellos fuegos inexorables, donde no hay demonio que no les dé su tizonada. . .Y sería muy acertado pensar cómo sufrirán el incendio del fuego eterno los que en verano no pueden sufrir el calor del sol, sino en sótanos regalados.[2]

This visualization of a dramatic scene, replete with vivid and concrete detail, is familiar to us from knowledge of sixteenth-century meditative practice[3] and it is not surprising to find preachers using such a technique to animate their hearers' flagging imaginations, engage their sympathetic attention, and control their emotional temperature. Fray Luis de Granada, in the section of the *Retórica Eclesiástica* which deals with *amplificatio* and *affectus*, gives the preacher the following advice: 'que cuando tratando de un asunto queremos conmover los ánimos de los oyentes, mostremos ser en su género de grandísima importancia, y si lo sufre su naturaleza propóngamosle *como patente a los ojos'.*[4] All the circumstances and detail of the scene are recreated and often antithesis is used to intensify the 'feeling' (emotion or sensation) which

[1] *Cien oraciones fúnebres*, fo. 326^V.
[2] Murillo, *Discursos predicables [Quaresma]* , i. 220. See also Ramón, *Conceptos*, p. 114: 'Poned los oídos en un agujero del Purgatorio y oiréis los clamores y voces que dan [las almas], puestas entre aquellas espantosas llamas de fuego.'
[3] Although, under the general term 'composition of place', this technique has been most frequently associated with St. Ignatius Loyola, it is common practice in mental prayer and use by Fray Luis de Granada, St. François de Sales, and countless others: see Louis Martz, *The Poetry of Meditation* (Yale Univ. Press, 1954; rev. edn., 1962), Ch. 1. Something similar is found in mnemonic methods from Aristotle to Giordano Bruno: see Yates, *The Art of Memory*. Memory 'places' were particularly used to produce unusual similitudes for the vices and virtues, together with more 'abstract' ideas and concepts.
[4] *Retórica Eclesiástica*, p. 547 (my italics). Under *De affectibus* the Jesuit theorist Cipriano Soares stresses the importance of *amplificatio*, especially definitions, similes, and examples, in arousing the emotions: see *De arte retorica* [1561] Salamanca, 1577), i. xxxii. 39. A more precise term, which subsumes the 'making present' quality of *imago, similitudo,* and *comparatio*, is *tractatio*.

the preacher hopes to produce. For example, Fray Diego de la Vega presents the incident of the shepherds arriving at the stable in Bethlehem in a way that not only makes the hearer/reader intimately concerned, as though present himself at the scene, but also uses the contrast between heavenly and earthly majesty to make a theological point. Christ's first palace on earth was:

un establillo lleno de basura; la tapicería de seda y oro, las telas de arañas que estaban colgando; la gente de guarda, la mula y el buey; el trono real, el pesebre; la investidura del Rey, unas mantillas pobres. Veen a la Virgen, que a veces le ponía en el pesebre, y del heno hacía mantillas con que abrigarle. Era al punto de la medianoche, el frío había entrado muy recio, el mundo estaba lleno de hielo y escarcha, el portal destechado, y sin abrigo ninguno. La Virgen venía desapercibida de las cosas necesarias al parto. No había allí fuego, no cama, no silla, no ropa, no tapices, no regalo ninguno. Tiembla de frío aquél de quien solía temblar el infierno; llora aquél que era el alegría de los Angeles, y de verle llorar, llora también la madre. Levántale del pesebre, y desnuda el pecho, y dásele para acallarle.[1]

The coldness of Earth at the time of Christ's Nativity is a traditional allegory, used in the *Vita Christi*, the exegetical work by Ludolph of Saxony which inspired much fifteenth-century Spanish narrative religious poetry.

In a similar way, Fray Tomás Ramón seeks to make his congregation aware of the full meaning of Christ as the Good Shepherd, and he does this by describing in some detail the hardships of a recognizably 'real' shepherd. Here we are moving towards simile and *comparación*.

¿Qué es ver un Pastor una noche invierno, puesto sobre un canto en pie, metido su capirote o galleruza, rebozado con su capote, al agua, al granizo, al ventisquero, a la nieve, toda la noche en vela mirando a las siete cabrillas, la vuelta del carro, y el movimiento de la bocina, el oído atento a si hacen ruido las ovejas, o si viene el lobo, o ladran los mastines? Y ¿ qué es verlo de día en medio del estío, estándose tostando al sol, y friéndose como en una sartén en medio de la dehesa, gustando de la música que allí suena, levantando su tenor con la cigarra, sin ningún refrigerio, y con trabajos muchos?[2]

'¿Qué es ver?' introduces the transposition to a figurative mode. The preacher is, in fact, recreating Christ's own activity as metaphor-maker and declarer of the sacred mysteries, and he does it with the special emphasis he feels is needed for *his* congregation, born in a particular place and time.[3] Many of the similes and comparisons used by preachers

---

[1] *Parayso*, i. 123–4.

[2] *Flores nuevas*, ii. 129–30.

[3] The concept of God can only be reached by a series of analogies and it has been the perennial task of preachers to expound the analogies found in the Bible and to invent their own: 'Symbol language is the mother-tongue of faith', G. Aulén, *The Drama and the Symbols* (in Swedish, 1965; London, 1970), p. viii.

in the Golden Age have a long history behind them and originate in
the Scriptures or in homilies of the Fathers, but to be effective they
must have an air of immediacy and freshness about them that carries
conviction. They are intended to 'make more real' the difficult propositions of the Faith, and, in so far as the aim of preaching has always
been to bring the Gospel to the people, such figures of speech are a
way of ensuring that the message reaches as many as possible and is
transmitted in terms of their own experience: 'porque con un buen
ejemplo se entiende fácilmente la doctrina, y sin él todo se pasa por
alto'.[1]

I shall now examine the three main 'figuras de sentencias' which are
used for sermon illustration at this period, and attempt to distinguish
between them, although all fall under the blanket term 'homiletic
simile', and it is *simile* that most frequently appears in the margin of
printed sermons to designate them.[2] They are, for the purposes of our
discussion, the *exemplum*, the *comparación*, and the *concepto predicable*. These are all terms with which the seventeenth-century preacher
would have been familiar, and occur much more commonly in the text
of the sermons themselves than do *parábola*, *metáfora*, or *allegoria*,
used by Timoneda, Valdivielso, and Lope to indicate similar rhetorical
figures in their religious drama.[3]

(i) *exemplum*

This term has a long history in the context of popular preaching (it
only appears in sermons to the laity) and has given rise to numerous
definitions, all of which concur that it is a short, illustrative narrative
or story.[4] Welter, whose book is still indispensable on the subject, calls
the *exemplum* 'un genre narratif spécial', although he then extends this
definition to include 'tout le fond narratif et descriptif du passé et du
présent', which makes it far less specific.[5] The three essential components

---

[1] Ximénez Patón, *El perfecto predicador*, fos. 28ᵛ–29. Similar remarks about
the 'non-intellectual' appeal of *comparaciones* and *exempla* in Granada, *Retórica
Eclesiástica*, p. 592.

[2] This draws attention to the role of the printed *sermonarios* as models for
inexperienced preachers and as collections of 'preachable material' in convenient
form.

[3] See J.–L. Flecniakoska, *La Formation de l' 'Auto' religieux en Espagne
avant Calderón* (Montpellier, 1961), pp. 396–9.

[4] See B. Smalley, *The Study of the Bible in the Middle Ages* (2nd edn.,
Oxford, 1952), pp. 256–7; Owst, *Preaching in Medieval England*, pp. 299–302
and *Literature and Pulpit in Medieval England* (Cambridge, 1933; rev. edn.,
Oxford, 1966), pp. 149–50; T.F. Crane, *The Exempla . . . of Jacques de Vitry*
(London, 1890), p. xviii and several other works by same author (see List of
Works Consulted).

[5] J.–Th. Welter, *L'Exemplum dans la littérature religieuse et didactique du
moyen âge* (Paris and Toulouse, 1927), pp. 2–3.

of the *exemplum*, according to Welter, are a story, a moral, and the application of the moral. This, however, is the pattern of any kind of extended homiletic simile or *comparación*, and therefore if we wish to distinguish an *exemplum* from other sermon illustrations we must pay most attention to its narrative form. *Exempla* used in sermons include animal fables and tales of Oriental origin, such as may be found in the *Libro de los Gatos*,[1] *El Conde Lucanor*, and innumerable other medieval miscellanies or jest-books. They also embrace myths, historical events, episodes in the lives of the saints,[2] or anecdotes from the preacher's own experience ('A funny thing happened to me...'). While our preachers frequently refer to notable historical figures—Julius Caesar,[3] Cato,[4] Cleopatra,[5] and Charles V[6]—their own personal reminiscences are less often found in print, and theorists express their disapproval of this type of sermon illustration.[7] Terrones del Caño tells the preacher that: 'nunca ha de tratar de primera persona...ni diga casos que a él le hayan acontecido, si no fuese alguno muy raro y de gran edificación.[8] The attribution to a known (named) source, whether truthful or not, was deemed to lend dignity to the anecdote, and Fray Luis de Granada defines an *exemplum* as 'una proposición de algún hecho o dicho pasado, con nombre de autor cierto' (*Retórica*, p. 592).

An interesting distinction has been suggested between the earliest *exempla*, of the first few Christian centuries, and those of the thirteenth and fourteenth centuries in Europe.[9] The former, although undoubtedly a story ('exemplum historia est'), presents man as a symbolic figure in the struggle between good and evil, and is expected to illustrate what Tubach calls a '*summa* of religious principles', with actions measurable against an absolute metaphysical norm. He chooses to apply the term

---

[1] Based on the *exempla* of the English priest, Odo of Cheriton (1160–1247).

[2] In the *Vitae Patrum, Acta Sanctorum*, and Voragine's *Legenda aurea*. Alfonso de Villegas, *Flos Sanctorum* (Toledo, ?1585) had many additions and editions in the early seventeenth century.

[3] Suetonius' account of the death of Caesar, in Murillo, *Discursos predicables [Quaresma]*, ii. 401. Death of Caesar (no source given), in Rebolledo, *Cien oraciones fúnebres*, fo. 179[V].

[4] Suicide of Cato, in Fonseca, *Discursos predicables* (1614), fo. 61.

[5] Cleopatra and the Asp (Devil), in Ponce de León, *Discursos para diferentes Evangelios*, ii, fo. 51. Also with Cato, as in n.[4]. Cleopatra dissolves pearl in vinegar, in D. de la Vega, *Empleo y Exercicio*, ii. 1.

[6] Charles V and thief, in Ponce de León *Discursos para diferentes Evangelios*, fo. 152. Charles at Cadiz, in Avendaño, *Sermones del Adviento*, p. 571. At siege of Tunis, in Ramón, *Flores nuevas*, ii. 206. Also anecdote about Catholic Kings, in Vega, *Marial*, fo. 30.

[7] Olmedo, *Juan Bonifacio*, p. 188.

[8] *Instrucción*, p. 80. He himself refers a personal example anonymously: see above, p. 49, note. The first person is used to good effect by Lanuza in a sermon: see below, p. 126.

[9] F.C. Tubach, '*Exempla* in the decline', *Traditio*, xviii (1962), 407–17.

proto-exemplum to this type of narrative.[1] The *exemplum* proper, characteristic of the preaching of Dominican and Franciscan friars in the middle to late Middle Ages, is a story in which man as an individual personality is judged in accord with practical human wisdom and the social values of his age. His adventures hold up a 'mirror' to human life, and one which performs a dual function of edification and entertainment.[2] The 'decline' Tubach speaks of seems to be connected with the point at which the *exemplum* began to be only extremely loosely connected to the body of the sermon and when it appeared to have been included solely to raise a smile or as light relief.[3]

Although by the early seventeenth century the vogue for *exempla* had somewhat abated, it is still possible to find large numbers of this type of illustration in Spanish sermons of the period, alongside the more sophisticated *concepto predicable*, the emblem or the quotation from a Classical poet. We have, for example, the dramatic tale of a husband's vengeance on his erring wife, recounted by Fray Diego de la Vega in vivid detail, which summons up a 'cuadro de costumbres' which would not be out of place in the honour theatre of Lope or Calderón.[4] Although in the margin we find *simile* and the reference to Hosea (Chs. 1–3), which reminds us that the unfaithful wife is a traditional symbol of the People of Israel or the Christian Church, the passage is presented in a way which assumes that preacher and congregation hold certain views on marital fidelity which are very much of their own time.[5] The *exemplum* is an appeal to a contemporary response and an attempt to rephrase a traditional symbol in a 'modern' idiom: *accommodation*, in other words. The visualization of the guilty wife, awaiting the return of her husband, has great dramatic effect:

Tiene un hombre una mujer, la cual ama tiernísimamente. Dále el vestido rico, el bordado, la gala, la joya; no ha venido el buen bocado a la plaza, la golosina, la fruta temprana, y lo demás, que luego no se lo trae; que anda con ella a que qui (sic) es boca, adivinándole los pensamientos para cumplírselos. Y si ésta no le guardase lealtad, sino que con otro le cometiese adulterio: *no es cosa llana que, en sabiéndolo, había*

---

[1] This corresponds to S. Kahrl's definition of the allegorical *exemplum* in 'Allegory in Practice: a study of narrative styles in medieval *exempla*', *Modern Philology* lxiii (1965–6), 107.

[2] Tubach, '*Exempla* in the decline', 415.

[3] See K. Whinnom, 'El origen de las comparaciones religiosas del Siglo de Oro: Mendoza, Montesino y Román', in *RFE* xlvi (1963), 283.

[4] *Empleo y Exercicio*, i. 34–5 (my italics).

[5] The same preacher elsewhere (*Marial*, fo. 136) presents a more 'balanced' view, which stigmatizes 'el traidor del marido, públicamente amancebado todo el año, y que tenga en su casa los hijos de la amiga', who normally escapes the judicial punishment for adultery. The Spanish legal code to this day (1976) applies different penalties for *adulterio* (by the wife) and *amancebamiento* (by the husband), and the treatment of an erring wife is the more severe.

72   THE PREACHER IN ACTION

de procurar de volver por su honra, y vengarse, y que así a él como a
ella ha de procurar de quitarles la vida, sin que basten intercessores ni
ruegos de nadie? Y decidme, si este hombre agraviado viniese a la media
noche a su casa, y la mujer la estuviese aguardando con la cena aderezada,
la mesa puesta, con sus cuchillos y servilletas, vasos de vidrio, con dos
candeleros, y en ellos dos candelas ardiendo, y en entrando en casa
diese un empellón que los estrellase por las paredes: decidme, la mujer,
por quien todo aquello se hace, que es la causa de su cólera y saña,
¿no tendría razón de temer y temblar? ¿quál os parece que estaría
entonces? ¿qué lágrimas derramaría? ¿qué pensamientos tan tristes
serían los suyos, como por momentos estaría aguardando la espada que
le ha de atravesar las entrañas?

'¿No es cosa llana...?' speaks directly to the assumptions and prejudices
of a known group, and forms a striking contrast with the spelling-out
of the analogy which follows. This analogy is founded on the juxtaposition of a *prothema* (*Non parcet in die vindictae*, Proverbs 6:34)
with the main text for the First Sunday of Advent ('Erunt signa in
Sole, et Luna, et stellis, et in terris praesura gentium,' Luke 21:25−7).
Together these texts furnish the Apocalyptic imagery of the *exemplum*,
which is expounded by the preacher in the next few lines of his sermon,
in order to leave his congregation in no doubt that he is really speaking
about the retributive justice of God and the overthrow of the firmament at the Second Coming, figured in the overturning of tables and
chairs: 'ese hermoso aparador de los cielos, darále un vaivén, que dará
con todo en el suelo'. Similarly, the Sun and Moon as 'esos dos candeleros' which will be extinguished on the Last Day, when Christ, the
Bridegroom, returns to judge His Bride, the Church, or the sinful
human soul.[1] This illustration, in fact, throws Tubach's definitions into
confusion because it fuses together the symbolic *summa* and the
realistic *speculum* to make an *exemplum* that is both allegorical and
topical: both general and particular.

There are a number of other quite lengthy narratives of a popular
character used by preachers in their sermons to both explain a point
and provide light relief. One of these is introduced, in the margin of
a sermon on Nuestra Señora del Carmen, as a 'Chiste que sucedió a un
caballero Italiano' and it is applied, ingeniously, to the 'stratagem' of
the Immaculate Conception, whereby the Devil was to be deceived
with a surprising similarity between Christ and his mother. The story
goes as follows:

[1] A husband's vengeance on an unfaithful wife, 'cuando le volteó la honra en
los cuernos del toro', is also given by Fray Cristóbal de Avendaño to illustrate
the story of Moses and the Golden Calf. However, not only does he acknowledge
his debt to St. John Chrysostom for the illustration, but also makes the point
that Christ does not kill the guilty lovers but pardons 'mayores agravios', *Evangelios
de la Quaresma* (Madrid, 1622), i, fo. 33ᵛ.

Es de advertir que un Caballero tenía dos criados confidentes, ambos
dormían en su antecámara, en una cama. Una noche el uno, cuando le
parecía que dormía su amo, se levantó con sumo silencio, y pasando
por el mismo aposento iba, o a solicitarle una hija, o a abrirle un
escritorio. Sintióle el amo y levantóse al punto. El criado, que sintió
su señor se había levantado, volvióse a la cama muy aprisa, por no ser
conocido. El dueño no dio voces por no deshonrarse, o deshonrar sus
hijas. Parecióle que había de ser dificultoso el conocer al delincuente,
porque estaban los dos criados juntos en una cama. ¿Qué sería bueno
que hiciese para conocer al desleal? Puso la mano sobre el corazón
de ambos, pareciéndole que él que de los dos diese saltos, inquieto,
aquél era el culpado. Por aquí conoció al ladrón, o desleal; tomó unas
tijeras y, para conocerle a la mañana, cortóle un poquito del cabello que
le caía sobre la frente. El mozo, viéndose perdido, y que había de ser
conocido a la mañana de su señor, hizo para deslumbrar al compañero
que dormía con él, cortóle otro tanto cabello de la misma parte, sin que
lo sintiese. Venida la manana llamó el señor sus criados, que le diesen
de vestir. Cuidadosamente levantó los ojos para ver el culpado, y como
les viese ambos cortado el cabello, quedóse perplejo, sin saberse deter-
minar. Y así se escapó el mozo del delito que había cometido, y su
señor siempre vivió admirado de la sagacidad con que se libró, y perplejo cuál de los dos fuese el delincuente.[1]

There is quite a similarity between this story and the shorter *patrañas*
of Juan de Timoneda, and as the source is probably Italian it may well
have come from a collection of *novelle*, or a jest-book based on such
novelle.[2] It belongs to that type of *exemplum* in which the moral
point has to be supplied by the preacher's explanation, since it is not
self-evident in the tale itself and there is no sign of any allegorical sense
which would place it immediately within a religious context, nor of the
personification of theological concepts. The conceptual link with the
rather difficult dogma it illustrates is one that we must take on trust
from the preacher himself.

In the same category is the 'gracioso picón', or joke played by
Jupiter on jealous Juno, retold by Fray Pedro de Valderrama to make a
point about the repentance of Mary Magdalene. A wooden dummy is
placed beside that well-known philanderer Jupiter when he goes out to
drive in his carriage and Juno, deceived by the rich robes and jewels in
which it is decked, takes it for another of her husband's 'ninfas', and
attacks it both verbally and physically—'con lo cual descubrió que no
era mujer de carne, sino de palo, que ni con los ojos veía, ni con la
boca hablaba, ni tenía sentimiento'. The Christian interpretation

---

[1] Avendaño, *Marial*, fos. 209–209ᵛ.
[2] There is a very similar story, although with more explicitly sexual over-
tones, in Boccaccio's *Decameron*, Day iii, novel 2. See also D.P. Rotunda, *Motif-
Index of the Italian Novella in Prose* (Bloomington, 1942), K 415, for other
possible sources and variants.

follows immediately afterwards: 'O Fariseo loco y zeloso indiscreto, ¿pensáis que Christo está con una ramera, y que hace gran tiro a la santidad y oficio de Profeta? Pues llegaos y veréis: esta mujer no es la que vos pensáis, es otra muy diferente. No es ya mujer de carne sino de palo.'[1] This interpretation seems a little far-fetched, as there seems a wide divide between Jupiter's rather cruel joke, to conceal previous misdemeanours, and the effects of Christ's saving grace on the penitent Magdalene. The preacher himself appears to see the *exemplum* as 'gracioso' rather than illuminating.

The marginal note *Eleemosynae exemplum* introduces an even longer narrative passage, or 'sabroso cuento', as the preacher Fray Diego de la Vega describes it, based on a tale from a book entitled *Prado espiritual.*[2] The moral is: 'El que hace limosna al pobre, a Dios le da a logro',[3] and the plot is a familiar one in many mythologies: a treasure 'lost' turns up in the belly of a fish, served at the table of the rightful owner, just in the nick of time.[4] This tale is too long to be quoted in full,[5] but it deals with a Christian woman and her unbelieving husband, both very poor, who decide to invest their money at interest. The wife claims that 'el Dios de los Christianos' offers the best rate, and shows her husband his agents ('oficiales'), who are in fact the beggars at the church door. They therefore 'invest' their money by distributing it. After a while the husband grows impatient and hungry:

Comenzó a afligirse, y dijo a la mujer: "Señora, no veo que vuestro Dios nos paga el interés de nuestro dinero; lo que veo es que morimos de hambre, y sin remedio ninguno." Dijo ella: "Yo sé cierto que no dejará de cumplir su palabra. Id al lugar donde dimos el dinero, que yo fío que nos remediará." Fue a la puerta de la Iglesia y, andando mirando por una parte y por otra, no veía sino pobres que estaban allí pidiendo limosna. Pero a caso mirando bien, hallóse en el suelo una de aquellas monedas que él había repartido.

With this coin, on his wife's advice, he buys a fish, and inside it is a precious stone. 'Llevóla el marido al contraste si la quería comprar, y conociendo su valor, dijo que le daría por ella cinco escudos. Pensaba que le burlaba, rióse. El fue pujando hasta que vino a dar por ella trescientos ducados, o numismas, que era la moneda de entonces.' Delighted with this outcome, and with the munificence of 'el Dios

[1]   *Exercicios espirituales [Santos]*, ii. 637.
[2]   This is the Byzantine collection of *exempla, Pratum spirituale*, attributed to St. Sophronius and translated into Spanish by J.B. Santoro (Saragossa, 1578). The *exemplum* itself ('flores de la limosna') is the first in the book: fos. 1–3^V.
[3]   Proverbs, 10:17. No. lxx (p. 464) of the *Libro de Enxemplos*, ed. Gayangos (Madrid, 1884) is headed *Elemosynam facere non est perdere sed ad usuram dare*, but the story is different.
[4]   S. Thompson, *Motif-Index of Folk-Literature* i (Copenhagen, 1955), no. B 5482.
[5]   *Empleo y Exercicio*, ii. 44–5.

de los Christianos', the good man is converted and baptized. The efficacity of alms-giving is hereby illustrated, and its 'returns' are seen to be both financial and spiritual. No adaptation or application is required to make this a Christian illustration, even if the moral is not a very subtle one. The characters in it are personalities in their own right, not symbols of something else, and the purpose of the *exemplum* is that of agreeable consolidation of a known truth, rather than the exposition of something new and difficult, in terms 'accommodated' to the congregation.

(ii) *comparación*

A *comparación*, on the other hand, is fundamentally an expository form, a making visible of invisible realities, and it traditionally chooses the familiar, the natural, and the commonplace to 'figure forth' a mystery. The definition given by Martín Alonso, in his *Enciclopedia del Idioma*, is 'un símil retórico, que consiste en comparar expresamente una cosa con otra, para dar idea viva y eficaz de una de ellas'.[1] The more concrete, visible term of the comparison illuminates the abstract, invisible one, and therefore we find this device used frequently in religious writings, particularly those dealing with the Mystical Way. Sta Teresa de Avila, in her writings about mental prayer, which are addressed to nuns and novices, and especially in *Las Moradas*, is very fond of using *comparaciones*. She accompanies and explains the central image of the castle with subsidiary *comparaciones*, or similes: a spring, a silk-worm, a king's antechamber, wax candles, light entering a room through two windows, and many others.[2] Juan Pérez de Moya, in his *Comparaciones o símiles para los vicios y virtudes* (Alcalá, 1584), which is directed at preachers, uses predominantly country imagery of bees, vines, and weather conditions, all with a moral or devotional second term. The *comparación* is usually much more compact than the *exemplum*, and its illustrative character is never lost sight of. The spelling-out of the *correspondencia* between the two terms of the comparison is never overlooked, as sometimes in the case of *exempla*, but becomes the climax and *raison d'être* of the illustration. No special premium is set on originality, unlike the *concepto predicable*, and the terms of the comparison are unambiguously set out, and yet the result

---

[1]   3 vols., Madrid, 1958, i. 1145b. Covarrubias, *Tesoro*, ed M. de. Riquer (Barcelona, 1943) does not have a separate entry for *comparación*, except as a grammatical term; *comparar* is 'hazer cotejo de una cosa con otra en razón de semejanza' (p. 343). The *Diccionario de Autoridades* [1756] facsimile edition (Madrid, 1963) has the words 'parangón', 'cotejo', and 'similitud' in its definition of *comparación*.

[2]   *Obras completas de Santa Teresa de Jesús*, ed. Efrén de la Madre de Dios and Otger Steggink (Madrid, 1967), 2nd edn. *BAC*, pp. 367–8, 385–6, 395–6, 415, 441.

is a form of wit; according to Baltasar Gracián: 'Siempre el hallar correspondencia entre los correlatos es fundamento de toda sutileza'.[1] It is usually introduced by 'así como...así...,' or clearly labelled *simile* or *comparación* in the margin, and it seeks to convince by its own natural appositeness, rather than by the arguments of logic or by the props of scriptural cross-reference. Most of Pérez de Moya's *comparaciones* are short and pithy. For example:

Así como al vino aunque le echemos la mayor parte de agua le llamamos siempre vino: así conviene que la hacienda y la casa se nombre del marido, aunque la mujer haya traído lo más. (fo. 12^V)

Como la lluvia hace salir los gusanos y producir la hierba, así la palabra de Dios hace salir los pecados del alma y producir buenos propósitos. (fo. 31).

Fray Cristóbal de Fonseca employs two *comparaciones* for a 'corazón duro' which are so short as to seem only blueprints for a later development: 'como el yunque que con los golpes queda más duro' and 'como el arena, que con el agua se tapia'.[2] The image does not need to be original, and Fray Cristóbal de Avendaño borrows a short *comparación* from Tertullian which presents the soul as a sword in the scabbard of the body: 'Supuesto, pecador, que tu alma es la espada de tu cuerpo, ¿por qué no la das cada día un tiento a ver si está en disposición de salir? que hay almas que se toman de orín, y se pegan a la vaina del cuerpo.'[3] This particular *comparación* is carefully prepared for by the preacher and he spells out its implications so that the point about the dangers of rust is not lost.

A *comparación* can be considerably longer, but not really any more complex, since all the author can do is examine, turn by turn, the qualities of the things compared, so as to find more and more illuminating similarities or striking contrasts. 'Likeness' is valued above 'unlikeness', although, in accordance with the rules of *amplificatio*, a certain amount of dissimilarity may be introduced to add piquancy.[4] However, it is the relationship between the terms of the comparison which is all-important, as may be seen in Fray Tomás Ramón's description of the taking of the Dominican habit by a young novice, which

---

[1]   *Agudeza y arte de ingenio*, ed. A. del Hoyo (Madrid, 1960), discurso vi, p. 265. This treatise (in its expanded form of 1648) underlines the importance of witty figures of speech with quotations from preachers as well as poets of sixteenth- and seventeenth-century Spain.

[2]   *Discursos predicables [Quaresma]*, fo. 2^V.

[3]   *Sermones de Quaresma*, i. fo. 4^V.

[4]   'Estas son las agradables proporciones e improporciones del discurso, concordancia y disonancia del concepto; fundamento y raíz de casi toda la agudeza ... porque, o comienza o acaba en esta armonía de los objetos correlatos', *Agudeza*, v. 259.

he compares to a snake sloughing off its old skin after the winter hibernation. The passage occurs in the *salutación* of the sermon and follows quite closely the ritual of the ceremony, underlining its spiritual significance. Incidentally, it seems to echo a passage in Virgil, favourite poet of many Spanish preachers at this period:

¿Qué cosa es ver una serpiente en medio del invierno, desamparada del fuerte y picante calor del Sol, hecha un ovillo, con mil ñudosas vueltas, retraída y escondida en su oscura cueva, y espantosa caverna? Si acaso sale alguna vez fuera, verla héis encogida y débil, y que con su cuerpo flaco va arrastrando por el suelo: y que la que antes era tan espantable a todos, ahora viene a ser juguete de los mismos niños. Pero cuando después por el ordinario curso de los planetas se torna el Sol a nosotros, y con sus calurosos rayos hace retoñecer los árboles, refuerza los brutos, purifica los aires, fertiliza la tierra y renueva el mundo. Luego la serpiente rebulle y se alegra, cobra su antigua fuerza y vigor, sale de su caverna, deja en su puerta el vestido roto y viejo, vistiéndose de otro plateado, refriégase por las piedras y puesta contra el Sol, se pule y afeita, y como que levantada contra el Cielo, le amenaza con tres lenguas, y dando temerosos silbos, soberbios y orgullosos, hace temer a los pasajeros, y atemoriza los corazones, aunque sean de los más fuertes hombres y caballeros armados.[1]

We wait, in some suspense, for the 'application' of this image and are then presented with the figure of the postulant, who has robed himself in his shining white habit and now prostrates himself before his new Superiors, begging admission to the Order. The preacher addresses him thus:

¿Qué tal estabades, N., en esa caverna oscura y lóbrega del mundo, enroscado y envuelto en vuestros gustos y placeres, sin luz del Cielo, ni gracia de Dios, flaco, desmedrado, débil y sin rastro de virtud, por estar alejado de vos, N., el divino Sol de Justicia, no tocaros con sus rayos poderosos? Qualquier tentacioncilla del demonio os sujetaba y rendía, y hacía burla de vos, pero volvió el Sol sus ojos, apareció y derribó los rayos de su santa vocación sobre vos, y apenas os hubo tocado cuando os hizo salir de la caverna en que estabades. Desnudaros de la piel antigua y viejo Adán, vestiros de aqueste plateado hábito. N. derribaros por el suelo, y como que fregaros por esas piedras, meteros por estos agujeros sagrados y cavernas divinas de la Religión con tanto brío y denuedo que a los más cuellierguidos del mundo ponéis espanto.

---

[1] *Aeneid*, ii. 469–75.

    Vestibulum ante ipsum primoque in limine Pyrrhus
    exsultat telis et luce coruscus aëna;
    qualis ubi in lucem coluber mala gramina pastus,
    frigida sub terra tumidum quem bruma tegebat,
    nunc, positis novus exuviis nitidusque iuventa,
    lubrica convolvit sublato pectore terga
    arduus ad solem, et linguis micat ore trisulcis.

See also Ch. IV below, esp. pp. 103–6.

Y con un silbo que dáis, pidiendo misericordia de Dios y destos Padres que en su caverna os reciben, hacéis estremecer a los demonios del infierno y les quitáis las fuerzas.

The second description is managed in such a way as to send the reader or hearer constantly back to the first, so that the composite picture of the snake/friar gives us a fresh and ingenious insight into the meaning of Sin and Grace.[1] The illuminating power of Christ, the 'Sol de Justicia', has brought about this metamorphosis. The novice has become a new man, having cast off the old Adam, just as the snake has sloughed off its skin, and both are stronger and more formidable in consequence. This is a transformation, as Ramón comments later, 'más maravillosa que la que hizo Moysen, convirtiendo la piedra en agua; el agua en sangre; la vara en culebra; y que las que cuentan las fábulas mentirosas de los poetas, que convertían la Ninfa en árbol, el cazador en ciervo, y las otras doncellas en estrellas' (p. 354). At the same time it is a *comparación* based on a commonplace yet amazing event in nature: this in itself may tell us something about Grace.

Several extended *comparaciones*, together with *exempla*, are used to satirical effect in sermons of this period. In a later chapter we shall see the pool at Bethseda being used in this way (below, p. 134).

(iii) *concepto predicable*

The dividing line between a *comparación* and a *concepto predicable* is analogous to that which separates a *simile* and a *conceit* in poetry: it is neither entirely clear nor completely impermeable. Both types of figure seek to establish a convincing degree of parity between two poles (in Gracián's words, 'dos cognoscibles extremos'), be they ideas, concrete images, or a mixture of the two, and to yoke them together in such a way that the appositeness of their conjunction prevails over any initial impression of dissimilarity.[2] With a *comparación* or *simile* likeness wins an easy victory over unlikeness, and the consonance between the two terms is evident to the eye, whereas the *conceit* requires a forging of conceptual links between apparent contraries, or an 'acto del entendimiento' which at times looks like a leap of faith. Quite often this takes the form of a fallacious syllogism, in which the starting premiss is true only in one respect, and manifestly false in every other. Sometimes the link is one of sound rather than sense, as in the pun or spoonerism. The *concepto predicable*, like its secular counterpart,

---

[1] It is perhaps interesting that the World and the Order are both compared to caves, and how the sun can be present *inside* a cave might exercise the minds of the Dominican Fathers, if the image is to be pursued to its logical conclusion.

[2] See T.E. May, 'Gracián's idea of the *concepto*', *HR* xviii (1950), 15–41 and essays by Joseph A. Mazzeo in *Renaissance and Seventeenth Century Studies* (New York, 1964).

cultivates strangeness, surprise, 'far-fetchedness'. It is, to quote one of
its earliest apologists Emanuele Tesauro, 'un Argomento ingenoso,
inaspettato, e populare'.[1] The 'Argomento' is, in fact, the justification
of an image, and this justification may be based on the slenderest
evidence.[2] The American critic Joel Spingarn describes the technique
thus: 'the symbol selected seemed so far from the purpose that the
mind received a shock of surprise when the preacher appeared to
justify its selection by argument and by sacred authority'.[3] The appeal
of a *concepto predicable* is akin to the suspense aroused by a witty
conundrum to be solved, together with a pleasurable sense of com-
plicity between author and reader once the solution is reached: in both
cases difficulty heightens the pleasure.[4] (See also below, p. 106, for
similarity with emblematic technique.)

When we light on choice examples of *conceptismo* in sermons by
contemporaries of Góngora and Quevedo it is tempting to speculate
about 'cross-fertilization' or, some would say, 'contamination' of the
sacred by the profane and vice versa.[5] There are, of course, many
parallels and similarities to be found, as I suggest in my chapter on the
preacher as moralist, but it would be as well to remember that our
preachers have their own tradition of allegory and 'metaphysical' wit
stretching back to St. Augustine and beyond, and this tradition includes
the use of puns, riddles, and conceits. The Jesuit critic Walter J. Ong,
commenting on the wordplay in St. Thomas Aquinas's hymn *Pange
Lingua* ('verbum caro panem vero / verbo carnem efficit'), points
out that:

This is the same theology of the Word which has proved a limitless
source of conceits, not only for medieval theologians but also for
patristic rhetoricians [St. Augustine], for 17th century Englishmen
[Lancelot Andrewes] and for the contemporary poets interested in
the metaphysical tradition [T.S. Eliot].[6]

There seems to be a tendency in the Christian religion, as in many
others, to couch revelation in mysterious language, which somehow
preserves it intact and untouchable: 'the whole of the Christian economy

[1] *Il Cannocchiale Aristotelico* [1654] (5th edn., Turin, 1670), p. 65.
[2] Lucien-Paul Thomas speaks of 'des rapprochements sentimentaux ou
poétiques d'habitude plus apparents que fondés' and stresses the fact that scholastic
proofs and reputable erudition are discarded in favour of striking but unsubstantial
'connections' between passages of Sacred Scripture in *Le Lyrisme et la préciosité
cultistes en Espagne*, xviii, p. 60.
[3] *Critical Essays of the Seventeenth Century*, i (Oxford, 1908), xxxvii–xlviii.
[4] Fonseca, *Discursos predicables para la Quaresma*, fo. 2ᵛ.
[5] See Introduction. Paravicino and Góngora have been linked in this way by
countless critics and there is, moreover, the contemporary topos of 'Los gustos
están estragados' to confirm this approach.
[6] 'Wit and Mystery: a revaluation in medieval Latin hymnody', *Sp* xxii
(1947), 317.

80 THE PREACHER IN ACTION

is dominated by what may be called, with all reverence, super-paradox' (p. 339). S.L. Bethell has gone further and claims that direct influences have been at work: 'I believe that it will sometime become clear that the whole European movement of "baroque wit" or "metaphysical conceit" originated in a Jesuit revival of patristic wit—first appearing in Spanish sermons of the sixteenth century, I imagine.'[1] It is difficult to know how one might prove or disprove this theory conclusively, even by studies of readership, based on availability of editions and evidence of their presence in the library of individual authors.[2] The chief similarity is one of function: the expression of religious truths in vivid everyday terms by means of an extended metaphor or conceit.

The *concepto predicable* has been called a Spanish invention by Italian critics, but it is one which quickly spread to Italy where *concetti napolitani* became synonymous with *il gusto spagnuolo*, which in turn came to mean 'bad taste'.[3] The Franciscan historian Zawart, however, claims that the Italian Franciscan Franceso Panigarola (1594) was the originator of *concetti e pensieri predicabili*,[4] and that the traffic was in the opposite direction. There is certainly no doubt that the sermons and preaching theory of Panigarola were well known in Spain by the beginning of the seventeenth century.[5] Other critics, including A. Soria Ortega, claim that the Valencian preacher Fray Melchor Fuster, whose career spans 1640 and 1660, was the first to use this type of illustration and that the first instance occurs about 1645.[6] Until Fuster's *Varii conceptus morales praedicabiles* (Lyons, 1672), however, the only sermon collection to include *concepto* in its title is Fray Tomás Ramón's *Conceptos extravagantes y peregrinos*

[1] 'Gracián, Tesauro and the Nature of Metaphysical Wit', *Northern Miscellany of Literary Criticism* i (1953), 21. This echoes the point made by E. R. Curtius, *European Literature and the Latin Middle Ages* (New York, 1953), p. 282.

[2] Both E.M. Wilson ('Spanish and English Religious Poetry of the Seventeenth Century', *Journal of Ecclesiastical History* ix (1958), 38–53) and P.E. Russell ('English Seventeenth-Century Interpretations of Spanish Literature', *Atlante* i (1953), 65–77) have produced evidence of the widespread diffusion of Spanish religious literature, both in the original and in translation, in seventeenth-century England. However, E.M. Simpson, in 'Donne's Spanish Authors', *MLR* xliii (1948), 182–5, suggests that Donne owes more to French and Italian sources than to Spanish.

[3] Tesauro, in his *Cannocchiale Aristotelico*, ed. cit., p. 503, and Croce, *I predicatori italiani del Seicento e el gusto spagnuolo*.

[4] 'A History of Franciscan preaching and of Franciscan preachers', in *The Franciscan Educational Conference*, ix (New York and Washington, 1927), 389. Also mentioned by Tesauro, *Cannocchiale Aristotelico*, p. 502.

[5] Suárez de Figueroa's *El Passagero*, alivio iv, contains almost word for word Panigarola's treatise *Il Predicatore* (Pub. Venice, 1609).

[6] *Fray Manuel de Guerra y Ribera y la oratoria sagrada*, pp. 12–15 and 45. He simultaneously confesses that 'Este es recurso de los oradores de todos los tiempos'..

(Barcelona, 1619).[1] *Conceptos espirituales* and *conceptos divinos* are used in the early 1600s to designate collections of *a lo divino* poetry, and it would appear that these were not altogether divorced from the pulpit when we read Fray Juan de Arenas's introduction to Alonso de Ledesma's *Conceptos espirituales* (1602) in which he recommends the book as an essential companion to preachers who want to be up to date:

que le leyeren, no passen de paso, sino que reparen y tanteen todos sus dichos, y *hallarán muchos conceptos no predicados*, como los que ahora se escriben, *sino para predicar*, que cayendo en hombres versados en Escritura los sabrán acompañar con tales lugares y tan a propósito que sean muy agradables al auditorio, con cuyos sainetes abrirán la gana tan perdida y apetito prostrado a las cosas Divinas, engolosinándole con las curiosidades que el libro a cada paso tiene.[2]

This passage steers an uncertain course between applauding Ledesma's book, rendering it 'respectable' in the eyes of potential critics, and paying lip-service to the topic of disdain for the 'gusto depravado' of the age which makes such books necessary in the first place. It is difficult to glimpse a 'historical reality' behind such a wealth of commonplaces, but this is in itself symptomatic of an age in which the legitimacy of wit and rhetorical subtleties was being debated by both churchmen and humanists. The debate ranged much more widely than just whether the *concepto predicable* could be used in the pulpit, as we shall see in the following chapter, but Fray Diego de la Vega, who is adamantly opposed to 'retruécanos y consonantes y sus juguetes' in sermons, speaks for a large number of preachers when he says:

Lástima bien para llorar es ver que se les pasen horas enteras algunos predicadores, sin tomar una reprehensión en su boca, ni proponer un concepto moral al auditorio, sino que todo se vaya en flores y agudezas de ingenio, en palabrillas y razones compuestas y afeitadas, más que une novia, con lo cual ahogan el espíritu y le quitan a la palabra de Dios la fuerza y virtud que había de tener.[3]

He is, however, speaking of the *mis*use of certain rhetorical devices and, although seventeenth-century theorists claim to disapprove of the use of *similiter cadens* and other forms of *agudeza verbal* in any kind of prose, let alone sermons,[4] we still find quite conservative preachers using 'retruécanos', 'consonantes', and 'equívocos' in their sermons.

[1] Fray Francisco de Ontiveros entitles a collection of commonplaces *Conceptos predicables, políticos y morales* (Madrid, 1674) but these are not sermons.

[2] Prólogo al Lector, sig. ¶¶^{v} (my italics).

[3] *Discursos predicables [Quaresma]* (Alcalá, 1622), Prólogo al Lector.

[4] Ximénez Patón, *Eloquencia española*, fos. 59^v–60 speaks of Fray Antonio de Guevara's excessive use of the former: 'tanto que se pone a peligro de hacer coplas'. Guevara was, of course, a *Predicador del Rey* and *similiter cadens* a classical technique of oratory, akin to internal rhyme.

For example, Fray Cristóbal de Avendaño opens his sermon for the Feast of St. John the Evangelist with a *prothema* which derives from a pun on *Pia mater* and *niñas de los ojos*, set in the 'mystical body' of the Church.[1] Fray Basilio Ponce de León, in one of his Lenten sermons, gives us this sobering definition of man as microcosm: 'era un cero, que un cero es una O, y una esfera es una O; lo mismo es ser cero y ser esfera. Bien que sea uno mayor el otro, una O más grande que otra o, pero en fin todos son de una misma naturaleza y linaje.'[2] Both these preachers, in their use of word-play, could be criticized by contemporaries as either 'old-fashioned' (harking back to Guevara and the quibbling scholastics), or as 'new-fangled' and 'contaminated' by *conceptista* poetry. These judgements bear out the theories of continuity advanced by Curtius, Ong, and Bethell (see above, p. 79), but suggest an equally constant opposition down the centuries between 'plain' and 'flowery' preaching. Pulpit wit and secular wit are similar enough to stand side by side in Gracián's *Agudeza y arte de ingenio*, since both depend on the discovery of the 'universal analogy' of Christianized neo-Platonism and, as Gareth Davies has pointed out, the seventeenth-century conceit 'was the product of a period in which the perception of order and relatedness was regarded as a fundamental principle of art'.[3]

When we look at the two examples that follow we shall see that a *comparación* becomes a *concepto* when a good deal remains 'between the lines' and the reader, or hearer, is challenged to pick up the conceptual clue by himself, with a sense of discovery. The first example appears, initially, to be little more than a homely simile drawn from a country remedy:

como la madre, cuando la avispa pica al niño acude aprisa con lodo, que viene a resolver el hinchazón: así picándonos las avispas del infierno y escupiendo en nuestro pecho el veneno de su arrogancia, acude nuestra madre la Iglesia con ceniza.[4]

In the second term of the simile we are still not very much further away from the 'visualization' of the first. We have the verb 'picar', the devils are called 'avispas del infierno', pride is a 'veneno', and the Church is, familiarly, our 'Mother'. The metaphors are retained to form a continuity rather than a contrast between the first two terms, and the conceptual link between the *lodo* of the first, with its connotations

---

[1]   *Otro tomo de sermones de Santos*, fo. 1. St. John and Christ are the 'apples' of the Virgin's eyes and that 'tender mother' is the membrane of the eye. There is an implicit reference to John 19. 26–7.

[2]   *Discursos para los Evangelios de la Quaresma*, i. 111.

[3]   *A poet at court: Antonio Hurtado de Mendoza (1586–1644)*, (Oxford, 1971), p. 66.

[4]   Fonseca, *Discursos predicables [Quaresma]*, fo. 2ᵛ.

of human clay, and the *ceniza* of the second, directly related to the ritual of Ash Wednesday, is the suppressed word *polvo* [*quia pulvis eris*], reminding us of our earthly origins and our final end. This conceptual link is the crux of the *comparación*, which is otherwise merely picturesque, and turns it into a *concepto predicable* with an implicit allusion to the sermon's *thema*.

The second example is more obviously biblical and is in fact the 'solution' of a paradoxical image in the Song of Songs (8:10—'I am a wall and my breasts like towers'), which corresponds to Tesauro's definition of the *concetto predicabile* as 'un Argutia simbolica, leggiermente acevvata dell' ingegno Divino: leggiadramente svelata dall' ingegno humano; e rifermata con l'autorità di alcun Sacro Scrittore'.[1] The conceit, framed as a *duda*, is found in Fray Diego Murillo:

¿Hay cosa más blanda, más muelle, más delicada, que los pechos de una mujer? Y por el contrario, ¿hay cosa más dura, más fuerte, y más terrible, que una torre, hecho para defensa de una ciudad? Pues en esto está el misterio de la comparación: Porque en eso se da a entender que la suavidad y blandura de los castísimos pechos de la Vírgen es el muro y torre de nuestra defensa: porque si ella no fuera tan suave, y tan blanda, y sino tuviera un pecho tan tierno, y tan lleno de caridad, no hubiera tomado a su cargo el defendernos con tantas veras.[2]

Here the preacher does not invent the conceit—it is given to him readymade in the poetry of Solomon—but he does make it into a *concepto predicable* by expounding the *ponderación* which brings the contraries together and links them in fruitful concord. He does, however, make as much as possible of the 'difficulty' in reconciling extremes of softness and hardness, and only when the softness becomes 'softness of heart' can he resolve the contradiction.[3] Here again he anticipates Tesauro: 'Et principalmente se ostentando nella lettera un senso contradicente di primo incontro, e difficile a strigare' (ibid.).

In both these examples the paradox springs from the text—indeed from the letter of the text—and in this respect is not 'far-fetched' in the sense that a *concepto* which equates the penitent Magdalene to a book censored by the Inquisition might seem to be. The breaking of the flask of precious ointment is compared to the destruction of the wooden moulds ('moldes') into which the type is cast, 'porque fueron instrumentos de una cosa tan mala'.[4] The same author, in a sermon

---

[1]   *Il Cannocchiale Aristotelico*, ed. cit., p. 65.

[2]   *Vida y excelencias de la Madre de Dios*, i. 410.

[3]   This is what Gracián calls a *transposición ingeniosa* (discurso xvii), in which there is an 'extremada transmutación en dar diferente causa al efecto de lo que parecía'. See *Agudeza y arte de ingenio*, p. 313.

[4]   Murillo, *Discursos predicables [Quaresma]* , ii. 127. A similar conceit, more elaboratedly expounded, may be found in Fray Manuel Guerra y Ribera's sermon on the Magdalene in M. Herrero García, *Sermonario clásico*, pp. 176–9.

on the conversion of St. Paul, picks another unlikely image, that of an octopus, whose special properties he swiftly outlines for the benefit of his congregation. The *concepto predicable* takes shape before their eyes:

No sé si habéis oído, señores, lo que escriben autores graves, y se experimenta cada día, de un pescado que se llama pulpo. Tiene unas colas muy grandes que le sirven como de piernas, y si acaso llega a donde está alguna peña, de tal suerte se afierra que no hay poder desasirlo della, sin hacerlo pedazos. Sólo un remedio han hallado los pescadores para poderlo desasir, que es echar aceite por todas partes, para que vaya calando entre él y la peña, y con esto lo desafierran y lo apartan con mucha facilidad.

Considerad, pues, aquí dos pulpos y dos peñas: el uno pulpo es el demonio, que estaba agarrado de Pablo, más duro que no parecía posible poderle desaferrar. *Tenebit praedam* (dice Dios por Isaias, aunque a otro propósito) *et amplexabitur, et non erit qui eruat* [Isaiah 5:29]. Y cuádrale maravillosamente al demonio, que cuando hace presa en un alma, de tal suerte la afierra que nadie se la puede quitar sino sólo Dios. Tal tenía al alma de Pablo, y así con razón le comparamos al Pulpo, y decimos que Pablo era, por la dureza, peña a que estaba agarrado.

El otro pulpo era el mismo Pablo, y la peña era Christo, a la cual estaba aferrado estrechísimamente, no por amor, sino por aborrecimiento, con determinación de no dejarle un momento hasta hacerle pedazos. ¿Qué remedio, pues, para que el demonio deje a Pablo, y Pablo deje al ruín afecto con que está asido de Christo? El remedio es que se tome aceite y se derrame sobre esos pulpos. Y ese oficio hace el santísimo Nombre de Jesús, a quien la Esposa llama aceite derramado, diciendo: *Oleum effusum nomen tuum* [Song of Songs 1:2].[1]

This example fits the category of *agudeza* which Gracián calls the *careo condicional* (discurso xv), and it is a *careo fingido* in which the same characteristics are attributed, turn by turn, to the Devil and St. Paul (the two *pulpos*), and to St. Paul and Christ (the two *peñas*). What is more, Gracián adds that 'Los sacros suelen fundarse en algún lugar de la Sagrada Escritura, aunque después el picante del concepto se ayude de las demás circunstancias',[2] and in this example Murillo clinches his conceit by a second text, having established and characteristic or 'condition' of the Devil by the first. Both texts are, however, very clearly taken out of context and are hardly sufficient authority to guarantee the credit-worthiness of the conceit.[3]

[1] *Discursos predicables [Adviento]*, p. 612.

[2] *Agudeza y arte de ingenio*, p. 306.

[3] At this point it might be as well to observe how frequently the properties, real or legendary, of animals, real or fabulous, are used in the fabrication of *conceptos predicables*. The Younger Pliny is the source of many of these, and they range from how a hedgehog gives birth (Murillo, *Discursos predicables [Quaresma]*, ii. 142–3) to whether the tears of the deer are sweet or salty (B. Ponce de León). The elephant, crocodile, ostrich, and unicorn are most frequently used to exemplify some vice or virtue, as in the medieval bestiaries.

Scripture both offers mysteries to the reader and helps to unfold them. For example, Fray Tomás Ramón takes a paradox from Matthew 23:37, and explains the apparently discordant elements by reference to events related elsewhere in the Scriptures. The first *reparo*, and axis of the conceit, is that: 'mientras el Señor vivió en la tierra con los hombres, hizo oficio de gallina; mas empero cuando se subió a los Cielos, hízole de Aguila, animando a sus polluelos a que le siguieran en su vuelo'.[1] In addition to the disproportion between the humble, timorous hen[2] and the soaring, majestic eagle, there is the equally astonishing difference between the eggs and the hen—a difference which the preacher exploits in order to illustrate the wonder of the Incarnation:

Quien ve el huevo antes que la gallina lo empolle y fomente, no imaginara que del puede salir una gallina, porque ¿qué tiene que ver la blandura, la blancura y la delgadez de la cáscara del huevo con lo demás que en sí encierra, con la gallina que tiene carne, plumas y huesos?. . . Pero si la gallina lo mete en bajo sus alas, foméntalo, dale calor, comunícale su sustancia, y en pocos días sale un polluelo vestido de plumas, armado de carne y huesos, y tan otro de lo que antes era, que en nada se asemeja al huevo. Así se hubo Dios con el hombre.

Once God has assumed human nature, that nature is transformed: 'aquesta carne flaca, desmedrada del hombre, unida al Verbo Eterno, quedará endiosada, fuerte y valerosa'. Were it not for the personal intervention and protection of Christ, who 'anduvo treinta y tres años como que empollándolo, comunicándolo su divina sustancia y dotrina, con el calor de su divina gracia' and, like the pelican, 'desentrañándose y desangrándose por darle vida', mankind would never come anywhere near even the most elementary conception of God, let alone be empowered to ascend and sit at the right hand of the Father Almighty. The final touch to the conceit (perhaps the last straw) is provided by reference to the stable of the Nativity as a 'gallinero' and the manger where Christ was laid as 'algún nido, forjado de heno y pajas', in which God and Man became one, so that 'ya el hombre es semejante a Dios'. This conceit is a powerful one which encapsulates the whole of Christ's ministry on earth, and its transforming effect on men, from the Nativity to the Ascension.

Bird imagery is the basis of another *concepto predicable*, this time by Fray Cristóbal de Avendaño, and here the scriptural scaffolding is both more complex and more clearly visible. The preacher is explaining

---

[1] *Vergel de plantas divinas* (Barcelona, 1629), fos. 72ᵛ–73. The eagle image comes from Deuteronomy 32. 11.

[2] Paravicino, who uses a similar conceit, remarks: 'Pero estraña es la metáfora de la gallina, que así han de amar los mayores: pues no parece de gallinas saber amar con riesgos': *Oraciones Póstumas divinas y humanas* (Madrid, 1766), p. 52. Preached 1624.

why the disciple John was particularly beloved by Christ and he turns
to falconry for his parallel:

Costumbre es de los cazadores de volatería, cuando ven la garza, ir
soltando pájaros para que la den alcance: un halcón, un girafalte, un
sacre, un neblí, y el que de todos éstos la derriba, por fueros estab-
lecidos en la caza, aquél se cena en el corazón de la garza. Desearon los
Padres antiguos, y todo el género humano, que se diese alcance a
aquella garza hermosa voladora de la divinidad de Dios. Soltaron un
halcón de un Ieremías, para que la diese alcance. Volvió diciendo,
á, á, á, Domine nescio loqui [Jeremiah 50:6]. Vuele otro pájaro: vuela
Esayas, y tampoco la da alcance, porque volvió diciendo, *generationem
eius, quis enarrabit?* [Isaiah 53:8]. ¿Quién podrá hablar de la Encar-
nación del Verbo, ni dar alcance a tan encumbrado misterio? Vuele
S.Pablo, éste que voló más alto, cuando le levantaron hasta el tercer
cielo. Cuando pensamos que había dado alcance a la garza, baja, diciendo
que los misterios que había visto, *neque oculus vidit, neque auris
audivit, neque in cor hominis ascendit* [1 Corinthians 2:9]. Vuele
Juan, que es más ligero que todos. Vuela este ligerosísimo sacre, da
alcance a la garza, cuando dijo: *In principio erat verbum* [John 1:1].
Derriba la garza cuando dijo: *Verbum caro factum est* [John 1:14]. El
verbo se hizo hombre. Pues él fue el que apeó el misterio, y derribó la
caza, justo es que se cene en el corazón de Christo, que por derecho se
le debe.[1]

This is manifestly an allegory of successive attempts to formulate in
words the mysteries of the Godhead and the hypostatic union, built
up on appropriate cross-references from Prophets and Apostles. The
image of hawking a heron has precedents in *cancionero* poetry and is,
of course, divinized by San Juan de la Cruz in his 'Tras de un amoroso
lance'.[2] The identification of each of the prophets mentioned with a
different type of hawk may originate in a homily by one of the Fathers,
or it may merely be prompted by the birdlike sounds of Jeremiah's
stammerings. There is, also, the traditional identification of St. John
the Evangelist with the eagle of the Apocalypse (Revelation 4:7) as a
possible starting-point.

The *conceptos* we have seen so far are legitimately *predicables* in
so far as they derive from a scriptural image, however far-fetched,
and are directed at elucidating a difficult point of doctrine. There are,
however, numerous examples of witty writing and florid metaphor
where the main intention seems to be to impress rather than to edify.
In a sermon on St. Mary Magdalene, Fray Basilio Ponce de León plays
upon the discernment of tears, true and false, and speaks first of Dido's
'costoso desengaño' which followed the discovery of Aeneas' crocodile
tears: '¿a quién no engañaran unos ojos hechos fuentes, hechos ríos,

---

[1] *Otro tomo de Santos*, fos. 5–5v.
[2] See D. Alonso, *Poesía española* (4th edn., Madrid, 1962), pp. 242–4.

hechos mares?' He develops the image more fully in the following passage, and in so doing treats the original hyperbole with a certain amount of humour: the *mares* and *ríos* have become *manantiales* and *encañadas*, which have slightly less currency as metaphors.

También hay arte de llorar como de escribir y bien hablar. Cuántas veces en una despedida se ven lágrimas que bañan la cara, y no son más que lágrimas de cumplimiento. En fin hay unas lágrimas verdaderas, otras falsas, unas de bien sentir, otras de buen parecer, unas naturales, otras de artificio, unas manantiales, otras encañadas, sacadas con la bomba del finjimiento, unas lágrimas vivas, otras muertas; unos lloran por naturaleza, otros de cartilla; hay unas lágrimas frías y otras calientes.[1]

This approaches the technique used by Quevedo in his sketch of the 'hablador plenario' in *La Hora de Todos*, although it is rather more stilted and mechanical.[2] Ponce de León, in the same sermon, finds another *concepto* in the *ojos-ríos-mares* sequence, only this time there is rather more of a theological undercurrent: 'La Magdalena arroja ríos de lágrimas por los ojos que salen del mar de su pecho. Mantiénese de sus lágrimas, que le acompañaron toda su vida, y es volverlas al mar, para que vuelvan a salir por los ojos, y nunca faltan lágrimas en abundancia (p. 287).' The preacher then reminds us that the sea is a traditional symbol of baptism and the tears of penance mark the sacrament of reconciliation and renewal of life. The passage is, however, made ponderous by being weighed down with numerous snippets of natural history from Plutarch and St. Ambrose and what began as a flash of *ingenio* is glossed and explained until it becomes merely tedious. This is, perhaps, the inevitable consequence of the traditional method of compiling *conceptos* or *reparos* in the form of concordances or miscellanies, like the medieval anthologies of similes which were still very popular in the Spanish Golden Age,[3] to judge by the fortunes of such works as Pedro Mexia's *Silva de varia lección* (Seville, 1540).[4] This contains heterogeneous 'facts' with authorized moral interpretations from which many preachers freely borrow, acknowledging only the name of the first begetter of the 'conceit', be he St. Bernard, Pliny, or Aristotle, and suppressing all reference to the intermediary. At the end of almost every printed sermon collection we find not only a concordance of the scriptural passages quoted in the sermons but also an index of topics or *conceptos*, arranged in like manner. For example, under the heading 'Cosas notables', Fray Pedro de Valderrama

---

[1] *Discursos para diferentes Evangelios*, ii. 286.
[2] In *Los Sueños* (Clásicos Castellanos, 1917), ii. 89.
[3] Used by the Dominican order in the reform of preaching: see Yates, *The Art of Memory*, pp. 95–6.
[4] It went into 33 Spanish-language editions as well as appearing in French, Italian, and English translations.

lists a number of *reparos* from which future preachers can draw and
elaborate conceits.[1] Under *Cabeza* he arranges the following:

En la del buey se engendran las abejas (p. 601)

En la del León muerto también (p. 347)

Una cabeza de buey está estampada en las entrañas de las abejas
(p. 517)

En la del hombre hay unas letras hebreas escritas (p. 605)

In the same way he can group together all references to horses, hawks,
or handsaws that he has found in his reading, be it of the Psalms,
Plutarch, or some 'modern' writer that he would rather not name.
The result is a rich mine of metals for the forger of conceits, and a
tribute to a mode of thought which is not new to the sixteenth or
seventeenth centuries, but has a respectable origin in the Fathers and
the Schoolmen.

We should not, therefore, be too surprised to find preachers in-
venting, or repeating, witty conceits in their sermons. The transference
of typological conceits first used in exegesis to *secular* poetry and
prose is potentially more surprising, although even this is apparent in
Spain as early as the fifteenth century in the paradoxes of troubadour
love poetry or the *cancionero* tradition. When the two traditions run
together, in the first quarter of the seventeenth century, even the most
conservative preachers find themselves overtaken by fashion and,
maybe despite themselves, parallel the *conceptista* school. The more
self-conscious among them, however, like Paravicino, positively profit
from the confluence and coincidence of preacherly and poetic styles.

---

[1] *Teatro de las Religiones* (Seville, 1612). Preachers advertise their works as
containing 'copiosísimas tablas' of this shredded information, which make the
sermonarios doubly useful to the apprentice preacher.

IV
ELOQUENCE SACRED AND PROFANE

In his introduction to Terrones del Caño's *Instrucción de predicadores*, Félix G. Olmedo outlines the history of preaching theory in Spain in terms of the quest for a specifically Christian eloquence.[1] Although *artes praedicandi* of the period reiterate many of the rhetorical precepts formulated by Aristotle, Cicero, and Quintilian, Spanish preachers of the later sixteenth century seem concerned to evolve rules which apply exclusively to the business of preaching, removed from any taint of worldliness.[2] Fray Luis de Granada, whose monumental and fundamentally Ciceronian *Eclesiasticae Rhetoricae* was first published in Lisbon in 1576,[3] admits in his preface that he has been forced to compromise, and whereas most of his illustrations are taken from the homilies of the Fathers, especially St. Cyprian, and from the Prophets, the rules and figures they accompany are no different from those to be found in any classical textbook of rhetoric. Drawing attention to this point, he writes:

Y querría yo, que no sólo los ejemplos, mas también los preceptos mismos, perteneciessen únicamente a la facultad de predicar, y que nada hubiese en esta obra, que tuviesse resabios de las letras de los gentiles. Pero habiéndose sacado toda esta doctrina de las fuentes de los retóricos que la inventaron para tratar las causas judiciales, no fue posible dejar de mezclar en esta obra preceptos y ejemplos de decir, que parecían menos pertenecientes a nuestro propósito. . .Y quizá habrá otro que se halle más desocupado, y según es fácil añadir algo a lo inventado, acabe más llana y felizmente esta obra que nosotros empezamos, y nos haga la misma retórica, por decirlo así, de todo

---

[1] pp. lvi–clvi. This survey enumerates, and in many cases summarizes, most of the important preaching treatises published by Spaniards between 1564 (Villavicencio) and 1617 (Terrones), although precise bibliographical identification is often lacking. See also M. Herrero García's 'Ensayo' to the *Sermonario clásico* and P. Sagüés Azcona's foreword to Estella's *Modo de predicar*, i. 226–67, which also contains some inaccuracies of dating. A. Martí, in an inconclusive article in *Hispanic Review* (1970), attempts to link sacred and profane oratory through the rise of *conceptismo*, although in doing so he falls into the trap of confusing theory and practice.

[2] This was no new attempt. H. Caplan discusses the medieval background to this question and particularly William of Auvergne's *Rhetorica divina* ('a rhetoric of prayer') in 'Classical Rhetoric and the Medieval Theory of Preaching', *Classical Philology*, xxviii (1933), 73–96.

[3] *Ecclesiasticae Rhetoricae* (Olysippone, Antonius Riberius, 1576). There were four more editions outside Spain before 1600 and the work was first translated into Spanish in 1770, and published at Barcelona in 1772. This edition forms the basis of the *BAE* edition from which I quote.

punto cristiana.[1]

Similarly, at the beginning of the first book he praises Jerónimo Vidas,[2] 'famoso poeta', for having 'llevado al río Jordan a las musas, de haberlas limpiado de la suciedad que se las pegó de los poetas gentiles, y de haberlas consagrado a la historia evangélica y a la alabanza de los santos'.[3] This approach to 'divinización', or 'spoiling the Egyptians', is in line with the attitude of St. Augustine, whose image of the two keys of eloquence, sacred and profane, is frequently invoked by Spanish preachers of the Golden Age.[4]

A thoroughgoing sacred rhetoric, as opposed to a preacher's handbook, appears not to have been published in Spain during the sixteenth century, although Olmedo is prepared to hail the Dominican Fray Juan de Segovia, whose *De praedicatione evangelica* appeared at Alcalá in 1573, as the author of the first 'verdadera retórica eclesiástica'.[5] What Segovia chiefly contributes is a change of emphasis: he lays great stress on the teaching ministry of the preacher, which must be founded on a thorough knowledge of the Scriptures and on his own spiritual development. Discussion of the graces, natural and infused, which equip the preacher for his role also plays an important part in the earlier works on preaching published by Villavicencio[6] and García Matamoros,[7] however, which detracts from Segovia's reputation as an innovator. The Gospel ('Evangélico') nature of the preacher's ministry receives great attention in these treatises, and is a reflection, if not a cause, of the 'reform' of preaching introduced by Fray Dionisio Vázquez, Sto. Tomás de Villanueva, San Juan de Avila, San Francisco Borja, Fray Alonso de Orozco, and Fray Luis de Granada himself, in the middle decades of the sixteenth century.[8] This reform

[1] *Retórica Eclesiástica, BAE* iii. 491.

[2] Marco Girolamo Vida (1485–1566), the Italian author of a religious epic poem *La Cristiade* (1527): see *Enciclopedia Italiana*, xxxv. 313. Reputed to have 'shocked' Erasmus.

[3] Op. cit. 494a.

[4] *De doctrina christiana*, IV. xi. 26; Migne, *PL* xxxiv. 100: 'Quid enim prodest clavis aurea, si aperire quod volumus non potest? Aut quid obest lignea, si hoc potest?' See Ponce de León, *Discursos para diferentes Evangelios de Quaresma*, p. 175. For the Augustinian conception of Christian eloquence, favoured by Catholic preachers at this period, see D. Quinn, 'Donne's Christian eloquence', *Journal of English Literary History* xxvii (1960), 276–82.

[5] Terrones, *Instrucción*, pp. lxvi–lxxii.

[6] Fray Lorenzo de Villavicencio, *De formandis sacris concionibus seu de interpretatione Scripturarum populari libri iv* (Cologne, 1575), Earliest identified edition (in three books) is Antwerp, 1564 (Bodl. 8° V 23 Th). Villavicencio has adopted to Catholic requirements the work of the same title by Hyperius of Marburg (Andreas Gerardus), published at Dortmund in 1555.

[7] *De arte concionandi* (Alcalá, 1570) (BL.011805 de. 15).

[8] D. Gutiérrez, *Los agustinos desde el protestantismo hasta la restauración católica* (Rome, 1971), pp. 219–21. 'Evangelismo' is here treated as an international phenomenon c. 1530.

had strong scriptural tendencies and a reliance on inner spirituality, as Robert Ricard has observed:

Uno de los rasgos esenciales de esta reforma, aparte de la purificación interior que exige del mismo predicador, es su carácter escriturario, y más especialmente evangélico y paulino: el orador sagrado debe ante todo predicar a 'Jesús crucificado' inspirándose muy particularmente en San Juan y en San Pablo.[1]

The Pauline precept most often invoked is twofold: 'And my speech and my preaching was not with enticing words of man's wisdom, but in demonstration of the Spirit and of power (*non in persuasibilibus humanae sapientiae verbis, sed in ostensione Spiritus et virtutis*)' (1 Corinthians 2:4).[2] 'Spirit' and 'power', or 'virtue', each taken in a special sense, are the two indispensable requisities for an effective Gospel preacher and are translated by Fray Tomás Ramón as 'la virtud y eficacia del espíritu interior'.[3] We also find the Jesuit General Vitelleschi recommending to the Aragonese Provincial in 1621 that 'nuestros predicadores prediquen con más espíritu' rather than 'con ostentación de su lengua e ingenio'.[4]

In Segovia's treatise, and in those which followed it, a distinction is drawn between two kinds of spirit, the natural and the supernatural. His translator, P. Félix G. Olmedo, expresses it thus: 'El natural es el don de persuadir que tienen algunas personas. El sobrenatural lo da Dios a los predicadores evangélicos para que, oyéndolos, se conviertan los pecadores, y los justos se justifiquen cada vez más.'[5] Spirit is what moves the hearers, and in more than one sense it moves, or moves in, the speaker.[6] On the first level it means 'nacer con cierta gracia en la acción, con cierta energia en la pronunciación, con cierto énfasi en el habla',[7] equivalent to the natural 'brío' with which some men are born, and which can neither be learned nor simulated.[8] It characterizes the 'natural' orator who, despite his lack of book-learning, is infallibly persuasive: '. . .algunos hay que con menos caudal de sabiduría, tienen más abundancia de espíritu y de otras gracias: los quales aprovechándose de trabajos ajenos, sustentan su familia más lucida y más gruesa

---

[1] *Estudios de la literatura religiosa española*, p. 215.
[2] Also frequently quoted is 1 Corinthians 1.17–24.
[3] *Flores nuevas*, i. 241.
[4] M. Batllori and C. Peralta, *Baltasar Gracián*, pp. 157–8.
[5] In the fourth book of his treatise. Quoted in introduction to *Instrucción de predicadores*, p. lxvii.
[6] Horace in his *Ars Poetica*, vv. 101–3, says that the orator who wishes to move his audience must be moved himself, and this is taken up by Estella, *Modo de predicar*, ii. 6 and Terrones, *Instrucción*, pp. 22–5.
[7] Suárez de Figueroa, *El Passagero*, p. 196 (Alivio iv refers specifically to the preacher).
[8] Joseph, *Elizabethan Acting*, p. 7.

que los que con más ciencia tienen menos espíritu para comunicarla.'[1]
At the same time it appears to be synonymous with that part of rhetoric
known as *actio*, which is concerned with the delivery of the oration.
Ximénez Patón speaks of 'la acción, que por otro nombre se llama
espíritu, o brío, o pronunciación',[2] as does Juan Huarte: 'Esta gracia es
tan importante en los predicadores, que con sólo ella, sin tener invención
ni disposición, de cosas de poco momento y vulgares hacen un sermón
que espantan al auditorio, por tener acción, que en otro nombre se
llama espíritu o pronunciación.'[3]

Theologically speaking, it is a divine (infused) grace, *gratia gratis
data*, bestowed on a man so that he may co-operate in the justification
of another.[4] The Holy Spirit uses the preacher as an instrument,
endowing him with effective speech, *gratia sermonis* by which he can
teach, please (i.e. attract to God's Word), and move his hearers (to love
what the Word signifies). Aquinas shows in this exposition how
Christianity has annexed the Ciceronian *sic dicere ut doceat, ut delectet,
ut flectat*, by way of St. Augustine (*De doctrina christiana*, IV. xii,
27) and that the right use of 'human' rhetoric was no new problem to
the Church in the seventeenth century.

The final perfection of the work of sanctification within the souls
of the hearers belongs to the Spirit, and not to the preacher (*Summa
Theologica*, 1–2, q. 177, i), which brings us back to St. Paul: 'So
then, neither is he that planteth anything, neither he that watereth;
but God that giveth the increase' (1 Corinthians 3:7).[5] This prompts
an anti-rhetorical stance by many preachers of all periods, but particularly Fray Luis de Granada, who says, in a letter to Fray Bartolomé
de Carranza:

Bien podrá ser muy gran letrado y predicar; pero convertir ánimas ni
es de letras ni es de ciencias, ni es parte para esto sino sólo Dios; que él
no obra este efecto por letrados hinchados, sino por siervos humildes,
como si hubiese Dios de tomar de retóricos para ministros de un tan
gran ministerio como su Evangelio y su espíritu.[6]

A preacher's most sure recourse, according to this line of thought, was
not to a handbook of rhetoric or a *florilegium* of fables and pre-digested

---

[1] Murillo, *Discursos predicables [Adviento]* , sig. *7–7[V], where he justifies
the publication of sermons in the vernacular.

[2] *El perfecto predicador*, fo. 27[V]. In the earlier *Eloquencia española en arte*,
fo. 4, he defines 'espíritu' as 'las palabras acomodadas a deffecto [sic] que quieren
causar', which is rather different, although it too is the means of 'moving'
(*flectere*) the hearers. See above, pp. 60–69.

[3] *Examen de Ingenios*, ii. 232.

[4] St. Thomas Aquinas, *Summa Theologica*, 1–2, q.111, i–iv.

[5] Carolus Regius, *Orator Christianus*, sig. *4[V]: 'Facultatem recte . . . atque
cum animarum fructu concionandi non esse humanae industriae opus, nec ab artis
cuiuspiam praeceptionibus manere, sed Dei esse donum.'

[6] Ricard, *Estudios de literatura religiosa española*, p. 216, n. 22.

erudition, but to prayer, meditation, and a more faithful discipleship. We are reminded of San Juan de la Cruz on preaching: 'Aquel oficio más es espiritual que vocal... Que comunmente vemos que (cuanto acá podemos juzgar) cuanto el predicador es de mejor vida, mayor es el fruto que hace...porque del espíritu vivo se pega el calor.'[1] In this context *in ostensione virtutis* becomes more meaningful both as 'virtue' (perfection of life) and 'power' (of prayer). Terrones del Caño is explicit on this point, when he describes the properties of the effective preacher thus:

Las calidades infusas son necesarias; más que todo todas las virtudes: mucha y continua oración; grande y vivo espíritu de nuestro Señor; ardiente deseo de ganarle ánimas; don sobrenatural de mover, conforme a aquello que está escrito de Cristo nuestro Señor, *potens in opere et sermone.*[2]

The imitation of Christ is likewise recommended to the preacher by Bartolomé Ximénez Patón in the fifth chapter of *El perfecto predicador* (fos. 31 ff.). Indeed, the very title of the work is significant, standing both for St. Paul himself and for the ideals of Christian 'perfección', a word which in the Spanish Golden Age carries strong connotations of the mystical way. Fray Tomás Ramón, twenty years later, insists that the preacher be always 'en la cumbre de la perfección evangélica',[3] and Fray Plácido Mirto Frangipane maintains that 'el Predicador ha de salir del piélago de una profunda contemplación'.[4]

If prayer and the cultivation of the interior life help the preacher to speak fervently, truthfully, and prudently, the other virtues, which are the fruits of perfection, will also be a speaking witness. Fray Diego Niseno claims that: 'No hay sermón como una vida santa. No hay Predicador más eficaz que unas costumbres loables; un exterior devoto es una voz que callando advierte, arguye, y corrige.'[5] The topic of 'Practise what you preach', which is invariably found in the *artes praedicandi* of all periods, is summed up for his generation by Fray Diego de la Vega:

Tal ha de ser el verdadero y perfecto predicador, que junte el púlpito con el altar, las obras con las palabras, la oración, devoción y santidad con el sermón...De tal manera había de vivir un predicador, que cuando le viessen ir por la calle, dijessen: véis allí el sermón puesto por obra.[6]

---

[1] *Subida del Monte Carmelo*, III. xlv. 4, in *Biblioteca Mística Carmelitana* (Burgos, 1929), ii. 375.
[2] *Instrucción*, p. 19.
[3] *Nueva premática de Reformación*, p. 332.
[4] *Fama póstuma de Fray Agustín Núñez Delgadillo* (Madrid, 1631), fo. 8[V].
[5] *Asuntos predicables para los domingos, miércoles y viernes de Quaresma* (Barcelona, 1634), fo. 169[V].
[6] *Empleo y Exercicio Sancto*, i. 356–7 and also 115–9. Also Ponce de León, *Discursos para diferentes Evangelios de Quaresma*, p. 299 (wrongly numbered as 199) and Ramón, *Flores nuevas*, i. 233: 'tomar la hoz de la palabra de Dios en la mano y no en la boca'. Ximénez Patón, *El perfecto predicador*, fo. 9.

Finally, as a commonplace, it finds itself among Juan Rufo's apoph-
thegms: 'Preguntáronle cuál era el mejor predicador de la Corte. Dijo
"que el mejor religioso; porque los eloquentes y no ejemplares dan a
comer frío y lavan sin jabón".'[1]

The moral character of the preacher, his holiness and spirituality as
described in the preaching manuals, may, however, also be seen as an
adaptation of the classical definition of the orator, attributed to Cato:
vir bonus dicendi peritus.[2] Ximénez Patón establishes the connection:
'en nuestros tiempos el predicador es el orador, y así en él son necesarios
los requísitos que pone Cicerón en su perfecto orador'.[3] Fray Diego de
la Vega reinforces it with a quotation from Quintilian:

Quintiliano en el principio de sus Instituciones Oratorias dice: Insti-
tuimus illum perfectum oratorem, qui esse, nisi vir bonus, non potest;
ideoque non dicendi modo eximiam in eo facultatem, sed omnes
animi virtutes exigimus. Aquel llamamos perfecto orador que juntamente con el don de la eloquencia tiene virtud, y que junta el bien
hablar con el buen obrar, en quien se requieren todas las virtudes del
alma. . .y si tanto como esto se requiere para un orador pagano, ¿qué
será necesario para el Christiano? cuya perfección ha de pasar tanto más
adelante cuanto la doctrina que persuade es más dificultosa y perfecta.[4]

Here we see the Christian spokesman standing firm on a difference
of *degree* rather than of essence. Although the concept of 'spirit' adds
a supernatural dimension to the preaching ministry, there are enough
similarities between pagan and Christian eloquence for there to be both
purpose and profit in juxtaposing them. Any implied contrast is between
the scholastic philosopher and the classical orator, who had become,
since the age of Petrarch, the hero of Renaissance humanism.[5] However, when it came to a decision for or against the human helps of
rhetoric in a basically 'spiritual' situation our preachers and theorists
seem to divide into two main camps.[6]

On the one hand, the apostolic ideal leads to the conclusion that
sincerity and plain-speaking are the only acceptable forms of Christian

---

[1] *Las seiscientas apotegmas* (Toledo, 1596; ed. A.G. de Amezúa, Madrid,
1923), p. 154. Fray Basilio Ponce de León wrote an *aprobación* to this work,
praising his 'maravillosa eloquencia'.

[2] Quintilian, *Institutio oratoria*, XII. i. 1–3 (Loeb edn., iv. 354–7).

[3] *Eloquencia española en arte*, fo. 4. Cicero, *De oratore*, I. ix. 35–6 (Loeb
edn., i. 26) says: 'oratorem in omni genere sermonis et humanitatis esse perfectum', which refers to his rhetorical skill and erudition, rather than to his moral
character.

[4] *Empleo y Exercicio Sancto*, ii. 504–5. The quotation is from *Institutio
oratoria*, I, Proemium, 9 (Loeb edn., i. 8–9).

[5] See H.H. Gray, 'Renaissance Humanism: the pursuit of eloquence', *Journal
of the History of Ideas*, xxiv (1963), esp. 500–4.

[6] In practice, in their sermons, the divisions are by no means so clearly drawn
and some preachers appear positively inconsistent.

preaching, and that all the rest is dangerous sophistry. The original Apostles stand as an example:

que recibieron don de lenguas, mas no para que con estilo elegante y muy retórico predicassen, ni para que con sus cortadas y compuestas razones llevasen embelesados los oyentes, si bien para que con un estilo llano y ordinario, llana y simplemente enseñassen la verdadera doctrina del cielo.[1]

Christ did not choose as His disciples, Ramón continues, twelve Demosthenes, twelve Ciceros, or twelve Homers to preach His Gospel, and we are thereby to conclude that the human arts of oratory did not figure in the divine purpose and consequently are not needed by the preacher whom God Himself has called and will inspire. Thus Balaam's ass and the cock that crew three times for St. Peter are both excellent preachers.[2] Among the advocates of biblical language at its plainest is Fray Diego Murillo, who maintains that: 'esta sencillez con que os decimos las verdades, sin adorno de eloquencia profana, hallaréis después una hermosura increíble: porque echaréis de ver que la verdad Evangélica ha de ser sin afeite y desnuda'.[3]

On the other hand, if one looks back to the Fathers one finds quite another kind of eloquence, and even elegance. According to Fray Cristóbal de Fonseca:

los santos, que son los espejos en que nos hemos de mirar. . .escribieron con tanta gala, que los Tulios, y los Demóstenes no los hicieron ventaja. Y en San Jerónimo y en otros muchos santos se hallarán cláusulas que juzgadas por las leyes de Retórica, por la demasía de la eloquencia, casi parecen viciosos.[4]

St. Paul himself, although paramount as *vir apostolicus*, has a style which is far from artless. He quotes from the playwright Menander (1 Corinthians 15:33) and from Epimenides (Titus 1:12), according to Fray Diego de Estella, who reinforces this example with that of St. Jerome, without, however, recounting the well-known anecdote in which the holy hermit repudiates Cicero and all his works.[5] Ximénez Patón, too, observes that: 'pues yendo con cuidado de no adornar las oraciones, hallamos sus escritos tan adornados que he dicho muchas

[1] Ramón, *Flores nuevas*, i. 241.
[2] Here Ramón is reproducing an extreme view, which has many antecedents in the Early Church: his own style is considerably more elaborate.
[3] *Discursos predicables [Quaresma]* i. 409.
[4] *Primera parte de la Vida de Christo* (Barcelona, 1597), Al Lector.
[5] *Modo de predicar*, ii. 130–1. Similar arguments are used by Erasmus in Chapter 2 of his popular *Enquiridion* (first published in Spanish Alcalá, *c.* 1526; ed. D. Alonso and M. Bataillon, Madrid, 1932; repr. 1971), pp. 132–3. The topic appears to originate in St. Jerome, *Epistolae, PL* xxii, p. 665 and is commented upon by Don Cameron Allen in *Mysteriously Meant: the Rediscovery of Pagan Symbolism and Allegorical Interpretation in the Renaissance* (Baltimore and London, 1970), p. 21.

veces que me atrevería a hacer toda una arte de Retórica exemplificada en tropos, y figuras y color retórico en solas las obras de San Pablo'.[1]

Fray Basilio Ponce de León makes a case for the cultivation of pulpit style, also quoting precedents:

Bien confieso que no es razón que el predicador sea grosero ni diga las cosas cruda y toscamente, ni sea bárbaro; que pues los santos hablaron con tanto primor, agudeza y elegancia, que la de ahora comparada con aquella es asco, es barbarismo, no es falta de ser bien hablado y elegante. Que no se hizo el buen romance y la agudeza solamente para la copla y el billete, sino mucho más para servir a la divina Escritura, pues la sabiduría divina siete criadas tenía. . .[2]

There is, moreover, at this period a pragmatic argument for disregarding St. Paul's strictures against preaching *persuasibilibus humanae sapientiae verbis*. In a situation where the Faith is long established, not directly threatened by heresy, and where there is no pressing need for dogmatic or catechetical instruction, Bartolomé Ximénez Patón recommends a certain amount of rhetorical embellishment to revive enthusiasm for a familiar creed:

Y aunque en aquél tiempo [the time of St. Paul] estuvo bien ir con aquél cuidado de el poco adorno en el decir, para diferenciar los caminos de Dios de los del mundo: *ya recebida la fe y de tantos años pasados*, bien se permite predicar con lugares retóricos y aprovecharse del buen decir y hablar. . .Antes vemos que hace más provecho el predicador que tiene las condiciones del buen orador, y le sigue más gente que a él que no usa de ellas. Y está muy en razón, porque si los antiguos oradores hacían entender al pueblo las cosas falsas por verdaderas (aprovechándose de sus preceptos y reglas) mejor se convencerá el auditorio Christiano, *persuadiéndole con artificio aquello mismo que tiene ya entendido, y creído.*[3]

The congregation is not merely supposed to be theologically literate but sophisticated enough to respond to figures of rhetoric and to appreciate calculated effects of style in the pulpit ('con artificio'). The topic of 'los gustos están estragados' is not far away when we find preachers perplexed as to how to 'pescar al oyente'. Juan Rodríguez de León puts the point:

Los auditorios siguen a los santos, pero no dejan a los doctos, y salen del sermón con hastío si les falta deleite con novedad; causa para que la predicación moderna no se juzque por la modestia antigua: que aunque la verdad no se ha mudado, el estilo está diferente, y como la malicia es

---

[1] *El perfecto predicador*, fos. 18^V–19.
[2] *Discursos para diferentes Evangelios de Quaresma*, pp. 174–5. The reference is to the maidens whom Wisdom sends out to bring people to her dwelling place (Proverbs 9.3) and whom Aquinas calls *ancillae Theologiae* (*ST* Ia, q.1, a.5). A connection is assumed, perhaps, with the seven liberal arts. Also Murillo, *Discursos predicables [Quaresma]*, ii. 36–7.
[3] *El perfecto predicador*, fo. 19^V (my italics).

entendida, quiere sutilezas que la enmienden, no bastando desengaños
que la convierten: llegando a tanto desahogo los gustos humanos, que
fundan en el estilo singular el séquito común, y juzgan que falta a lo
importante del púlpito, el descuidado en lo selecto del lenguaje, siendo
axioma de muchos, que predica mal, quien no habla bien.[1]

In the phrases 'el estilo está diferente', 'sutileza', 'estilo singular',
'novedad', we seem to be skirting the even more acrimonious debate
over *culteranismo* and *conceptismo* in the pulpit. Yet, although this
treatise is printed in 1638 the same dilemma was already being voiced
in 1580, and is probably coterminous with the existence of a preaching
ministry in any country, at any time.[2] For example, in his preface to
Herrera's annotated edition of Garcilaso's poetry, Maestro Francisco
Medina speaks of Fray Luis de Granada (who was then still alive),
arguing that this 'divino orador arrebatado en la contemplación de la
cosas celestiales' has misled writers into thinking that the Christian
message had no need to deck itself in 'el aparato de las disciplinas
humanas', and has had the effect of turning the public towards 'libros
fabulosos', in search of 'esta perfección de lengua que nosotros echamos
de menos'. However, these very novels of chivalry and pastoral romances
are soon found to be 'defectuosos en la elocución; disformes y mon-
strosos [sic] en la invención', and are incapable of providing good
models of style for vernacular writing. He concludes:

Dos linajes de gente hay, en quien debiéramos poner alguna esperanza:
los poetas y los predicadores...Los predicadores que, por haber en
cierta manera sucedido en el oficio a los oradores antiguos, pudieran
ser de más provecho para este intento, se alejaron del, siguiendo dos
caminos bien apartados. Unos, atendiendo religiosamente al fin de su
ministerio, contentos con la severidad y sencillez evangélica, no se
embarazaron en arrear sus sermones destos deleites y galas, y así
dejaron la plaza a los otros, que con más brío y gallardía quisieron
ocuparla; los cuales, en vez de adornarse con ropas tan modestas y
graves, cuanto convenían a la autoridad de sus personas, se vistieron
de un traje galano, pero indecente, sembrado de mil colores y esmaltes,
pero sin el concierto que se demanda.[3]

Although Medina goes on to qualify this criticism of contemporary
preachers by referring to 'algunos insignes Ministros de la palabra de
Dios' who come near to realizing his ideal of dignified decorum, this
appraisal of the Spanish preaching scene is one which could apply to
any decade of the Golden Age, even prior to the advent of Paravicino.
At least two styles of preaching—the 'evangélico' and the 'culto'—are
seen to coexist, if rather uneasily, but are not presented as part of

[1]   *El Predicador de las Gentes* p. 97.
[2]   See Introduction and Ch. III, pp. 79–82.
[3]   *Obras de Garcilaso de la Vega con Anotaciones de Fernando de Herrera*
(Seville, 1580), p. 4 ff.

a chronological development or a chain of action and reaction.

A topic which serves the partisans of both sides in their debate about rhetorical or non-rhetorical language in the pulpit is the eloquence of the Bible itself. Those who set their face against 'worldly' rhetoric can still make the point that the Scriptures contain a treasure-house of every kind of stylistic device and ornament, thus rendering superfluous human *artes praedicandi*. Fray Hernando de Santiago speaks of 'la elegancia secreta que en las sagradas letras hay (que vence infinitamente la de Cicerón)',[1] and Fray Alonso de Cabrera, dwelling upon the phrase 'Mulier per singulos dies molesta erat adolescenti' (Genesis 39:10) exclaims: '¡O retórica del Espíritu Santo! Si Cicerón quisiera decir esto gastara un almacen de palabras y no dijera nada'.[2] In the same vein, Fray Diego de la Vega praises the opening of the third chapter of Luke's gospel: 'Describe aquí el Evangelista San Lucas el principio de la predicación de San Juan, y de camino el que tuvo la de Christo y su reino, con tanta majestad y gravedad de palabras que deja muy atrás al *Arma virumque cano* de Virgilio, y al *Regia solis erat* de Ovidio.'[3]

The innate superiority of biblical language over the eloquence of pre-Christian orators is a distinctly two-edged commonplace. Any comparison between the two presupposes a comparability or similarity of kind, and may therefore be enlisted as an argument by those who wish to justify the use of figured and poetic language in sermons.[4] God has, after all, chosen to speak in a human idiom, as Fray Diego de la Vega points out:

Esfuerza esta verdad ver que la sinceridad de la Sagrada Scriptura, la cual tiene al mismo Dios por autor, aunque de ordinario procede con lenguaje y estilo fácil y llano, pero algunas veces se acomoda con el de las ciencias seglares, y lo que más es, habla el mismo lenguaje de los Poetas.[5]

He then refers specifically to a passage in the Book of Job (21:33) which appears in the Vulgate as '*Dulcis fuit glareis Cocyti, et post se omnem hominem trahet, et ante se innumerabiles*' and which he interprets as

---

[1] *Consideraciones para la Quaresma*, Al Lector. Here he is echoing St. Augustine, *Confessions*, iii, 5 (Loeb edn., i. 112) and implying a very special 'secret' eloquence: 'incessu humilem, successu excelsam, et celatam mysteriis'.

[2] *Sermones*, first pub. 1601 (*BAE* iii, ed. M. Mir, Madrid, 1906), p. 76.

[3] *Empleo y Exercicio Sancto*, i. 108. Also Murillo, *Discursos predicables [Quaresma]*, i. 452.

[4] Or even in a wider context: see Luis de Carballo, *Cisne de Apolo*, ed. A. P. Mayo (2 vols., Madrid, 1958), i. 123. First pub. Medina del Campo, 1602.

[5] *Empleo*, i. Prólogo, fo. 16^V, sig. ¶¶4^V. See also Fray Juan de Arenas' preface to Alonso de Ledesma's *Conceptos espirituales* (Madrid, 1602; ed. E.J. Martínez, Madrid, 1969), i. 15: '. . . el Espíritu Santo habló en poesía por David y por Job . . . [poesía] que tiene más primor que la de los muy primos'.

an allusion to the river of the Roman Hades.[1] Disregarding the pro-
bability that this reading only entered the text at the time of its translation into Latin, Vega concludes that the Holy Spirit is well grounded
in pagan mythology and prosody, supporting his contention with
quotations from Homer and Seneca.[2] This provides a precedent for the
Christian preacher:

Luego conforme a esto, si el Espíritu Santo, que era él que movía las
lenguas de los Profetas, no se desdeñaba de tomar en la suya sentenciosas fábulas de los Poetas, acomodándolas a nuestras costumbres, no
hay para que nosotros tengamos por tan descomulgado su lenguaje
como algunos lo tienen, pareciéndoles totalmente entredicho y prohibido
al predicador *mezclar lo humano con lo divino*, lo profano con lo
sagrado, y los dichos de los Filósofos con las verdades sinceras de los
Profetas.[3]

Almost imperceptibly, we have made the transition from a consideration of style alone to the more weighty question of subject-
matter ('las verdades sinceras de los Profetas'), involving the preacher's
attitude to pagan philosophy as well as to pagan rhetoric. Picking up
a few key words in the passage quoted above, we find 'fábulas', which
introduces criteria of truth and falsehood ('poetic feigning'), and
which is qualified by 'sentenciosas', stressing the didactic contribution
these 'fábulas' can make by means of their poetic elaboration. Vega
seems to wish to extend the scope of the sacred to include the erstwhile
profane, even at the risk of creating an initially shocking hybrid.
Cervantes, in his prologue to the first part of *Don Quijote*, seems to
consider contemporary preaching as a 'mixed' genre:

. . .ni tiene para qué predicar a ninguno, *mezclando lo humano con lo
divino*, que es un género de mezcla de quien no se ha de vestir ningún
cristiano entendimiento. . .no hay para qué andéis mendigando sentencias de filósofos, consejos de la Divina Escritura, fábulas de poetas,
oraciones de retóricos, milagros de santos.[4]

This impression is confirmed, later, by Juan Pérez de Montalbán who
justifies his miscellany *Para Todos* (1632) thus: 'cosa que también
sucede en el púlpito, con ser lugar tan sagrado, pues en el se toca la
fábula, la moralidad y la historia a vueltas del Evangelio Divino y
Sagrada Pasión de Christo Nuestro Señor.'[5] The position taken by
perhaps the majority of preachers at this period is summed up succinctly

---

[1] AV has 'the clods of the valley'. Terrones comments on the same text as
'una fábula poética del río del infierno', *Instrucción*, p. 84.
[2] This approach to Scripture originates in the early Fathers: Philo, Clement
of Alexandria, Origen, and St. Augustine. See P.O. Kristeller, *Renaissance Thought:
the Classic, Scholastic and Humanist Strains* (New York, 1961), pp. 75–7, and
Hugo Rahner, *Greek Myths and Christian Mystery* (London, 1963), p. 12.
[3] D. Vega, *Empleo*, i. fo. 17^V, sig. ¶ ¶ ¶^{V} (my italics).
[4] *Don Quijote*, ed. cit., pp. 24–5 (my italics).
[5] Fo. 4 of preliminaries, no sig.

by Terrones del Caño: 'Aborrescamos, pues, en ellos [pagan authors],
no su elegancia sino sus errores.'[1] This attitude is supported by the
frequently repeated statement that 'hurtábannos los Filósofos Gentiles
nuestras verdades: fundaban en ellas sus mentiras, y creyendo sus
mentiras, no creían nuestras verdades', and that it is therefore the duty
of the Christian preacher to reclaim his rightful inheritance.[2] This is
an idea which is to be found most forcefully in St. Augustine, applied
specifically to Platonism and neo-Platonism: 'Philosophi autem qui
vocantur, si qua forte vera et fidei nostrae accommodata dixerunt,
maxime Platonici, non solum formidanda non sunt, sed ab eis etiam
tamquam iniustis possessoribus, in usum nostrum vindicanda.'[3] In the
middle of the second century Christianity began to emerge from the
isolation of communal life and to make literary propaganda for itself.
Justin Martyr and others use trains of reasoning current among the
Hellenized Jews to demonstrate the conformity of Jewish law with
Greek philosophy.[4] This was no longer necessary when, under Con-
stantine, Christianity became the state religion of the Roman Empire.
However, the venerable debate on the legitimacy of 'pagan' philosophy
used as a corroboration of the Christian faith was not concluded by
the beginning of the seventeenth century, and when it finally disappeared neither side had won a total victory. The reason might be
that the same old arguments appeared over and over again, each time
supported by the name and authority of a different Church Father, and
they were inconclusive because, as R.R. Bolgar explains:

Each saying was elevated into a principle of wide application and
indiscriminately applied. The results were somewhat confusing. Patristic
authority could be quoted for almost any attitude between total
rejection and a very generous acceptance of the classical heritage.
Every Humanist and every non-Humanist could find a text to support
his case.[5]

Perhaps the oldest and most common metaphor used by the humanists
is that of the female captive, who must be tamed and trimmed before
she can become a useful and obedient Christian wife.[6] Provided that
the pagans are always kept in subjection and only allowed to perform
menial tasks, it is safe to admit them to the Christian citadel. A distinction is drawn by the majority of preachers between proof and

---

[1] *Instrucción*, p. 83.

[2] Fonseca, *Discursos predicables para la Quaresma*, fo. 102. Parallels are
drawn between the story of Jonah and myths of Hercules and Arion.

[3] *De doctrina christiana*, II. xl. 60 (Migne, *PL* xxxiv. 63). Estella, *Modo de
predicar*, ii. 129–30.

[4] Curtius, *European Literature and the Latin Middle Ages*, pp. 550–2.

[5] *The Classical Heritage*, p. 57.

[6] Deuteronomy 21.11–14. Murillo, *Discursos predicables [Quaresma]*, ii.
36–7 and Vega, *Empleo y Exercicio Sancto*, i. fo. 16^V.

illustration, in such a way that the pagan authorities take second place
to scriptural or conciliar revelation. Terrones del Caño reports an Easter
sermon by St. Gregory of Nyssa in which 'dice que las fábulas no sirven
para probar las verdades, sino para declararlas'.[1] In short, the allegorical
method, used for illustration, is the only legitimate one here. The
dangers of syncretism and Gnosticism seem to have retreated slightly
when Fray Cristóbal de Fonseca writes:

Verdad es que las verdades de nuestra Fe no se han de probar con los
Sénecas, Platones, Quintilianos, Epanimondas, sino con la Sagrada
Escritura, Concilios y santos, pero después podrá venir el historiador
profano, el orador, el poeta, el arte del bien decir, para que se vea las
costumbres y verdades de nuestra religión son conformes a la razón
natural.[2]

Fray Diego de la Vega also speaks of 'los Filósofos, alumbrados de la
luz de la razón natural',[3] which though necessarily less bright than the
light of Grace, is none the less able to illumine certain areas of Christian
doctrine and practice, making them accessible and agreeable to sinful
man. Horace's dictum *'Omne tulit puntum qui miscuit utile dulci'* is
frequently invoked by preachers, accompanied by the image of themselves as doctors 'gilding the pill'.[4] Sometimes they employ more
martial metaphors, as does Fray Pedro de Valderrama when he compares his strategems to those of Judith with Holofernes:

Este, pues, verdaderamente es mi intento, y debe ser el del predicador,
derribar la cabeza de los pecadores, y quitarles la vida que tanto daña
a la Iglesia, pero porque diciendo sin aderezo y gala las cosas, no se
aficionan los ojos de estos tales, muchas veces es permitido, y aun
según lo que habemos dicho conviene, ir a los libros de los Gentiles y
autores profanos, a buscar sus telas y recamados para que çebados con
esto, los ojos más desaficionados se paguen más de la doctrina, y les
parezca hermosa (lo que sin nada desto, si tuvieran sano juicio, les
había de parecer bellísima, como en efecto lo es) y asi desapercebida-
mente les corte la espada y alfanje de la palabra divina la cabeza. Por
este fin me he alargado a usar de algunas humanidades, guardando en
ellas el consejo que da San Basilio, *lib. de Legendis Gentilium libris.*[5]

Secular and sacred eloquence are here given two entirely separate but
co-operative roles: the initial attraction of the senses and the intellect
belongs to the colours and tropes of human rhetoric, the telling myth
or *sentencia* of the pre-Christian authority, while the subsequent

---

[1] *Instrucción*, p. 82.
[2] *Primera parte de la Vida de Christo*, Prólogo, no sig.
[3] *Parayso de la Gloria de los Santos*, i. sig. ¶4, Dedicatoria.
[4] Murillo, *Discursos predicables [Quaresma]* i. 271 and Terrones, *Instrucción*,
pp. 66–7. Also J. Pérez de Moya, *Comparaciones o símiles* (Alcalá, 1584), fo.
28ᵛ, uses both the images of the surgeon and the 'píldoras doradas'.
[5] Valderrama, *Primera parte de Exercicios espirituales para la Quaresma*, i, Al
Lector, sig. ¶ ¶2ᵛ.

penetration of the heart (in this case decapitation of the sinner), reforming the will and conquering sin, is left to the two-edged sword of the Word of God. Both functions are felt to be equally necessary; the former particularly so in a post-lapsarian society in which sin has already vitiated the judgement. The topic of 'los gustos están estragados' may be discerned here but, as in previously quoted examples, I feel that it refers less to a particularly 'spoiled' generation of Spaniards, fed on too rich a diet of plays and poetry, than to a general human propensity for 'lo ameno' and 'lo halagüeño'.

A spokesman for the considered use of rhetorical 'flowers' in the pulpit is Benito Carlos Quintero, who paraphrases Lactantius:

Y esta Eloquencia por dos causas es razón que la desee el púlpito, y la estudien sus profesores. . .La primera, para que vista la verdad Evangélica colores tan fuertes, que aun hacen creída la mentira, que con la persuasión compuesta de las voces gana engañosamente lo que perdiera por sí misma desnuda. Lo segundo, para vencer los Filósofos presumidos, que a fuerza de Retórica procuran desbaratar la entereza de nuestra fe, con sus mismas armas, que es la gala valiente.[1]

He continues that the preacher must not flinch from employing 'la Eloquencia usada, de las voces cultas, puras, sonoras, recebidas en el aplauso común; however, he counsels great moderation and circumspection:

Muy bien está que el Predicador asee su sermón, le pula, le remire, y examine; pero no tan artificioso como el Poeta, tan afectado, demasiadamente, que llevándose la atención toda su elegancia, no saquen los oyentes más provecho de una hora de sermón que el regalo del oído, la curiosidad del ingenio, y el aire de las voces.[2]

The *culterano* preachers, who call the clouds 'Archijardineras' and quote whole lines of Góngora's *Soledades* in a sermon[3] are then lambasted for their previous neologisms ('lustro, precipicio, joven, deliquios, rosicleres'), most unseemly in the pulpit. They are also ridiculed for their pleonastic use of synonyms ('unívocos'): 'Pues por remate de un sermón, o contera (como dijera alguno) entran por *alegrías, gustos, suavidades, dulzuras, sosiegos* y *felicidades de gracia en esta vida y en la otra de la gloria* etc., acabando a un tiempo más la paciencia que el sermón.'[4] Fray Pedro de Valderrama is equally scathing about preachers

---

[1] *Templo de la eloquencia castellana* (Salamanca, [1629]), discurso último, fo. 38[V] Cf. *Divinae Institutiones*, III, i (*PL* vi. 348–9).
[2] Ibid., fo. 39.
[3] Ibid., fo. 40. See also Lope de Vega's sonnet no. 307:
¿Quién dijera que Góngora y Elías
al púlpito subieran como hermanos
y predicaran bárbaras poesías?
(in *Obras no dramáticas de Lope de Vega, BAE* xxxvii, 1856).
[4] *Templo*, fo. 40[V].

who strive for effect by introducing neologisms which are in fact merely
archaisms: digging in the past they are 'gañanes' rather than 'galanes',
and when they try to 'adelgazar las razones que dicen. . .por adelgazarlas
las tuercen como la que hila, y es cosa muy afeminada y de mujeres'.[1]
One could continue almost indefinitely with scornful comment directed
by our preachers at the so-called *cultos-ocultos*, but Fray Tomás Ramón's
'Del lenguaje culto y su mal uso' in *Nueva premática de reformación*
(Saragossa, 1635) is the most useful compendium of such topics,
examined earlier in Chapter I.

POETRY IN THE PULPIT

Setting aside the question of the preacher's own sermon style, how
far was it acceptable for him to quote directly from professional poets,
be they ancient or modern, in the pulpit? Here we must distinguish
between theory and practice: the former is far more predictable than
the latter. For instance, Fray Diego de Estella warns us that: 'Es la
poesía en el púlpito como la fruta en la mesa, la cual se pone allí no
para que se harten, sino para abrir el apetito; pero el estómago hase de
henchir de manjares de substancia y provechosos.'[2] 'Doctrina de gentiles'
should take second place to Scripture, and not only should it be invoked
in moderation but also modestly. Terrones del Caño recommends that
poets, when quoted, should remain anonymous, and this is especially
true of near contemporaries and vernacular writers: 'Bastará decir "allá
vuestro poeta", o "el otro en sus devaneos"; aunque, si fuesen Virgilio,
Homero, Horacio, podríanse nombrar con algún encogimiento y un
poco de desdén, y no enjuagándose la boca con ellos, como si citaremos
a San Jerónimo.'[3] Certainly, those writers whom Benito Carlos Quintero
lists—'el lascivo Propercio, el enamorado Ovidio, el mentiroso Apuleio y
el presumido Luciano'—are considered unworthy of a place in any
sermon.[4]

Nevertheless, all these names, with the exception of Apuleius, are
acknowledged by Fray Hernando de Santiago in the *Index Autorum*
to his *Consideraciones sobre los Evangelios de los Santos* (Lisbon,
1617). Apuleius is accredited by Fray Tomás Ramón in the *Registro
de los Autores* to his second volume of *Flores nuevas* (Barcelona,
1612), and by 1634 the climate of opinion has changed so much that
Fray Diego Niseno is able to introduce the legend of Narcissus (which
he uses to explain part of a prayer used at the Eucharist: *Sacrificium
illud offerimus*) with an invocation to the poet Ovid as 'el padre y

[1] *Exercicios espirituales [Quaresma]*, i, sig. ¶¶3ᵛ. Also *Instrucción*, pp.
130−1.
[2] *Modo de predicar*, ii. 131.
[3] *Instrucción*, p. 87.　　　　　[4] *Templo*, fo. 48ᵛ.

Maestro del profano amor'.[1] In fact, it would seem to be a reversion to an earlier acceptance of Ovid, through the fourteenth-century *Ovidius moralizatus*, and Niseno's phrase echoes the 'doctor egregius' conferred on the poet by nuns and priests at the fictional love-court of Remiremont as early as 1150.[2]

Of the ten preachers I have selected for special study, most feel entitled to 'season' their sermons with choice Latin tags. However, Fray Diego de la Vega, who compares 'las cosas de humanidad' to salt and makes them necessary in moderation ('dos granos') in the prologue to *Empleo y Exercicio Sancto* (1604),[3] performs a volte-face later in the same volume and the word 'moderación' is overwhelmed by invective: O ceguedad grande, y no se diga locura o desvarío, de algunos predicadores deste tiempo, tan dados a la curiosidad y sutilezas de ingenio, que todo el discurso de su sermón se les pasa en hacer alarde de aquesto. Hasta el escribir tiene el demonio ya profanado, sabiendo que de la pluma ha de ir la doctrina a la lengua, y del libro al púlpito, donde se enseña y predica, y veremos sermones llenos de fábulas, de Ovidio, Virgilio, y Homero. Que aunque no condeno esto, cuando es con moderación y modestia Christiana, pero no lo apruebo cuando es con demasía. ¿Quánto mejor parecerá en un sermón Isáias que Tulio? ¿Ieremías que Homero? ¿y los versos de David que los de Ovidio? (pp. 288−9)[4]

In another volume of sermons, the second volume of *Parayso de la Gloria de los Santos* (Medina del Campo, 1604) he none the less quotes from Ovid's *Tristia* (p. 25) and from the *Metamorphoses* (p. 157), but as a rule his reliance on 'Gentile' poets is not excessive.

Fray Cristóbal de Avendaño is the only preacher of the group who is consistently opposed to any recourse to the poets and he is the only one to practise what he preaches. He illustrates his sermons with anecdotes and unattributed *exempla*, although on one occasion he is found to paraphrase the description of the battle of the bees from *Georgics* IV, summing up with a direct quotation from Virgil ('Qué bien lo dijo el Mantuano. . .').[5] In his prologue to *Otro tomo de Sermones de los Santos* (Valladolid, 1629) he banishes even such 'respectable' writers as Plutarch, Cicero, and Seneca from the *introducción* of sermons: 'pues sabemos que están en el infierno, y no es justo que den principio a acciones tan graves y de tanta importancia' (sig. ¶¶6). Earlier in the same prologue he had praised the resolution of his co-religionist Fray Agustín Núñez Delgadillo to preach only Scripture:

---

[1]   *Asuntos predicables [Quaresma]*, fo. 54ᵛ.
[2]   See Dorothy M. Robatham, 'Ovid in the Middle Ages', in *Ovid*, ed. J.W. Binns (London, 1973), p. 198.
[3]   Fo. 16, sig. ¶¶4.
[4]   Similar sentiments are expressed in his *Discursos predicables de la Quaresma*.
[5]   *Sermones de Quaresma*, ii (Madrid, 1623). fo. 20.

que a todo amparar y a todo defender defienda y ampare la Sagrada
Escritura contra muchos Predicadores que totalmente la van olvidando
y dejando, haciendo introducción a sus sermones, unos con Plutarco
en los Morales, otros con el Príncipe de la Eloquencia Cicerón, y el
más virtuoso entre éstos con Séneca; y camina tan a lo despeñado esta
corruptela, que vivo temeroso si ha de haber alguno tan deslumbrado
y tan dejado de la mano de Dios que introduzga su sermón con algún
epigrama de Marcial, o con Ovidio *De arte amandi* (sig. ¶ ¶ 5ᵛ)

In fact, Núñez Delgadillo himself quotes from Ovid's *Ars amandi*
on at least one occasion,[1] as well as from Seneca's *Hercules Oetaeus*,[2]
and at one point he follows an Alciati emblem with four lines from
Ovid, two lines from Juvenal, and eight lines from Menander, in quick
succession.[3] So much for 'sola Scriptura'.

Even the Franciscans follow the fashion for *humanidades* and
classical quotation. Fray Diego Murillo is not afraid to endorse the
doctrinal points of his sermons with the myths of Jupiter and Gany-
mede, Hercules and Atlas, Arion, Orpheus, Perseus, Minerva, Cadmus,
and Vulcan, while Fray Luis de Rebolledo ponders the force of the
word *hodie* in Terence's 'O populares, et quis me vivit hodie fortunatior?'
with quite as much earnestness as if it were Scripture itself.[4] The
Dominican Fray Tomás Ramón quotes Catullus, 'Nam simul te Lesbia
aspexi', with its *amens/amans* pun,[5] but by far the most popular poet
is Virgil, closely followed by Ovid and Seneca. Even when he is not
actually named we sense his presence:

Cado uno vivía debajo de su parra, y de su higuera, no porque todos
tuviessen parras y higueras, sino porque se podían echar a dormir
descuidados y seguros, como pinta el Poeta a los pastores Titeo y
Melibeo, recostados a la sombra de la haya, que decían, *Deus nobis
haec otia fecit.*[6]

Fray Basilio Ponce de León calls him 'el Príncipe de los Poetas Latinos'[7]
and Fray Diego de la Vega says that he is 'igual en la eloquencia a
Homero'.[8] Virgil was, of course, rendered respectable by the medieval
tradition which read his *Eclogues* IV as a foretelling of the birth of
Christ. Among the 'moderns' Jorge Manrique (often unnamed) is
perhaps the most popular, as in Fray Tomás Ramón: 'él que dijo
nuestras vidas son los ríos que van a dar en el mar de la muerte'.[9] We

---

[1] *Minas*, fo. 33: *Militia species amor.*   [2] *Victoria de los Justos*, fo. 55ᵛ.
[3] *Minas*, fo. 213.
[4] *Primera parte de cien oraciones fúnebres*, fo. 102.
[5] *Puntos escripturales* (Barcelona, 1618), ii. 140. A similar pun (attributed to
Seneca) is in Murillo, *Discursos predicables [Christo]*, p. 275.
[6] Fonseca, *Discursos predicables [Quaresma]*, fo. 60.
[7] *Sermón de Sto. Tomás de Villanueva* (Salamanca, 1620), p. 39.
[8] *Empleo y Exercicio*, i. fo. 6, Dedicatoria.
[9] *Flores nuevas*, i. 222. Also Murillo, *Quaresma*, ii. 40.

also find a reference to Garcilaso (*Egloga tercera*, v. 40) in Fray Cristóbal de Fonseca's elaboration on Alciati's emblem of co-operation
between the blind man and the lame man: 'A Iulio Cesar, maestro del
arte militar, pintaron los Romanos una mano en el libro, otra en la
espada. . .que es lo que dijo el Poeta español: *tomando ora la pluma,
ora la espada.*'[1] Dante's *Inferno* is quoted, in Latin, by Ponce de
León,[2] who, of all the preachers chosen, is perhaps the fondest of
poetry in the pulpit.

It should be borne in mind that many of the longer Latin quotations that we find in the *sermonarios* of this period may have been
added after the initial preaching, as part of the 'polishing-up' process
which preceded the appearance of the printed sermon. Fray Tomás
Ramón, for instance, permits himself a 16-line passage from *Georgics*
III (vv. 322–37) as part of a description of the Good Shepherd, and
follows it up with two cross-references to *Eclogues* V and VII, which
would probably never have been tolerated in the sermon as it was
first delivered.[3] Fray Basilio Ponce de León includes a 9-line quotation from *Aeneid* IV—a simile of an oak-tree—in one of his sermons,[4]
but I have yet to find the original of the preacher, satirized by Fray
Cristóbal de Avendaño, who after inviting 'los críticos' to his sermon
preached 'cuatro sonetos desleídos en una perversa prosa, sacando
el romance castellano de sus quicios'.[5]

EMBLEMS AS SERMON-EMBELLISHERS

Some of the longer passages of poetry found in the printed *sermonarios* accompany descriptions of emblems taken from Alciati,
Paolo Giovio,[6] Giovanni Pierio Valeriano,[7] Sambuco,[8] Otto van
Veen,[9] and 'los dos Orozcos'.[10] All these compilers of emblem books
are recommended by Juan Pérez de Montalbán in the chapter on
preaching which is found in his *Para Todos* (1632) with the words:
'Este linaje de letras es muy deleitable para el púlpito' (p. 305). Fray

---

[1] *Quarta parte de la Vida de Christo*, p. 57.
[2] *Discursos para los Evangelios de Quaresma*, i. 526.   [3] *Flores nuevas*, ii. 129.
[4] *Discursos para diferentes Evangelios*, ii. fo. 9.
[5] *Sermones de Santos* (Valladolid, 1628), fo. 169.
[6] His *Dialogo dell' Imprese Militari et Amorose* (Rome, 1555) was translated
into Spanish by Alonso de Ulloa and published at Lyons in 1561. His Spanish
name is Jovio.
[7] *Hieroglyphica sive de sacris Aegyptiorum aliarumque gentium literis* (Basle,
1556).
[8] Hungarian humanist whose *Emblemata* were first published at Antwerp by
Christophe Plantin in 1564, and went into numerous editions.
[9] Venio or Vaenius, *Amorum emblemata* (Antwerp, 1608).
[10] Juan de Horozco y Covarrubias, *Emblemas morales* (Segovia, 1589) and
Sebastián de Covarrubias Orozco, *Emblemas morales* (Madrid, 1610).

Diego de la Vega had already spoken appreciatively of 'la viveza de ingenio que la pintura o Hieroglífica encierra dentro de sí',[1] and the ingenuity required of an emblematist was akin to that which forged preacherly conceits, as we see from Ponce de León's *Relación de las honras de Antolínez* in which the devices adorning the catafalque were 'invented' by the *Predicador mayor*, 'con su agudeza y variedad de buena lición'.[2] However, at an earlier period (*c.* 1580), Fray Agustín de Salucio had expressed strong disapproval of the use of emblems ('semejantes mendrugos') in sermons.[3]

In Italy the connection between emblem literature and the pulpit appears to have been more firmly established than in Spain. Mario Praz refers to Ilario Cavo's sermon 'interspersed with descriptions of devices' in 1618,[4] and, at the end of the seventeenth century, to Carlo Labia who produced *simboli predicabili* (Ferrara, 1692) based on the four Gospels, with forty-two pages of illustrated devices, and also a collection of *simboli festivi per le solemnità principali di Christo nostro signore, della Beata Vergine Maria, degl' Apostoli, e d'altri Santi* (Venice, 1698).[5] We should bear in mind that 'religious' emblems in seventeenth-century Europe can range from the obscurely cosmological and erudite productions of the neo-Platonic school to the equivalent of a *biblia pauperum*. Spanish preaching covers the full range: for example, Fray Basilio makes copious use of emblems in his sermons, most of them gleaned from Alciati and Sambuco and encrusted in a rich framework of epigrams taken from other sources. He briefly describes the well-known emblem of the boy and the bees (Alciati cxi (Lyons, 1550): *Dulcia quandoque amara fieri*) together with the 6-line verse from the Greek Anthology which makes up the original emblem, and then includes parallel passages from Plautus, Euripides' *Hippolytus*, and Catullus.[6]

On another occasion he is glossing the Song of Songs 7:8, '*Et odor oris tui sicut malorum*', which leads him from the first apple, that of the Fall, to the golden apple of discord and the apples stolen by Hercules, equated in Pierio with the three virtues of the wise man—'no enojarse, no ser codicioso, tener el ánimo libre de desordenados deleites' —from which he passes to the apple as a symbol of love in the poets, to Atalanta's golden apple, and finally to the *empresa* of the Sforza

---

[1] *Empleo y Exercicio*, i. fo. 16, sig. ¶¶4.

[2] Salamanca, 1629, p. 10.

[3] *Avisos para los predicadores*, ed.cit., pp. 206–7.

[4] *Predica del Molto Rever. P.D. Ilario Cavo Genovese Chierico Regolare sopra l'autenticatione della Dottrina di S. Tommaso d'Aquino fatta dal Crocifisso* (Venice, 1618). See M. Praz's bibliography of emblem-books in *Studies in Seventeenth Century Imagery* (2nd rev. edn., Rome, 1964), p. 302.

[5] Praz, *Studies*, pp. 391–2.

[6] *Discursos para diferentes Evangelios de Quaresma*, i. 120.

family.[1] By this time it is not clear if any doctrinal point has been made: the outline of the argument has been lost as the cornucopia of fabulous fruit spills over.

Ponce de León seems less concerned with the pictorial effect of the emblem than with the literary accretions that have already gathered round it in the form of Latin verses. Other preachers use emblems almost exclusively to introduce a detailed description of a 'visual aid', which will demonstrate an allegory or an unfamiliar idea beyond the scope of the traditional pulpit 'props': hourglass, crucifix, or even death's head. Fray Luis de Rebolledo gives us an emblematic picture which cannot be a complete emblem because it lacks a motto or device, but which can easily be visualized:

Los Griegos pintaban el tiempo en figura de un mozo hermoso, los pies con alas de puntillas sobre una rueda voluble, una navaja en la mano derecha, en la mollera un copete de cabellos, como lo traen los mozuelos adamados destos años. El cerebro calvo, y atribuíanle divinidad, porque la oportunidad del tiempo es en cierta manera omnipotente como Dios; pues vemos que en los negocios él es el que todo lo dispone y acaba.[2]

Fray Diego de la Vega frequently refers to emblems, of love, of justice, and of youth:

Galana fue aquella pintura de la juventud que ingeniaron los antiguos: como lo refiere Riciardo Brixiano en sus Symbolos, y que nos declara bien los muchos riesgos a que está sujeta esta edad. Pintaban un mozo desnudo, con una venda puesta en los ojos, atada la mano derecha, y desatada la izquierda; el tiempo venía corriendo tras dél dándole alcances: el cual cada día le iba quitando un hilo de la venda que llevaba en los ojos.[3]

The preacher then proceeds to elucidate each components part of the picture, bringing out its moral sense.

Even more detailed and complex is the emblem which Valderrama uses to illustrate Grace, and whch he takes from Sambuco (lxiv), the original title being *Imperatoris virtutes*.[4] The composite symbolism, the overloading of allegorical *minutiae*, is typical of the iconography of the age, particularly the school of Valdés Leal, in which each detail is a lesson in *desengaño*.

Iba un príncipe a caballo, y llevaba en la mano un Globo, que representaba el mundo: en los pechos del caballo llevaba colgado del petral

---

[1] *Discursos para diferentes Evangelios*, ii. 317.
[2] *Cien oraciones fúnebres*, fo. 120^V. Alciati cxxi (p. 133 of 1550 edn.) fits this description and is entitled *In occasionem*.
[3] *Empleo y Exercicio*, ii. 455. In the same volume (p. 116) he has a 'galano Geroglífico' of eloquence, also found in Erasmus, Pierio, and Alciati: Hercules with chains issuing from his mouth. Cf. Alciati clxxx, (p. 194 of 1550 edn.).
[4] Sambuco, *Emblemata* (augmented edn., Antwerp, 1566), p. 64.

un Delfín [diligencia], en las ancas una cabeza de Buey [pereza y tardanza en los negocios]: llevaba en la otra mano una bandera, y en ella muchos Geroglíficos, porque llevaba el sombrero de Mercurio [elocuencia], el caduceo [deseo de la paz], con las dos culebras, junto a el un libro [la ley], y últimamente una pirámide [inmortalidad], pero los que más hay aquí que notar es que ese príncipe no traía acompañamiento sino solamente una doncella por paja. . .tras del caballo [Fortuna].[1]

The educative properties of emblems have been studied by several critics, notably Mario Praz in Chapter IV of his *Studies in Seventeenth Century Imagery*.[2] Their simultaneous appeal to mind and eye was considered, in the seventeenth century, to achieve that union of pleasure and profit (*utile dulci miscere*) so essential to serious art. The education emblems provide is, however, an education in subtlety: the true emblem is essentially enigmatic and composed of a set of secret relationships, which at first puzzle the beholder. Its meaning resides in the interaction of picture, motto, and verse, and for this reason it communicates itself in a flash of understanding, rather than at the end of a logical, linear argument, although 'líneas de ponderación' may be traced to justify the revelation, rather as one might explain arrival at the solution of a crossword puzzle by recounting successive stages of thought or guesswork.

The emblems so painstakingly reproduced in the *sermonarios* are, for the most part, rather disappointing as they sacrifice much of their enigmatic appeal to the cause of unambiguous didacticism.[3] Not only are they frequently overloaded with Latin tags and verses (in addition to those found in the original emblematists) but the preachers are frequently so anxious to extract every ounce of morality from their emblems that they do not allow the pictorial aspect to 'speak' for itself. Ideally the visual and the elucidatory elements should complement each other, and Fray Luis de Rebolledo describes the making of a rudimentary emblem in these terms:

De un santo Arzobispo de Milano, que alcanzaron nuestros días, se cuenta que tenía un retrato de la muerte con un cuchillo en la mano, y estimaba la pintura, no solamente por la mano, que era buena, pero porque entre los del arte la tenían por de Michael Angel. El santo Prelado, que en mirarla gastaba mucho tiempo, y en meditarla más,

---

[1] *Exercicios espirituales de los Santos*, pp. 530–1. The allegory is spelled out later in the sermon in the terms specified within square brackets in my quotation.

[2] pp. 169–203. See also R.J. Clements, *Picta Poesis: Literary and Humanistic Theory in Renaissance Emblem-Books* (Rome, 1960: *Temi e Testi*, vi).

[3] The transposition of the sermon from an oral to a literary mode may also have the effect of making the use of emblems less dramatically vivid, since the suspenseful pause between the enunciation of the mystery and its elucidation is removed.

llamó a un pintor y díjole: *Enmienda esta tabla, porque esta muerte no es Christiana.* Y preguntándole los pintores, ¿cómo se había de matizar? Mandó que en la otra mano le pusiesse una llave, y que tuviesse el cuchillo en la izquierda, y la llave en la derecha. Y su concepto era: porque la muerte de los amigos de Dios, en ley de naturaleza de Escriptura, no tenía más que cuchillo para cortar el hilo de la vida, y apartar los trabajos del trabajado. Pero en la ley de Gracia, los que mueren en ella, hace la muerte más que acabar su trabajo, porque les pone en possessión y entrega de descansos. Y así la muerte Christiana ha de tener cuchillo y llave juntamente, porque la llamó el Espíritu Santo descanso.[1]

The representational art is here endowed with the power to bridge the gap between two different, even fundamentally antagonistic, systems of ideas—the pagan and the Christian—by a simple transposition of detail and a few brush-strokes! The artistic 'sanctity' of a painting by Michelangelo is violated in order to make it serve a holier purpose. From the preacher's point of view, a 'pintura tosca' which contains a Christian message or a pious truth is a better painting than the 'lienzos lascivos' of the greatest artists. Fray Hortensio Félix Paravicino discourses at some length on the moral value of art in his funeral sermon for the Infanta Margarita de Austria, and is convinced that pictures have a strong effect, for good or evil, on their beholders:

¡O pueblo Fiel, y no Cristiano sólo, o los que imperan en el! No consientan, ni permitan en lugares públicos (ay, ni en el más retirado) esta nociva profanidad, este veneno insensible, que en mentiras animosas iguala tal vez la verdad, y más disimulado que en el oro, en el carmín, en las cenizas, y en el espalto, quita la vida a honestidades, que de la hermosura efectiva quizá se defendieran, o con la fuga, o con el valor. Confieso ingénuamente, se ha dicho sin ofensa de personas, ni casas (que no las miro) con odio, si grande deste exceso, que me duele, no acierto a discurrir, como en aposentos Cristianos penden estos lienzos gentiles, ¡o en cuántos más yerros que clavos penden![2]

Many examples of changes of heart produced by the sight of truly Christian art are adduced by Francisco Pacheco in his *Arte de la Pintura* (Seville, 1649), especially in Chapter XI, which is entitled 'De la pintura y de las imágenes, y de su fruto y la autoridad que tienen en la Iglesia Católica'. He draws frequent parallels between the aim of the Christian painter and that of the preacher, which is to 'persuadir al pueblo, llevarlo, por medio de la Pintura, a abrazar alguna cosa conveniente a la religión' (p. 143). However, profane art was still considered potentially dangerous, precisely because of its power over eyes and heart, and should therefore either be excluded altogether or 'divinized' into a worthy ally for the Christian preacher.

---

[1] *Cien oraciones fúnebres*, fos. 145–145ᵛ.
[2] *Oraciones evangélicas y Panegíricos funerales.* Preached 1633.

V

THE PREACHER AS MORALIST

A large part of the preacher's task is to admonish his flock, describing to them their besetting vices and showing the way to amendment and newness of life. The Rule of St. Francis expounds succinctly how this should be done: 'Moneo. . .Fratres, ut in praedicatione. . .sint examinata et. . .casta eorum eloquia, ad utilitatem et aedificationem populi, annuntiando eis vitia et virtutes, poenam et gloriam cum brevitate sermonis.'[1] Vices are seldom spoken of without reference to their corresponding virtues and at the same time they are set within a retributory scheme of reward and punishment, Heaven and Hell. The preacher's aim is a practical one: to inform and reform his congregation. *Cum brevitate sermonis* conveys this purposefulness, and yet, as I hope to show below, does not necessarily preclude certain witty and stylized techniques of satire (allegory, parody, travesty, etc.). I propose, therefore, to look first at the injunctions to the preacher to perform his admonitory role in a fitting way, then to identify the objects of attack, and finally the terms of attack, which at times constitute satirical 'fictions' and invite comparison with secular models.

REPREHENSIONES DEL PREDICADOR : COURAGEOUS YET DECOROUS

The preacher in his rebukes and reproaches to the People of God must be truthful, strong, and fearless:

Voz de trompeta, no de dulzaïna, ni clarín, ha de ser la del predicador en Quaresma; no ha de deleitar las orejas con la cláusula rodada, con la harmonía de las palabras elegantes y estudiadas, con la erudición de letras humanas, con el donaire del chiste y dicho picante: ha de asombrar y atemorizar, representando las penas eternas del infierno, el rigor de nuestras obligaciones, la necesidad de la penitencia y buenas obras, para no incurrir en ellas.[2]

Fray Tomás Ramón lays even more emphasis on the seeming harshness of the preacher:

los predicadores. . .han de escocer y picar, han de ser dientes agudos que despedaçen y desmenuçen a veces, y que aturdan al pecador y lo amedrenten. No han de ser de miel y azúcar los prelados y predicadores, no sólo florear en el púlpito y deleitar los oyentes. . .Han de rechinar y chispar como sal lanzada en el fuego, que abrasen los pecadores

---

[1] *Opuscula Sancti Patris Francisci Assisiensis* (Quaracchi, 1904), Regula II. cap. ix. p. 71. See Diego de Estella, *Modo de predicar*, ii. 13 and Diego Murillo, *Discursos predicables [Quaresma]*, i, Prólogo. sig. ¶ ¶ 7ᵛ.

[2] Juan Galvarro, *Glosa moral sobre los Evangelios de Quaresma*, p. 2.

y los enciendan en el amor de Dios.[1]

He continues to the effect that San Vicente Ferrer 'no predicaba otro que el juicio; no fábulas de Ovidio, ni Trofeos de Alejandro, sino espinas, hierro, cuchillos, llamas' (ibid.). The preacher must be cruel to be kind: 'Tiempos hay en que es necesario un término pesado, que escueza al oyente: y por ventura para enseñar esto llamó Christo a sus predicadores sal de la tierra, porque la sal escuece donde halla herida, y aunque causa dolor, da salud.'[2] In this respect the preacher is frequently compared to a doctor or surgeon. The life-giving effect of the operation, painful as it is, can only be appreciated afterwards: 'Con el cauterio de fuego suele blasfemar el enfermo del cirujano: Por Dios, un Turco no fuera tan despiadado y tan cruel. Pero después que ve atajado el cáncer y que goza de salud, dice: Gran oficial es Fulano.'[3]

The most frequent figure of the preacher in his reproving role to be used in seventeenth-century Spain seems to be that of the dog, symbol both of prudence and protection.[4] The shepherd's dog, barking and biting, drives away wolves from the flock, as well as keeping the sheep together on the right path: the analogy is an obvious one. 'También el predicador es como el perro que ha de ladrar, y aun morder a ratos . . . Desdichado del poderoso que con amenazas o promesas tapa la boca al perro contra el mandato de Dios.'[5] It is taken up by Mateo Alemán, also with Isaiah's 'dumb dogs' in mind, when he makes Guzmán say: 'Pues aun conozco mi exceso en lo hablado: que más es doctrina de predicación que de pícaro. Estos ladridos a mejores perros tocan: rómpanse las gargantas, descubran los ladrones. Mas, ¡ay, si por ventura o desventura les han echado pan a la boca y callan!'[6] These examples all imply that preachers may only too often be squeamish about speaking out, or may too easily be silenced by bribes and respectability. Fray Alonso de Cabrera, in a passage quoted by Félix G. Olmedo and Otis H. Green, gives a pessimistic picture:

Nunca el mundo ha estado peor que agora: más codicioso, más

[1] *Flores nuevas*, ii. 158.
[2] Murillo, *Discursos predicables [Quaresma]*, i, 272.
[3] Cristóbal de Fonseca, *Discursos para la Quaresma*, fo. 393[V].
[4] P. Valderrama, *Exercicios espirituales para la Quaresma*, ii. fos. 21[V]–22. However, dogs are also Cynics and their didacticism easily turns to 'murmuración': Cf. Cervantes, *El Coloquio de los Perros* (Clásicos Castellanos, 1952), ii. 232–3 and B. Gracián, *El criticón*, I. xii. 641–2 in Del Hoyo edition.
[5] Terrones del Caño, *Instrucción*, p. 65. He echoes Isaiah 56:10–11: 'His watchmen are blind, they are all ignorant; they are all dumb dogs, they cannot bark . . . Yea, they are greedy dogs which can never have enough.'
[6] *Guzmán de Alfarache*, I. ii. 3 (ed. cit. ii. 42). It is very frequently applied to preachers in earlier periods too, cf. Owst, *Literature and the Pulpit*, p. 246 [fourteenth century] A.J. Krailsheimer, *Rabelais and the Franciscans* (Oxford, 1963), p. 67 [fifteenth century].

deshonesto, más loco y altivo; nunca los señores más absolutos y aun
disolutos; los caballeros más cobardes y aun sin honra; nunca los ricos
más crueles, avaros; los mercaderes más tramposos; los clérigos más
perdidos; los frailes más derramados; las mujeres más libres y desver-
gonzadas; los hijos más desobedientes; los padres más remisos; los
amos más insufribles; los criados más infieles; los hombres todos más
impacientes y enemigos que los toquen ni aun los amaguen con la
reprensión. Y los predicadores, ¿vivimos en sana paz, estimados, queri-
dos, regalados, ofrendados, nadie nos quiere mal, todos nos ponen
sobre la cabeza? No hacemos el deber y no damos herida ni sacamos
sangre.[1]

This passage belongs to the Golden Age topic of present-day degeneracy
contrasted with a more innocent and admirable past. It leads directly
into the theme 'los gustos están estragados', harped upon by preachers
of every age, and otherwise termed *prurientes auribus*: 'Y porque si eres
buen predicador, que no les has de *rascar las orejas*, sino lastimarlos con
reprehensión dura y verdadera (y por eso te han de perseguir).'[2] Intimi-
dation by wealthy and important patrons, together with the temptation
to seek popularity rather than to speak the truth to sinners, are both
warned against by all our preachers: 'aunque se arriesgue la vida, no se
ha de adular sino decir verdades, aunque se pierda la vida en este
ministerio'.[3] In fact, it could often be dangerous to preach unpalatable
truths, as Terrones del Caño points out:

¡Cuántos predicadores se ha sorbido el mar de una ira de un principe o
de sus privados! ¡Cuántos han llevado al Santo Oficio, por oyentes
ignorantes o melevolos [*sic*], que, aunque los den por libres, salen
tiznados...Yo certifico, como Calificador que he sido en la Inquisición
de Granada y en el Consejo, que, si hubiesen los inquisidores de llamar
a todos los predicadores que son denunciados por oyentes ruines, no
habría ya quien predicase.[4]

Preaching at Court, in the presence of the monarch, is seen to present
special problems, requiring the utmost tact and circumspection. Again
Terrones speaks from personal experience:

Para donde es menester más prudencia son los auditorios de los reyes,
porque verdaderamente no han de ser reprehendidos en público ellos,
ni los prelados, de manera que el pueblo eche de ver sus faltas, porque
ellos se irritan, y no quedan aprovechados; y el pueblo les pierde el
respeto y se huelga, casi por modo de venganza, que les asienten en
el púlpito.[5]

---

[1] *Sermones del P. Fr. Alonso de Cabrera* in *BAE* (Madrid, 1906), i. 361a.
Also Terrones, *Instrucción*, p. 69.
[2] P. Valderrama, *Exercicios espirituales para la Quaresma*, i. fo. 14 (my
italics).
[3] Avendaño, *Sermones del Adviento*, p. 232.
[4] *Instrucción*, pp. 87–8.   [5] ·Ibid., pp. 94–5.

He goes on to enumerate several conciliar rulings on the matter and concludes that only if the sin of the prince or prelate is already so public as to give scandal, and only after his confessor has tried in vain to reform him in private, should the preacher rebuke him from the pulpit.

The question of preaching at Court is dealt with much more extensively by another well-known preacher of the period, the Augustinian Fray Juan Márquez, who, besides being *Predicador del Rey* to Philip III, was also the author of the anti-Machiavellian treatise *El Gobernador christiano* (Salamanca, 1612). In a manuscript guide for preachers, unpublished until the last century,[1] he begins by stating that if ministers of the Word are under an obligation to preach 'reprehensiones', then it follows that their congregations, even though they might include kings or bishops, have a similar obligation to listen to them. He does, however, distinguish between 'materias...notoriamente culpables' and 'otras no tan claramente culpables' in which a prince or prelate may offend. He dismisses the latter quite categorically, 'no porque no puedan ser materia de pecado...sino porque la reprehensión del Predicador ha de caer sobre materia cierta, y ésta casi nunca lo es' (p. 174). These matters include favouritism, extravagance, excessive taxation, 'juegos, Cazas, Comedias, y otros divertimientos tomados sin moderación y con detrimento del bien público', but they are not 'inescusables', and therefore should pass without comment. In more serious matters, however, the preacher has a moral duty to denounce the sin and rebuke the sinner, whoever he be, since if the sin is publicly known more scandal will be caused by the preacher's remaining silent.

None the less, Márquez proceeds to draw another distinction: this time between sins against the good of the State (heresy or the introduction of pagan practices) and 'las culpas personales de pasión o de flaqueza'. The latter, even should they become widely known ('públicas y escandalosas'), should not, he believes, be denounced in such a way that the sinner is immediately identifiable. 'Bien veo que esta doctrina no ha de caer en gracia del vulgo que, so color de la libertad del Evangelio, desea desquitar los sentimientos que suele tener de sus superiores' (p. 178). He is concerned to preserve the reverence due to persons in supreme authority, 'porque es precisamente necesaria para el bien de la comunidad, respecto de que el Príncipe que es menospreciado del pueblo no se puede reducir como convendría a la obediencia de sus órdenes' (p. 181). Finally, he maintains that 'el fin de los sermones no es la corrección de los particulares, sino la instrucción de todo el pueblo' (p. 259), thereby dodging the issue and recommending that

---

[1] P.F. Blanco García, 'Un manuscrito inédito del P. Márquez', *C de D* xlvi (1898), 172–87, 259–71.

all 'reprehensiones' should be of the most general kind: 'y no hallo materia en que sea necesario dar doctrina y aviso a los Reyes que no se pueda tratar por cláusulas generales sin hablar al descubierto con el Príncipe que está presente' (pp. 270–1). A certain amount of cynicism regarding the preacher's mission at Court is evinced by Fray Diego de la Vega. Using the story of Belshazzar as a starting-point, he sees an ironic relevance in the writing on the wall:

Misterio grande, que quiere Dios que en las casas de los Reyes hablen las paredes, donde los hombres no osan hablar, y que pues de ordinario tienen oídos, que tengan también lengua para reprender la insolencia de un Rey: porque justo es que hablen las piedras, donde enmudecen los hombres. Piensan los poderosos del mundo que todo les es lícito, y así nadie se atreve a irles a la mano en sus gustos.[1]

He speaks, indeed, of 'las casas de los Reyes' as 'reservadas' or exempt from the natural processes of criticism and correction: '. . .no ha de entrar alguacil, ni vara de justicia, por ser reservadas: así tampoco la verdad no ha de tener allí entrada'.

In all circumstances, not only at Court, the preacher must shun any kind of vindictiveness or lack of objectivity in the criticisms he voices from the pulpit. It should be clear that 'el predicador so color o celo de reprehender vicios no ha de vengar en el sermón sus injurias, ni manifestar sus pasiones, reprehendiendo, por jabonar a sus contrarios'.[2] This advice would seem to have been very necessary, as slanging-matches between pulpit and pulpit were not uncommon in seventeenth-century Spain: 'Y que negro de usado está ello, que en oyendo el pueblo que un predicador motejó a otro, si sabe que el motejado predica, se le hinche la iglesia para ver como se satisface! Mirad que buena manera de predicar a Jesucristo. . .'(ibid.). Fray Tomás Ramón uses the metaphor *dientes* as a figure of the preacher not merely in his satirical and castigatory aspect, but also to indicate that he should be united with fellow preachers: 'blancos, limpios, iguales, fuertes'. There is too much mud-slinging from the pulpit, too little solidarity.

subc el otro al púlpito y por ganar fama y crédito todo lo facilita, y mofa del que anda algo estrecho; éste burla del otro, pareciéndole pone las almas en libertad; ésta es lástima, y cuando se hiciese punto aquí sería menos el daño y el escándalo, pero es cosa digna de lágrimas que alcanzamos ya un tiempo que los púlpitos sirven más para escandalizar que para edificar, pues en ellos se desdoran unos a otros dentro de una misma ciudad, olvidados de sí mismos y del ministerio que llevan entre manos.[3]

Benito Carlos Quintero also warns preachers against 'hacer sátiras los

---

[1] *Empleo y Exercicio Sancto*, i. 58–9.
[2] Terrones, *Instrucción*, p. 78.
[3] *Flores nuevas*, i. 208. Also Murillo, *Discursos para la Quaresma*, ii. 213–14.

sermones y campo de batallas la paz serena de los púlpitos, whether it be through doctrinal differences of opinion or simply envy of another's popularity.[1]

Several historians of our period record incidents from the controversies over the Immaculate Conception,[2] in which both Dominicans and Franciscans turned to rabble-rousing from the pulpit.[3]

Siguió utilizándose también ahora el púlpito como arma y lugar a propósito para exponer a las multitudes la doctrina concepcionista. Las controversias y tumultos populares se suscitaron principalmente en Andalucía. Teatro de tan lamentables discusiones fueron las ciudades de Córdoba, Sevilla y Granada.[4]

Even after Alexander VII had pronounced in favour of the 'inmaculistas' (1662, *Solicitudo omnium Ecclesiarum*) the controversy continued, as may be seen from the anonymous criticism of a sermon preached against the 'opinión piadosa' by the Dominican Fray Diego Ramírez:

...de aquí han nacido las sátiras y libelos, que han puesto a los ojos del siglo las desgracias de algunas gravísimas familias Religiosas, la Religión sin decoro, huyendo los pueblos de los sermones de los Padres Dominicos, con decretos de Provincias, y señoríos, para que no prediquen.[5]

Leaving aside personal quarrels and feuds between different religious orders, the preacher is enjoined to a certain minimum decorum in his 'reprehensiones', and it is implied that the special prudence and moderation required of a preacher excludes certain techniques of satire which would be perfectly acceptable in any other context. Satire, according to the definition of Covarrubias, is 'un género de verso *picante*, el cual reprehende los vicios y desordenes de los hombres' (my italics), while for Alonso López Pinciano it is 'un razonamiento *maledico* y *mordaz*, hecho para reprehender los vicios de los hombres'.[6] These epithets fit exactly the two 'figures' of the preacher we referred to before: *sal* and *perro*. However, the preacher has to handle his weapons of irony, ridicule, and invective with great care to avoid scandal: 'no

---

[1] *Templo*, fo. 51.

[2] At their height in Spain between 1615 and 1617, and also in 1663. See Domínguez Ortiz, *La sociedad española en el siglo xvii*, ii. 97-8. See also Ch. VI, pp. 149.

[3] J.–F. Bonnefoy, O.F.M., 'Sevilla por la Inmaculada en 1614–1617', *A I–A* xv (1955), 7–33, esp. 9.

[4] Alejandro Recio, O.F.M., 'La Inmaculada en la predicación franciscano-española', *A I–A* xv (1955), 120–32.

[5] *El sermón de Peor está que estaua*, n.d. [Madrid, 1663] in BNM V Ca. 999 no. 28. We shall return to this subject in the next chapter, since the reign of Philip III marks an increasing popular interest in the definition of this dogma, despite the decrees of Pius V (1570, *Super speculum*) and Paul V (1616, *Regis Pacifici*) forbidding sermons in the vernacular which referred to the Immaculate Conception.

[6] *Philosophia antigua poetica* (3 vols., Madrid, 1953), iii. 234 (my italics).

han de ser tampoco las reprehensiones del sermón, como sátiras no más
para picar y notar y afrentar. Lo que fuere pecado claro remediable
háse de reprehender, pero sin infamar las personas, ni señalarlas con
libertad, *quasi de plaustro loquentes.*[1] Moreover, *picantes* meaning
'wittily amusing' or 'racy' was applied derogatorily to preachers of the
conceptista school: 'O si estos predicadores hubiera en Madrid muchos,
y que en lugar de *picantes* picaran las conciencias, y aun atravesaran
corazones, pues por eso se llaman las palabras de Dios saetas agudas y
encendidas.'[2] Facetiousness in the pulpit is especially to be discouraged
and it is particularly out of place when vices are being depicted and
condemned. Benito Carlos Quintero is severe with the preacher who
employs a 'licencia vana de decir gracias entretenidas para risa del
pueblo en lugar tan sagrado, siendo el fin principal suyo no ganar
aplausos con desperdicios de su autoridad, sino mover a lágrimas'.[3]
Similar sentiments are expressed by Fray Diego de Estella: 'el púlpito
es lugar de gravedad y majestad, y no de chocarrerías y donaires. Y
así se ha de guardar el predicador como del fuego del infierno de
decir palabras en el púlpito que provoquen a risa.'[4] The same preacher
is also anxious to preserve another kind of decorum of speech in pulpit
'reprehensiones': 'no le es lícito decir palabra descortés ni injuriosa. . .
Para lo cual no debe decir este vocablo "bellacos", ni "bellaquerías",
aunque fuese hablando de Lutero.'[5] Instead he advises the words
'maldades' or 'abominaciones'. Bartolomé Ximénez Patón tells his
preachers: 'Cuando han de predicar contra algún pecado torpe, usen de
palabras honestas, como lo hace San Agustín en el sermón que hizo
contra la Sodomía.'[6] The same principle of *decorum* applies when the
preacher has to find a middle term between that type of *reprehensión*
which causes scandal because it pillories an individual, be he king or
carpenter, and the type of satire which loses its point because it is not
particular enough in its aim. Commenting on sermons by Fray Hernando
de Santiago, Baltasar Gracián remarks that: 'La moralidad que tiene un
punto de satírica es muy gustosa, pero ha de ponderar en común para
ir segura.'[7] Here, it might seem, the preacher's role and the satirist's

---

[1] Terrones, *Instrucción*, p. 66 (my italics).
[2] Núñez Delgadillo, *Minas*, fo. 81^V. He accuses them of 'hipérboles falsos'
(Prólogo).
[3] *Templo*, fo. 49. Also Ximénez Patón, *El perfecto predicador*, fos. 76−76^V,
and Terrones, *Instrucción*, p. 88.
[4] *Modo de predicar*, ii. 132. The Jesuit rules for preachers give the advice:
'Caveant omnino ne facetiis aut inutilium rerum narratione concionem con-
temptibilem faciant, iisve auditores ad risum moveant', in *Institutum Societatis
Iesu*, ii. 17.
[5] *Modo de predicar*, ii. 82. See also *Instrucción*, pp. 131−2.
[6] *El perfecto predicador*, fo. 79.
[7] *Agudeza y arte de ingenio*, discurso xxvii, p. 361b.

part company. The satirist attacks his chosen target mercilessly and only incidentally does he expound a more general moral lesson. In order to satirize something he aims to detach his readers from it, both intellectually and emotionally, right from the start. The technique is initially 'Look at that silly fool/evil rogue' rather than "Look at your-selves, you silly fools/evil rogues'. This is not to deny that many, if not most, satirists hold a mirror up to their readers, but they are satirists rather than preachers because this almost invariably comes as a surprise, and is couched in the ironic fiction that 'we' were initially talking about 'somebody else.'

The preacher, on the other hand, does not want any section of his congregation to imagine that they are not being *personally* addressed: Y es muy ordinario no aprovechar lo que predicamos, porque cada cual echa mano del plato ajeno y deja el que es proprio suyo. El casado dice: ¡O qué bien ha reprehendido a las viudas! El mozo: ¡O qué bien ha asentado la mano a los casados! Y la viuda está muy contenta de que riñeron muy bien a las doncellas: y desta manera nadie toma lo que a él le dice, y todos hablan de lo que dijeron al otro.[1]
He may, therefore, deliberately choose a more general term in which to illustrate his point, thereby sacrificing vividness and immediacy of impact to the desire not to be taken too literally.

Guárdese de decir, como neciamente lo hacen muchos, al reprehender el lujo y la prodigalidad en el comer y en el vestir: 'Tal es el estado de las cosas que hasta la mujer del zapatero vive ya tan suntuosamente y se adorna con aderezos y trajes de seda, de modo que por su elegancia y vestidos de diversos colores parece una princesa'. Esto es afrentoso sobremanera, y con ello se habla mal de los zapateros.[2]

OBJECTS OF ATTACK: SÁTIRA CONTRA ESTADOS

Elsewhere, however, it is the case that a sermon seeks to indict a whole class for a sin or failing to which its members are considered to be particularly prone; or a particular sin may be depicted in its different manifestations at different levels of society. Both these procedures appear to be a survival of the *sermones ad status*, or *ad omne hominum genus*, which are found in both English and French preaching in the Middle Ages.[3] Owst describes them as being addressed principally to

---

[1] Murillo, *Discursos predicables [Quaresma]*, i. 723.
[2] Estella, *Modo de predicar*, ii. 175.
[3] There is a parallel, and probably related, tradition in the Dances of Death and mystery plays of the late Middle Ages all over Europe. The tradition was given fresh impetus by Erasmus and his Spanish followers (Alfonso de Valdés, *Diálogo de Mercurio y Carón*) and includes several of Calderón's *autos sacramentales*. See I. Nolting-Hauff, *Visión, sátira y agudeza en los 'Sueños' de Quevedo* (Madrid, 1974), pp. 114–18. Also R. Mohl, *The three estates in medieval and Renaissance literature (Columbia, 1933)*.

clerical 'states' (prelates, lower clergy, religious, and clerks), but he did locate one manuscript collection of *sermones varii ad mercatores*, although he was not able to date it or to attribute it to a named preacher.[1] T.F. Crane quotes the *proemium* to Jacques de Vitry's *sermones dominicales*, in which he enumerates the different *sermones ad status* as follows: 'Ad Praelatos, ad Sacerdotes in Synodo, ad Monachos et Moniales, et alias Regulares personas, ad Scholares, ad Peregrinos et Cruce-Signatos, ad Milites, ad Servos et Ancillas, ad Virgines et Viduas et Conjugatas.'[2] He concludes that 'secundum enim varietatem personarum oportet non solum variare sermones, sed et sententias, et plerumque loquendi modum et scribendi stylum'.[3] The three 'estates' of political theory—clergy, nobles, and the common people—require three distinct styles: high (*alto*), middle (*ecuestre*), and low (*plebeyo*).[4] Although Spanish preaching in the Middle Ages is scantily documented,[5] it may be assumed that these distinctions of 'states' and 'styles' applied in some degree. Indeed, in the early seventeenth century Terrones del Caño tells us that: 'así, conforme el auditorio, se ha de templar la voz y modo de reprehender. Al vulgo, a gritos y porrazos; al auditorio noble, con blandura de voz y eficacia de razones; a los reyes, casi en falsete y con gran sumisión.'[6]

Quite apart from the need to accommodate doctrine to congregation, whether by style, 'tone', or degree of theological 'difficulty', we find in many of the sermons of this period a type of *sátira contra estados* which reminds us as much of the techniques of classical satirists (from Juvenal to Quevedo) as of the preoccupations of the preacher (to be all things to all men). The basic assumptions which this type of satire promotes are set out by Fray Cristóbal de Fonseca:

Tienen algunos Estados tan antigua posesión en el mal que se cree con dificultad el bien; en oficiales, mercaderes y tratantes alega prescripción el mentir. ¿Quántos años ha que dijo Salomon, que el mercader quando vende alaba su mercadería, y que el comprador la desalaba y la desprecia? *Bonum est, bonum est, dicit omnis emptor.* En Receptores, y Procuradores es negocio muy antiguo el pelar; en los que sirven adular; en los soldados, desgarros, robos y desafueros...así el soldado no se puede vivir sin pecar.[7]

---

[1] *Preaching in Medieval England*, pp. 247–65, esp. note to p. 264.

[2] *The Exempla... of Jacques de Vitry*, note to p. xxxix.

[3] See Ch. I, pp. 11–14.

[4] Twelve 'states' or 'estates' within the Church are listed in *Dormi secure* (Paris, 1538). They are Pope, cardinal, bishop, abbot, religious, priest (*presbyter*), emperor, king, prince, baron, knight (*miles*), and lawyer.

[5] A.D. Deyermond, review of Owst's book in *Estudios lulianos*, vii (1963), 233–5.

[6] *Instrucción*, p. 151.

[7] *Discursos para la Quaresma*, fo. 24^V. A misquotation of Proverbs 20:14, where '*Malum est...*' should be substituted for *Bonum est*.

Particularly harsh treatment is meted out, working on these assumptions, to all officials and 'middlemen'–'Alguaciles, Escribanos, Almotacenes, Denunciadores, y todos los demás que se sustentan del alcabala del Infierno'[1] –and this appears to reflect the traditional unpopularity of such people, who fit rather uneasily into the social hierarchy and are frequently accused of injustice to those below them and disloyalty to those above. Social antipathy, as Professor John Hale has pointed out, was frequently founded on the fear that lawyers and mercenaries could, and would, abuse the trust placed in them: 'So could millers and tanners [and tailors], both universally reviled as men who were needed to process others' products, but who could set aside or snip aside part of these products with little fear of detection.'[2]

The medical profession, so heavily satirized in most literatures for its mumbo-jumbo and kill-or-cure remedies, hardly suffers at all at the hands of preachers during this period in Spain, to judge by the sermons I have selected.[3] I have, however, found one quite wittily elaborated description of a charlatan doctor, in which he is compared to a fortune-telling gypsy:

. . .como una Gitana que llega a decir la buena dicha, y mira a la otra las rayas de la mano, y si ve que es moza en casa grande, y tiene padres ricos, dirá que la sirven muchos, y que uno se adelanta en quererla, y otras cosas que barrunte por las apariencias que se ve: acertó a tener un padre, o de mala condición, o un poco tiniente de manos, y por no desembolsar el dinero, se le despinta el casamiento a la hija, y queda la buena dicha burlada y sin efecto. Entra un gitano de un médico en vuestra casa, esperando a que le ofrezcáis el real de a cuatro, y no a deciros la buena sino la mala dicha, toma el pulso, toca la lengua, hace un interrogatorio más largo que un Alcalde de Corte cuando examina un testigo, ve la calentura que os abrasa, manda sangraros aprisa, fue acaso vuestro mal de resfriado, y el despacho de las sangrías fue despachar con vuestra vida.[4]

There is also, in Fonseca, a condemnation of 'los médicos del cuerpo, que por tenerse por Apolos y Esculapios, se desdeñan de visitar a los pobres'.[5] 'Médicos del alma', confessors, are often no better.

In many sermons it is the officers of the law who are attacked for their venality and hypocrisy. They accuse the poor of dishonesty while themselves perpetrating 'hurtos de marca mayor', as in this dramatized passage from Fray Cristóbal de Avendaño:

[1] Ibid., fo. 243[V].
[2] J.R. Hale, *Renaissance Europe, 1480–1520* (London, 1971), pp. 192–3.
[3] Spanish satire on doctors in other literary genres has been studied by Y. David-Peyre, *Le Personnage du médecin et la relation médecin-malade dans la littérature ibérique du xvie et xviie siècle* (Paris, 1971).
[4] Ponce de León, *Discursos para diferentes Evangelios de la Quaresma*, i. 20–1.
[5] *Discursos para la Quaresma*, fo. 30.

Llega el Regidor a la frutera, y porque faltó en el peso un maravedí hácela una causa, y reprehéndela con grandes voces, que es una ladrona. Bien pudiera la frutera responder: Señor Regidor, ¿cómo se admira V.M. tanto que yo hurté un maravedí, y no le admiran sus hurtos, pues cuando le envia el Regimiento a una comisión hurte los cinco y seis mil ducados?[1]

He continues with similar observations about *alguaciles* and *escribanos* and their ill-gotten gains—topics familiar to us from our reading of Quevedo.

The attitude towards the merchants class which manifests itself in the sermons is also a traditional one, as Fray Diego de la Vega indicates in a sermon for the Feast of St. Matthew, beside the marginal note *Locus pro mercatoribus*. After interpreting the lion image in Psalm 9:9 as a picture of the predatory merchant, seeking to lure the poor man into his lair—

¿Qué (veamos) es un mercader codicioso cuando está escondido en su tienda y sentado en ella, sino un león emboscado y puesto en asechanza. . .? En pasando el labradorcito, el hombre bozal, a quien pretende engañar y chuparle la sangre, sale luego a él, atráele con palabras halagüenas y blandas.[2]

—he continues, with a show of mock reluctance, to quote other images used in Scripture to denote merchants ('thieves' and 'crows'):

Ahora mirad, Christianos, lícito es el trato de los mercaderes y la granjería, y no lo sería el querer yo condenar a bulto todos los que se ejercitan en ello en la república: pero está esto tan estragado y hácese de ordinario tan mal, que de ahí nace que los tratantes y mercaderes no tienen muy buen nombre en la Escritura.

He then expands the comparison between merchants and thieves thus:

Pues, ¿qué tiene que ver ladrón con mercader? Mas, ¿qué no tiene que ver? El mercader engañoso que vende el gato por liebre, y lo que vale cuatro por diez, y él que vende al fiado más que al contado, vendiendo el tiempo y la necesidad dél que compra, ¿qué tanto os parece que le falta para ladrón? (p. 358)

The merchant is seen as being doubly dangerous: firstly, because he sells substandard goods at excessive prices, and secondly, because he makes a policy of encouraging his customers to get into debt by giving them unlimited credit, on which, it is implied, he charges interest. The connection between merchants and money-lenders is not explicitly spelled out, but enough is said to indicate that the age-old problem is still a pressing one.

Fray Basilio Ponce de León, commenting on a passage from Pliny (*Latifundia perdidere Italiam*, lib. xviii. 6), elaborates on this kind of social injustice and the exploitation of the common people by officers of the state, seeing it as a spreading sickness of the body

[1] *Sermones de la Quaresma*, i. fos. 161^v−162.   [2] *Parayso*, ii. 357.

politic: '¿Qué pensáis que es la causa de haber tantos pobres?' The old
order is giving way before a brash new class of professionals and semi-
professionals, parvenus who are viewed with disdain, and at times
apprehension, by the traditional aristocracy, as well as by the poor:
'. . .que si hasta agora había grandes en España, y hay otros mayores,
que son Oydores y Letrados, pues éstos les compran las haciendas, que
ellos venden por verse empeñados, y cuando nos las compran las chupan
dulcemente'.[1] Ponce de León here appears to be speaking from the
point of view of a specific interest group, the old aristocracy, to which
he belongs (although illegitimate), rather than from the more detached
and lofty standpoint of the preacher.[2] He speaks with great distaste of
'escribanos, notarios, oficiales, gente de papeles' (p. 297) and while he
criticizes their behaviour towards the poor, there seems at the same
time to be a shadow of class antagonism of a different kind.

Entró un Corregidor en un pueblo con menos de capa de bayeta; a
pocos días está su casa como colmena, su mujer en coche, y sillas
sobradas en casa, y negros que la lleven, pajes, criados, lacayos; y
cuando sale de lugar va rico, y lleva que comer toda la vida. ¿De dónde
tanta riqueza tan presto? Fácil es de adevinar: del cohecho, del soborno,
del abrir las manos, de decir *adueniat* a todo cuanto viniere, aunque
la justicia se arrastre, de puras vejaciones y condenaciones de pobres;
pues de la hacienda dellos se enriquece aquéste. (p. 147)

The preacher has previously 'exposed' the *oydor* and the *letrado* in just
this way and now proceeds to an *amplificatio*:

Id discurriendo desta suerte en el mercader, tesorero, depositario,
alguacil, escribano, procurador, regidores, obligados, tenderos, y oficiales,
como tan ricos con tanto oro a buchado, tratándose como príncipes.
Porque es a costa de otros, que es fuerza que lo lasten: son bazos de
la república, que el hinchazón dellos es enfermedad de los que en ella
viven. (ibid.)

The conclusion is that 'la riqueza de los unos es causa de la pobreza
de los otros', and this statement is frequently expounded and illustrated
in sermons for Lent, the season of penance and alms-giving. A vice is
here being used to spotlight a virtue.

Poverty and riches are two such different 'states' of life that they
can hardly be addressed together, unless it is to point up a stark contrast between them. The poor man is depicted by preachers as being
so severely ostracized by the world that 'si el pobre dice que es pariente
del rico, no averiguarían el parentesco cuantos juristas hay en las
Universidades de España'.[3] The gulf separating Dives and Lazarus is

---

[1] *Discursos para diferentes Evangelios*, ii. 147.
[2] I do not wish, however, to lay undue stresss on the pronoun 'nos'. He
declared in 1610 that he was the natural son of don Rodrigo Ponce de León,
Conde de Bailén.
[3] Rebolledo, *Cien oraciones fúnebres*, fo. 189.

almost unbridgeable and the only consolation for the latter is a spiritual one: the poor are 'por la mayor parte, los más aventajados en el conocimiento práctico de Dios, y en la sequella de Cristo'.[1] Great emphasis is laid, as is to be expected in ascetical writing, on the vanity of worldly prosperity, which dazzles and blinds men to more real and lasting joys. This lesson of *desengaño* belongs particularly to the funeral sermons of Fray Luis de Rebolledo, who says that rich men 'son escuchados con tan gran admiración como si cada uno dellos fuera en hablar un Cicerón, en difinir un Platón, en disputar un Aristóteles, y en aconsejar un Séneca', and he concludes:

...en lo cual anda el mismo mundo tan engañado como los Indios cuando daban las perlas por el vidrio y el oro por cosas de poco valor. Y si esto era ser los Indios bozales entonces, el mundo lo está agora cada día más, pues tiene en más las riquezas que todos los demás bienes de fortuna, de naturaleza y aun de gracia.[2]

In another sermon the same preacher paraphrases a text from Ecclesiastes 10:19–'*Pecuniae obediunt omnia*' ('Todas las cosas obedecen al dinero')–linking it to the Golden Age topic '*Aurea sunt vere nunc saecula*' from Ovid's *Ars amandi*, ii. 277: 'Verdaderamente si los siglos pasados decimos que eran los dorados, éste es de oro, pues en el tanto se estima.'[3] He is, none the less, able to say of a money-lender, for whom he preaches a funeral sermon, that he feels that the money he employed in alms-giving has amply compensated for an excessive concern for the world's goods in his lifetime: 'Yo creo (vistas sus limosnas) que compró el Cielo a dinero, y que no sólo no le estorbó para subir a el, sino que antes hizo dél escalera de plata, y está a la puerta del Cielo, que es Purgatorio.'[4]

On the other hand, Fray Tomás Ramón shows us graphically how Dives can neglect his duty to show charity to Lazarus through a combination of avarice and vain extravagance:

Ya no sé qué ha de responder a Dios el día de la cuenta el rico, que no hace sino amontonar dinero y aumentar la renta, sin acordarse de las necesidades extremas de sus prójimos. El tiene los cofres llenos, funda casas y mayorazgos, y eterniza su nombre con gastos bien escusados, y el pobrecito, por no tener con qué pagar hasta veinte reales, está detenido en la cárcel, comido de los que entre la camisa y la carne se

---

[1] Murillo, *Discursos predicables [Quaresma]*, i. 243.
[2] *Cien oraciones fúnebres*, fo. 188; see also fo. 255: 'Engañamos a los negros en Caboverde, dándoles un bonete colorado y quitándoles la libertad. Engaña el mundo: dános la honrilla, y está en ella el abatimiento y la envidia.' This is capped by the sermonizing *Guzmán de Alfarche* (II. iii. 2; ed. cit. iv. 228): 'Ved quién somos, pues para los negros de Guinea, bozales y bárbaros, llevan cuentecitas, dijes y caxcabeles; y a nosotros con sólo el sonido, con la sombra y resplandor destos vidritos nos engañan.'
[3] *Cien oraciones fúnebres*, fo. 155.   [4] Ibid., fo. 111^V.

crían. La doncella se determina y abalanza por verse pobre, se acaba y pierde, y la pérdida no se reduce. El enfermo vuelto el rostro a la pared y la lengua apegada al paladar muere, por no tener quien dél se apiade. ¡O despiadados ricos! Esclavos de la avaricia, adoradores del dinero, cuán sin consuelo se hallarán sus ánimas al partir desta vida, y con qué desamparo en poder de los demonios, ardiendo con aquel otro ricacho en el fuego sempiterno, pues tan inhumanos fueron con los que debían amar como a sí mismos.[1]

This is the preaching of complaint rather than satire: the preacher seems to be using pathetic realism to launch an onslaught on a particular sector of society. However, when the faults which accompany riches—extravagance, affectation, false pride—are to be shown up we frequently find vignettes, or wittily sketched portraits, of particular individuals who incarnate them, and who thereby belong to a 'class' of sinner. Two examples are women (who stand as symbols of vanity and fickleness in both sexes) and *pretendientes* (who immolate their lives to false gods). Women often appear as the last group in the catalogue of 'estates' in medieval literature of the estates and their faults are enumerated.[2]

The female sex has always been unpopular with the preachers, and their attitude may be summed up by the frequently quoted text from Proverbs 7:10–12— '*garrula et vaga, quietis impatiens, nec volens in domo consistere pedibus suis*'.[3] Fray Diego de la Vega has his own word for 'mujeres andariegas': 'Que se hubo antiguamente un Cid en nuestra Castilla, que por renombre le llamasen Campeador, ahora hallaremos muchas mujeres a quien con justo título se les podía dar ese apellido campeadoras, callejeras, desasosegadas, que nunca se les cae el manto de acuestas.'[4] Women are depicted as both fickle and insatiable in all things: 'antojadiza y mudable' describes not only 'la mujer adúltera' but all her sisters, in the eyes of Fray Cristóbal de Fonseca:

Cuando una mujer da en golosa, en comer buenos bocados en secreto, y limpiándose los labios, da en decir que ayuna; cuando da en traviesa en sus rincones, y en ja[c]tarse en público: Nadie vive tan honradamente como yo, teniendo alquilada el alma al demonio, es negocio casi desafuciado [*sic*].[5]

The contemporary fashion for society ladies to eat clay, or pieces of pottery, in order to have an interestingly pale complexion is seized

---

[1] *Flores nuevas*, i. 59.
[2] Mohl, *The three estates*, pp. 20–1.
[3] Owst, *Literature and Pulpit*, pp. 375–404.
[4] *Parayso*, i. 324. In the *Empleo y Exercicio*, i. 60–1 he has more serious complaints of the 'malicia y crueldad de las mujeres', particularly their vengefulness.
[5] *Discursos para la Quaresma*, fo. 383. Murillo calls women 'multívolas' and 'sanguijuelas' in *Discursos predicables [Quaresma]*, i. 530.

upon by Vega, in order to demonstrate how the moral sense can become blunted and habitual sin become palatable: 'Mujeres hay que comen barro y yeso, y aun algunas hay que comen carbón (y lo que más espanta, que les sabe bien y se saborean en ello) y dicen: O qué bueno está esto; más me sabe que un pedazo de alcorza.'[1] Even more explicitly, Fray Cristóbal de Fonseca makes a similar point: 'Al quartanario es desabrida la pechuga del capón, y sabrosa la sardina, la cebolla y el salpicón de vaca. Al pecho lleno de tierra es fuerza sea desabrida la doctrina del cielo.'[2]

When extravagance in dress is being preached against, women provide an easy target, although Fonseca also draws attention to over-dressed fops and 'carpet knights', who have succeeded the hardy, hirsute warriors of old. He describes them as 'almidonados, alheñados, encopetados, engomados' and comments that 'entonces todos olían a pólvora: ahora muchos a ámbar, y todos a almidón'.[3] Women, in fact, have become the warriors in this degenerate age: 'Las mujeres con sus galas y con sus adornos, danzando y bailando, han hecho más guerra a los hombres que los ejércitos con picas, tiros y balas.'[4] Even widows, who might be expected to dress in a seemly fashion as dowdy *dueñas*, are, according to the preachers, excessively merry:

Las que se ponen tocas de seda cortas [instead of 'una toca plegada, tan larga como una sobrepelliz, de holanda'] y jubón de raso picado; sacan los cabellos rubios por las sienes, y enguantan las manos; andan olorosas y afeitadas; salen muchas veces de casa, y en la suya dan silla de buena conversación y entretenimiento; visten mantón de la villa, y faldellín de grana; por la melancolía hállanse en la boda y en el bautismo.[5]

Fray Basilio Ponce de León, preaching to the freshmen of Alcalá in 1599, unmasks the dangerous face of woman:

Estudiante novatillo, que, en este río de la Universidad que de continuo corre, poco sabidor del uso de las damas desta tierra, que son como zarzas en el camino para prender al que pudieren; te arrebaten los ojos y el corazón un tocado alto, unas nubecillas en el rostro de diferentes arreboles, unas razones muy cortadas y estudiadas de cartilla ...deténte, que esa que pretendes no desea tu bien, sino codicia su manto y su basquiña a costa de tu sangre y tu honor.[6]

The preacher who wishes to rebuke his female listeners for their frivolity

---

[1] *Parayso*, ii. 127. Also Avendaño, *Sermones de Quaresma*, i. fo. 6^V.

[2] *Discursos predicables para la Quaresma*, fo. 352^V.

[3] Ibid., fo. 61^V. See Góngora *letrilla* (1593): 'Al que de sedas armado'.

[4] Ramón, *Puntos escripturales*, ii. 645.

[5] Rebolledo, *Cien oraciones fúnebres*, fo. 102. See also Avendaño, *Sermones de Quaresma*, ii. fos. 39^V–40. R. Jammes gives several examples of the same satires against merry widows in his *Études sur l'œuvre poétique de Don Luis de Góngora* (Bordeaux, 1967), pp. 109–10.

[6] *Discursos para diferentes Evangelios de Quaresma*, i. 345.

may be caught unawares by changes in terminology. Fray Jerónimo Bautista de Lanuza gives us an anecdote, allegedly from personal experience:

Predicando, el año 1606, la Quaresma en el insigne Hospital de nuestra Señora de Gracia de la ciudad de Zaragoza, reprehendiendo algunas veces, con los Apóstoles S. Pedro y S. Pablo, el demasiado cuidado de las mujeres en su composición y ornato, nombrando algunas cosas de sus galas y dijes—el hurraco, la arandela, la trampilla &c—dijéronme con mucha gracia unas Señoras de título, que me imaginaban que venía como aquél de los siete dormientes, que yendo a comprar a la ciudad, sacaba monedas tan antiguas, que no estaban en uso, ni las conocían, porque totalmente eran otras las que corrían: porque las cosas de adorno de las mujeres que yo nombraba, aunque poco antes eran usadas, ya estaban del todo olvidadas, y eran nuevas cuántas ahora traían, y comenzáronmelas a nombrar con unos nombres que parecían compuestos para bernardinas o gerigonza, y que hubiera menester mucho días para tomarlos de memoria. . .Buen estudio sería éste de un predicador religioso: tan loco me probaría yo como ellas, si perdiese el tiempo atendiendo tanto a saber los nombres de sus galas, como ellas a inventarlas.[1]

His conclusion is by no means an admission of defeat. It is, rather, an intensification through ridicule and irony (the laugh seems at first to be on the out-of-date preacher) of the satire, and points up the vanity of a concern with fashion, even of the most 'academic' kind, since it is at best here today and gone tomorrow.

Insubstantial and transitory, too, are the goals on which the *pretendiente* sets his sights, and through the ludicrous picture of a servile opportunist—one of the many who flocked to the Court of Philip III in the hope of preferment—Fray Luis de Rebolledo satirizes a more general human failing. His treatment of the type, in a funeral sermon for a real-life *pretendiente*, is a comic caricature:

¿Qué es ver un pretendiente en la Corte de los Reyes; colgado de la cola del caballo del privado, arrimado al estribo del coche de la dama, hecho un camaleón, volviéndose de todos los colores que halla? Si habla con el triste, arruga la frente, baja los ojos, tuerce la cabeza, abemola ['lower the voice' (from *bemol*=flat [music]) which is another sign of his self-prostration]la voz, dice el pésame.[2]

The *pretendiente* has deliberately forfeited his personal identity and integrity in order to conform to his new environment, and in so doing he has become like a grotesque spider, 'con muchos pies y poca cabeza' (Isaiah 59:5–8). The image is continued because 'si todas las dignidades duran poco, las pretendidas y negociadas menos: porque, como telas

[1] *Homilías sobre los Evangelios de la Quaresma* (Barbastro, 1621), i. Prólogo, sig. e.3.
[2] *Cien oraciones fúnebres*, fo. 208.

de arañas, una mosca las rompe' (fo. 208^V). The sermon, in fact, appears
to be almost entirely satirical. Puns abound ('proveídos / pobres e idos')
and burlesque effects ('sus hijas, que ni eran pocas ni pequeñas, ni aun
pequeños ni pocos los trabajos y necesidades que habían padecido en
la ausencia de su padre'). Rebolledo is quite obviously tongue-in-cheek
when he describes his *pretendiente*'s lack of vices:

El pretendiente nunca puede ser soberbio al parecer, porque se anda
humillando a todos los que le pueden dar la mano. Ninguno hay mal
criado, porque gastan dos gorras más por año quitándola cada punto,
aun hasta a él que no la tiene. Puesto que a uno oí decir, que las gastaba
menos; porque el pretendiente siempre la trae en la mano. (fo. 206)

Here the preacher has moved from the particular to the general and
even beyond, into the fictional. The stock figure of the *pretendiente*
has by now entirely supplanted the man for whom the funeral sermon
was originally preached. The final, cynical, conclusion, which purports
to address itself to the individual rather than to the type, is that 'no
supo. . .ser buen pretendiente en la vida, porque no fue a pretender a
Madrid por el camino de la plata, que es llano, sino por la Sierra Morena.
No dio, y por eso no recibió' (fo. 207). There is, however, a more
general, and more preacherly, moral: that he should have aspired to
heavenly rather than earthly honours and not gone to Court at all.

'Ambiciones y pretensiones' are among those vices which, 'por no
ser castigados en el mundo, son tenidos por menos que otros', and
for that very reason should, according to Fray Diego de Estella, be
particularly preached against.[1] He also includes in this category the sin
of *murmuración*, which, although it might seem to be so widespread as
to transcend class barriers, is traditionally seen as the special province
of the lower orders and 'labradores' in country villages.[2] This may well
be linked with the topic of the envious *vulgo*, so frequent in the prologues to *sermonarios* as well as in secular works.[3] Fray Basilio Ponce
de León draws attention to the danger of listening to malicious gossip:
'Ni para con vos pierda honra aquél de quien oyeredes murmurar san-
grientamente, ni el crédito de aquél, ni la honestidad de la casa dáse
mella en vuestro pecho, si no véis que se prueba.'[4] However, he then
warns the victims of calumny to be sure to avoid scandal: 'Y si no
queréis que digan, no les déis ocasión para que digan, que tiznarán

---

[1] *Modo de predicar*, ii. 127.
[2] Ponce de León, *Discursos para diferentes Evangelios*, ii. 171 (quoted above,
p. 12). See also Martín de Azpilcueta, *Tratado de alabanza y murmuración*
(Valladolid, 1572).
[3] Valderrama, *Exercicios espirituales para la Quaresma*, ii. Dedicatoria,
sig. ¶4^V and Ponce de León, *Discursos para diferentes Evangelios de Quaresma*, i.
Dedicatoria, sig. ¶3. See also Cosme de Aldana, *Inuectiva contra el vulgo y su
maledicencia* (Madrid, 1591), stanzas xvi and xxxiii.
[4] *Discursos para diferentes Evangelios*, ii. fo. 285.

vuestra honra con sólo decirlo, aunque no sea muy fuerte la probanza'.[1]
The prudent man is careful to guard his reputation and to pay attention
to the *qué dirán*: 'El prudente Corregidor suele visitar disfrazado los
bodegones y las tabernas, codicioso de saber qué dicen de su gobierno,
que el freno que más a raya hace estar él que gobierna es lo que dicen y
dirán. . .No basta vivir con Dios, sino con los hombres.'[2] A good name
(*honra* or *buena fama*) is not only a precious jewel to its possessor but
it also edifies and inspires others, when it is rightfully won.[3] *Honra*
is not only 'patrimonio del alma' in the eyes of the preachers but it is
a powerful civilizing force in human society: 'sino fuese por la honra
muchos harían desatinos notables, sin tener respeto al temor de Dios'.[4]

On the other hand, it can have the purely negative connotations of
vanas honras, pundonor, and *negra honrilla.*[5] Fray Diego Murillo paints
a satirical picture of men enslaved by false honour:

Otros hay por el contrario tan honrados, que al parecer traen la honra
en redoma de vidrio, que cualquier golpecillo la quiebra, fundando
puntos de honra de cada palabrita, y espantándose de cada cosita que
dicen de ellos: tanto, que alguna vez por una palabrita vuelven atrás en
cosas que emprendieron de honra, y fuera bien pasarlas adelante.[6]

They neglect their real responsibilities for something imaginary and
become so touchy about trifles that they do less than justice to themselves and others. The wrong kind of honour can be not so much a
'freno' as a stumbling-block: 'los puntos de la honra son muchas veces
escándalos de las almas, y hacen incurable la enfermedad de la culpa'.[7]

Honra can, nevertheless, be a powerful motivating force for either
good or evil, as we see from Fray Basilio Ponce de León's illustrative
alegoría:

¿Qué poderoso es este idolillo de la honra? ¿qué dellos lleva tras sí
y arrastra lo que dicen pundonor en el mundo? ¿a qué peligros no se

---

[1] Ibid. Núñez Delgadillo, *Minas*, fo. 339 speaks of 'un airecillo [que] lastima
los ojos, y un rumor iniquo lastima la fama'.

[2] Fonseca, *Quarta parte de la Vida de Christo*, p. 17. Cf. *El médico de su
honra*, II. vv. 385−98 (ed. C. A. Jones, pp. 54−5) and *El castigo sin venganza*, I.
vv. 137−46 (ed. C.A. Jones, p. 31).

[3] Florencia, *Marial*, ii. 319 and Vega, *Parayso*, i. 300.

[4] Murillo, *Discursos predicables [Quaresma]*, i. 614 and Fonseca, *Discursos
predicables*, fo. 381: 'Entre nobles es la honra freno del vicio: y caso que no
profesan virtud, es gran negocio estimar la honra.' Here he follows St. Augustine
in speaking of the morals of the pre-Christian Greeks and Romans, *City of God*,
v. 13.

[5] Vego, *Empleo y Exercicio*, i. 92. Similar ambivalence about different kinds
of honour, including the 'negra honrilla', 'punto de honra', and 'provechos del qué
dirán', is to be found in B. Gracián's *El criticón*, ii. crisi xi.

[6] *Discursos predicables [Adviento]*, pp. 564−5.

[7] Fonseca, *Discursos predicables para la Quaresma*, fo. 324. He is commenting
on the story of Naaman the leper.

ponen? ¿qué dificultades y trabajos no engullen? un molino de viento,
quien le ve con tantas y tan grandes velas, tanta madera, y tan pesada,
tantas ruedas, tanto hierro y piedra no pensara que es caso posible
dar aquello una vuelta en un siglo; y un remusgo de aire que se levante,
le trae con una ligereza que espanta. Un navío como un palacio, que
tantos hombres apenas podrían menearle de su lugar, con un soplo de
aire vuela.[1]

Just as the breeze 'miraculously' sets both the mill and the sailing-ship
in motion, so the *vientecillo* of honour inspires men and drives them
to action:

¡Cuántos de su natural o perezosos, o poco diligentes, o para poco, o
embarazados de suyo, y que ruegos ni importunidades de muchos serían
poderosos para hacerlos dar un paso, y este soplo de la honrilla los hace
tan diligentes, solícitos, despiertos, entremetidos, que no parece asientan
en el suelo los pies! (Ibid.)

The implication is, unfortunately, that men will do for honour what
they are not prepared to do for God, and that in fact honour is itself
a false god.[2] The same preacher continues:

Honra pretendida por buen medio, y no pretendida por lo que ella es,
sino ordenada al servicio de Dios, digna es de estimarse: mas honra
deseada como fin nuestro, y que allí se piense de día y se sueñe de
noche, y por ella se afane a todas horas, y que a este Dios se ofrenden
los trabajos y cuidados, y a trueque de conseguirla, o conservarla, no
se repara en dar un vuelco en el infierno, mala honra, desordenada
afición, errado pensamiento. (p. 62)

What is being rebuked here is not a specific sin but a whole attitude
of mind, a corrupt set of values, which challenges the Christian ethic
through being a travesty of it.[3] It belongs to the preaching of *desengaño*
rather than the older *sátira contra estados*, and we shall examine other
examples of it below, after passing in review a number of satirical
'fictions' or 'set pieces' of different kinds.

TECHNIQUES OF SATIRE

Satire is an intention rather than a genre and manifests itself in a
varied set of stylistic techniques (wit, ridicule, irony, sarcasm, cynicism,
the sardonic, and invective) which originated in speech and still retain
much of their public and oral character. The convention implies an

[1] *Discursos para diferentes Evangelios*, ii. 60—1.
[2] *Lazarillo de Tormes*, Tratado III: 'Oh Señor, y cuántos de aquestos debéis
vos tener por el mundo derramados que padecen por la negra que llaman honra lo
que por vos no sufrirían.'
[3] The religion of honour is treated still more scathingly by Fonseca, *Discursos
predicables para la Quaresma*, fo. 245: 'Los Capitanes y soldados adoran en las
leyes del duelo, que examinadas bien son muy grandes necedades. Al mentís
palos; a los palos, cuchillada; a la cuchillada, muerte.' See also P.N. Dunn, 'Honour
and the Christian background in Calderón', *BHS* xxxvii (1960), 89.

audience and a tone of voice, and furthermore it has been observed that there is a close connection between satire and rhetoric, even when the satirist presents himself, directly or indirectly, as a plain speaker. The satirist is always acutely conscious of the difference between things as they are and things as they should be and, if he is to be successful, his audience (society) should at least pay lip-service to the ideals he upholds.[1] Members of a congregation gathered for worship share certain assumptions about desirable behaviour and attitudes. Consequently, the persona and professional competence of the preacher would seem to be ideally suited to satire. However, since the purpose of a sermon is not solely castigatory but also exhortatory and devotional, a preacher's satire is usually intermittent and concentrated around a few focal points. We have already quoted a couple of satirical 'portraits', which in the Theophrastan tradition seek to show foibles and vices as part of a living, human personality, however grotesque, rather than as allegorized figures or personifications.[2] It is a consequence of the 'mirror-up-to-nature' topic employed not only by satirists but by many other poets at the Renaissance.[3] Moreover, the techniques of sermon-illustration examined in Chapter III above—*simile, comparación*, and *exemplum*—are common currency in the satirist's trade.

A further development of these 'fictions' (all of which point up the significance of one reality by drawing attention to the existence of another) is the extended parallel. This is not just a *comparación*, used for a satirical purpose, but a stark juxtaposition of two 'realities' whose likeness-within-unlikeness is nothing short of shocking. The gypsy-doctor (p. 120) is one example of this sort of construction and another hybrid, the *halcón-escribano*, dreamed up by Fray Cristóbal de Avendaño, is even more damning in its implications:

Los halcones de Norvega ejercitan mucho las plumas y las uñas, porque en tres horas que tiene el día en aquella región, han de cazar para sustentarse veinte y una que tiene la noche. Hay un escribano en esta Corte, que se levanta a las once del día y por la tarde no está otra hora y media en su oficio, porque se va a la comedia: de modo que en tres horas ha de ganar para sustentar lo restante del día. Pues, ¿cómo es eso? Yo os diré: son como los halcones de Norvega que ejercitan las uñas, y en poco tiempo roban mucho. De dedos de semejantes escribanos hace Lucifer plato a los demonios.[4]

---

[1] A Pollard, *Satire* (London, 1970), p. 3.
[2] See above, pp. 125–6. La Bruyère's *Caractères* (1688) are probably the best-known examples of the genre, but perhaps closer to the style of our preachers are the *Characters* of Thomas Overbury (1581–1613).
[3] See J.H. Hagstrum, *The Sister Arts* (Chicago, 1958), pp. 70, 121 and 181–2.
[4] *Sermones de Quaresma*, i. 234^V–235. He attributes the idea to 'un discreto Cortesano'. Quevedo in *El Sueño de la Muerte* (written 1606–7; pub. 1627) uses the same pun 'volar con las plumas' to refer to *escribanos* and the Genoese. See *Obras completas*, i. 188b. 'volar' = 'desaparecer rápidamente'.

After a seemingly innocuous opening, in which the falcons are depicted as deploying assiduously both *plumas* ('wings') and *uñas* in their search for food under adverse conditions, a thoroughly damaging parallel is established with the habits of the hawkish notary, in which it is stressed that in the same space of time the *plumas* ('pens') are idle, while the rapacious *uñas* are only too much in evidence. The construction bears some resemblance to a syllogism and is crowned by an explicit conclusion of condemnation in which *escribanos* and *halcones* are further identified by the juxtaposition of *dedos* and *uñas*.

Other equally opportunist public servants receive similar treatment at the hands of Fray Agustín Núñez Delgadillo. This time the inspiration is the Gospel text: 'My house shall be called the house of prayer; but ye have made it a den of thieves' (Matthew 21:13). The symmetry, again, speaks for itself:

Están cuatro ladrones en su cueva escondidos y tienen quien ve a los pasajeros. Llega éste: —Señores, uno pasa.
—¿Qué hombres?—
—Un pobre a pie.—
—Estémonos quedos, ¿para qué hemos de salir a un pobretón?—
—Gente pasa.—
—¿Qué gente?—
—Dos hombres bien puestos a mula; parece que llevan dineros.—
—Pues, vamos a ellos.
Están cuatro Eclesiásticos en conversación, entreteniéndose.
Doblan en la Parroquia.
—Corre, muchacho, mira quién es el muerto.—
—Un pobre de la Parroquia.—
—Estémonos quedos, entiérrelo el cura.—
—¿Quién murió?—
—Don Fulano.—
—Vamos, que hay vela y dos reales.—
¿Qué es esto? Parece la Iglesia cueva de ladrones.[1]

The dialogue gives ample scope to the preacher to exercise his dramatic bent, and the parallel is knit together by a disingenuous question and answer, consolidating the satirical point.

Another device used by preachers for satirical effect is an extended metaphor, punctuated by a refrain. The whole might be termed a *gloss*, and an example of this form is found in Fray Cristóbal de Avendaño's sermon for the first Sunday of Advent. It forms part of a longer development on the text *Video mundum senescentum*,[2] in which all the members of society show the same signs of rigor mortis as the limbs

---

[1] *Minas*, fo. 87. See also Alfonso de Valdés, *Diálogo de las cosas ocurridas en Roma* [1527] (Clásicos Castellanos, 1956), p. 66.

[2] Isaiah 24:4: 'The earth mourneth and fadeth away' and Isaiah 40:6–8: 'All flesh is grass' seem to be juxtaposed here.

and organs of a dying man. This particular passage, however, picks up the image of the corn harvest, following the *Glosa interlinealis* on Psalm 115:11.

Todo hombre es mentiroso, como los trigos, que por Abril suelen prometer una gran cosecha, porque están lozanos y hermosos, y por Mayo le dio un poco de niebla, y venido el Agosto todo es paja. Dice David: *Omnis homo mendax*. Todo hombre es mentiroso, como los trigos.

Veréis un penitente a los pies de un Confesor, que por que le absuelva sus amancebamientos, puestas las manos, y arrojando suspiros al viento, se muestra muy compungido: ¡o qué bello trigo! Dios le bendiga: no es posible sino que de aquí ha de coger Dios una gran cosecha de penitencia. Por Abril es hermoso a los pies del Confesor, pero por Mayo, en pasando por cierta calle, le dará la niebla, y toda su penitencia y promesas al cabo será paja. *Ego dixi in excessu meo omni homo mendax*.

¿Qué es ver un tribunal de jueces? ¡Qué bello trigo! ¡qué de justicia cogerá de aquí su Magestad! Por Abril es hermoso el trigo en el tribunal, pero por Mayo, cuando en secreto se vota el pleito, le suele dar la niebla, y todas sus resoluciones suelen ser paja. *Ego dixi* &c.

Recebís en vuestra casa un criado. Los primeros días muéstrase muy servicial. ¡Qué bello trigo! No hay duda sino que se ha de coger muy buen servicio, acompañado con mucha lealtad. Por Abril es bello el trigo, los primeros días, pero por Mayo le da la niebla. Apenas estuvo quince días en casa cuando la robó, y descubrió ser paja todas sus promesas. *Ego dixi* &c.[1]

In the last two paragraphs we find ourselves back once more in the realm of *sátira contra estados*, where judges are, by profession, 'crooked' and servants, traditionally, dishonest and disloyal. Avendaño concludes, thereby linking the *gloss* to the main metaphor: 'O mundo, que tus pies, que son los inferiores, ¡qué helados y qué desleales para servir a los ricos! Acabarte quieres.' The stiffening corpse represents both society's malfunctioning and man's hardness of heart.

An extended passage in a sermon by Fray Pedro de Valderrama may also be classified as a *gloss*, since it takes as its refrain *Ecce Homo* and progresses through a series of situations in which the mocking of the Son of God by men, who dress Him as a worldly king (with crown of thorns, reed sceptre, and royal purple robe), is ironically reversed, and it is God's turn to discountenance the proud mockers:

. . .a los que se han querido hacer dioses, siendo hombres, los ha de hacer unos *ecce homos*, y exponerlos a burla y mofa del cielo y tierra, asomándolos a la ventana del mundo, para que con risa y gritería, viendo a cada uno con su corona de espinas en la cabeza, de las congojas que les punzaron los sentidos, con una caña hueca en las manos,

---

[1] *Sermones del Adviento*, pp. 76–7.

que les dará a entender cuán flaco y vacío ha sido todo aquello en que
estribaron, y de que hicieron confianza, con una ropa de púrpura,
teñida en la sangre de sus culpas y abominaciones.[1]

The *Príncipe*, the *Rico*, and the *Fraile* are all in turn exposed to God's
stern judgement, and all have to wear the insignia of their infamy. The
repetition of each part is inexorable and cumulative. Whereas the *Rico*
is warned of the vanity of his worldly prosperity in language which
hardly goes beyond the conventional *desengaño* of the contemporary
lyric,[2] the *Fraile*, on the other hand, is told that his purple robe is the
colour of the flames 'en que arderá para siempre'. There is great
emphasis on *homo*, human nature, as opposed to man's presumptuous
desire to rise above his destiny and 'faire l'ange'.[3] All men are demon-
strated, in this passage and by the use of the single symbolical situation,
to be equal before God, and to be equally 'not-God'. The painstaking
repetition of 'corona de espinas', 'caña hueca', and 'ropa de púrpura'
has the effect of both generalizing and intensifying the indictment.
Moreover, Valderrama uses the dramatic device of direct speech—God
to the sinner ('tratabas a las bestias como a hombres, y a los hombres
como a bestias'; 'ven acá, hipócrita, que predicabas virtud. . .')—which
he projects into the formidable context of the Last Judgement.

The Last Judgement also inspires the very common 'fiction', or
metaphor, of the theatre, which recurs in sermons of this period in a
way that recalls Calderón's *El gran teatro del mundo* or *No hay
más Fortuna que Dios*. Life is a *comedia* in which all men have to
play the parts allotted to them and 'acabada la farsa, todo se ha de
dejar'.[4] The preacher's irony is directed at those actors who think
that their costumes and 'properties' really belong to them, and therefore are loath to leave them in the 'vestuario de la Muerte'.[5] In his
funeral sermon for the Duquesa de Arcos, Señora doña Teresa de
Zúñiga, Fray Pedro de Valderrama gives a detailed and naturalistic
description of the performance of an *auto sacramental* in the streets
of Seville, 'o en otra Ciudad populosa', in order to convey the brevity
of life. The preacher asks us to visualize ('veremos', 'veréis') the preparations for the procession, the spectators decorating their balconies and the
four carts moving swiftly through the maze of streets: 'Representan el

---

[1] *Exercicios espirituales [Santos]*, i. 5–6.
[2] The *crown* of thorns 'christianizes' the poetic conceit of roses turning into
thorns (*abrojos*).
[3] Diego de la Vega, commenting on the words *Homini regi*, is even more
explicit: 'la dignidad Real . . . no los deshombrece' and 'no ha faltado en el mundo
quién con la dignidad Real se desvaneció tanto, que no se tenía por hombre, sino
que creyó de sí que era Dios', *Empleo y Exercicio*, ii. 576.
[4] Vego, *Parayso [Adiciones]*, p. 99. See also Núñez Delgadillo, *Minas*, fo. 231.
[5] Mateo Alemán, *Oración fúnebre . . . de García Gera*, ed. A. Bushee in *RH*
xxv (1911), 417.

primer Auto a los Cabildos eclesiástico y seglar, y con tanta prisa que apenas ha acabado el primer carro los últimos acentos mal pronunciados y peor oídos cuando dan prisa los alguaciles, "Vote el carro", y llega el segundo, y tras el segundo los demás, sin parar un punto.'[1] He divides the rest of the sermon up into *Actos*, addressing his moral message to (1) married people, (2) merchants, (3) lords, princes, and kings, and (4) the mourners actually present.

Another interesting extended metaphor or fiction used to satirical effect is the pool of Bethseda, used by Fray Cristóbal de Fonseca in one of his Lenten sermons to represent the Court. In fact it might be considered a double metaphor, since within its terms the Court is 'un mundo abreviado, por haber en ella cuánto hay por el mundo repartido, y esta piscina es estampa de la Corte': if the pool is a figure of the Court, the Court in turn is a figure, or microcosm, of the world.

Fonseca proceeds, systematically, to establish the terms of the comparison. First of all,
. . .en la piscina había gran muchedumbre de enfermos, de enfermedades desafuciadas [*sic*] : ciegos consumidos, tullidos, baldados, cojos, mancos . . .En la Corte hay muchedumbre de enfermos de varias enfermedades del alma. Una apoplejía cautiva todos los sentidos del cuerpo: una pretensión los sentidos del cuerpo y las potencias del alma.[2]
Pretendientes have come to Court to be cured of 'una enfermedad de pobreza', and not only do they make no attempt to cure themselves of their other, equally crippling, infirmities, but they are not even aware of them. '¿Quién, soplando prósperamente el viento de la ambición y pretensión, trueca el ropón del Consejo por la ropa de buriel y se recoge a una hermita? ¿Quién da arcadas con la privanza antes que con la vida? ¿Quién a la insaciable codicia de atesorar dice, Basta?' Like the invalids at the pool, the *pretendientes* and courtiers live in hope: 'El pretendiente espera que se revuelva el agua de la piscina de manera que le quepa alguna suerte venturosa; el ladrón, alguna presa que le saque de lacería; la doncella, algún encuentro dichoso.' The courtiers, like the invalids, are so intent on their own advancement that they trample on and injure their rivals in the rush to be first: '. . .estaban con suma vigilancia y atención como los alanos de la carnicería, que están rasgados los ojos, esperando la piltrafa. Y al que se atraviesa de sus compañeros le dan dentelladas, con que queda gimiendo un rato. . .El que en la piscina salía con su intento, tan pretendido y deseado, dejaba a los demás lastimados y envidiosos.' A further comparison, inserted into the main metaphor, heightens the impression of inhumanity and ferocity, as we are invited to visualize the invalid courtiers as dogs, squabbling over butcher's scraps. An even more damning point is made

---

[1] *Teatro*, p. 730.
[2] *Discursos para la Quaresma*, fos. 114ᵛ–116.

by contrast: 'un Angel solo movía las aguas de la piscina, pero las de la Corte son muchos Angeles, o por mejor decir, muchos demonios a moverlas'. He continues to underline the differences:

el Angel que venía a la piscina. . .era uno mismo; nunca aceptaba personas; a cada uno dejaba en las manos de su diligencia. . .Si fuera Angel de la Corte, algunas horas antes de su venida avisara, y quizás ganara albricias, no sólo del que había de sanar, sino de todos los que pretendían. Y no sería mal consejo que en la Corte fuese uno solo el que sanase, y no se mudasen tantos, porque los que salen quedan gordos, y los que entran, muy flacos, y muy hambrientos.

The corruption of the Court breeds flies ('moscas') that gorge on the flesh of the unfortunate, yet, the preacher argues, it is surely better to have a few sated, and therefore less importunate, flies, than a whole succession of hungry ones eagerly clustering round 'las llagas de los pobres'. The image arouses disgust and comes very near to open invective. It is clear that, despite the distancing of metaphor and simile, it is an identifiable aspect of contemporary affairs that is being evoked, yet at the same time the passage follows the form of a *declaración del Evangelio* (in this case John 5:1−9) which, first and foremost, illustrates the saving intervention of Christ. For the space of this passage, however, the satirical intention is allowed to predominate.[1]

DESENGAÑO

Each of these satirical 'fictions' has been aimed at disabusing the reader, revealing to him the awful discrepancy between things as they should be and things as they are. Ascetical style, the language of *desengaño*, has been described by Stephen Gilman as a deliberate contrast between the world 'vitally perceived' and the world 'logically cónceived': 'the infinite is constantly applied to the finite in order that the latter may suffer by the contrast'.[2] Whereas Gilman pursues his argument in order to account for the techniques of distortion and misleading perspective used by Quevedo and Gracián, I should simply like to draw attention to the constant use of antithesis by our preachers to point up the imperfections of mortal life without God. The following passage on the decay of beauty is an example of the kind of antithesis, joined to the 'intensification of loathing', that is typical of *desengaño* language:

Cada día que vive la dama más gallarda, va perdiendo de su belleza: y como que le comen una partecilla de su hermosura los días, con que se va desflorando y envejeciendo. Todos los puntos de su vida son daños y

---

[1] The same metaphor is found, without elaboration, in Gabriel Pérez del Barrio's *Secretario de señores* (Madrid, 1622), fo. 31^V: 'Porque siendo muchos los que siguen una misma pretensión, es forzoso ejercitarse el misterio de la probática piscina, haciéndose con uno el milagro'.

[2] S. Gilman, 'An Introduction to the Ideology of the Baroque in Spain', *Symposium* i (1946), 93.

menoscabos de su belleza y bizarría. No hay día ni hora que no desflore su mocedad, se amortigue su hermosura, se estrague su verdor, se deslustre su tez, y debiliten sus fuerzas, y dentro de breves años los ojos más bellos se cubren de nubes, la frente lisa y tersa (como decía el divino Jerónimo) se asulca, ara y arruga. Las mejillas que parecían unas rosas se decaen y marchitan, los cabellos dorados se platean con las blancas canas, los dientes que parecían perlas ensartadas se ennegrecen, desmoronan y caen, conque queda tan otra de su solía, tan fea y deslustrada, que la que era tenida por ninfa del cielo por todos sus aficionados, de puro fastidio no osan mirarla. Y ella misma, por no se ver al espejo y tan mal transfigurada, o lo arroja a un rincón, o lo consagra a la Diosa Venus, como a tan hermosa.[1]

The sonneteering conceits and commonplaces (Mejillas/rosas; cabellos dorados; dientes / perlas) reinforce the contrast between the vain pursuit of physical beauty and more enduring qualities. They culminate in 'ninfa del cielo', which is an ironic cliché and cautionary tale for those who worship too long at the altar of Venus, a goddess who cannot confer immortality, rather than bowing to the decrees of the eternal *Cielo*. The passage is constructed on a thematic and verbal polarity, reflected in the balance of nouns and parallel constructions: 'se desflore su mocedad; se amortigue su hermosura; se estrague su verdor; se deslustre su tez; y debiliten sus fuerzas'. Ternary groupings ('se asulca, ara y arruga' and 'se ennegrecen, desmoronan y caen') also reveal a rhythm familiar in ascetic style and reminiscent of the periods of Mateo Alemán.

Even more reminiscent of a passage in Mateo Alemán's most world-weary manner are these few lines from a sermon by Fray Luis de Rebolledo:

Una de las infelicidades desta vida es el peligro con que las cosas de ella se poseen, que es tan grande que podemos decir que se tienen y no se gozan. Si va el hombre al convite, en el halla la apoplejía, la indigestión y la enfermedad no pensada. Si bebe frío, en la bebida está el resfriado, el dolor o pasmo. Si duerme en el suelo, le ahoga la sangre.[2]

One could quote parallel passages *ad infinitum* without reaching any conclusion about the real relationship between the style of the sermons and that of contemporary novelists. Indeed, it may well be that there is no clear relationship of cause and effect, or mutual influence, despite what we have glimpsed of the preacher as a self-conscious stylist, aware of the rules of *decorum*, the springs of *admiratio*, and the human persuasions of eloquence in all its forms. The preacher of the seventeenth century has attempted to equip himself to speak to the men of his age in terms they can not only understand but also appreciate. Even his satire and rebukes are couched in the language of polite society, but

[1] Ramón, *Puntos escripturales*, ii. 604.
[2] *Cien oraciones fúnebres*, fo. 243. See *Guzmán de Alfarache*, I. i. 7 (ed. cit. i. 165–6).

none the less biting for that. It is therefore only to be expected that similarities will occur, but these merely reflect a common social reality, in which it is just as legitimate for the poet to preach as for the preacher to please. The very frequency with which sermons were preached does, however, explain the persistence and currency of certain timeless techniques of satire which are the prerogative of the preacher and yet can be annexed by the secular writer.

VI

THE PREACHER AS THEOLOGIAN

The ministry of preaching, according to the decrees of the Council of Trent, is to teach 'all that is necessary for salvation', in plain and simple language, 'leaving aside any useless disquisitions'.[1] Too much discussion of the subtler points of theology was discouraged, for fear of causing scandal, either through the inadequacy of the priest or through the ignorance and inexperience of the congregation: 'Cuando predicare entre gente ignorante y rudo vulgo, haga cuenta que canta a la medianoche donde las tinieblas y obscuridad están en su punto.'[2] It was firmly believed that a right emphasis on certain thorny subjects, such as Faith and Works, was essential if the Church's teaching was not to be misrepresented or dangerously distorted. This is borne out in St. Ignatius Loyola's counsel in *The Mind of the Church* ('ut cum orthodoxa ecclesia verè sentiamus') that in talking about Grace or Predestination 'our language should be such as not to lead ordinary people astray'.[3]

On the one hand, few preachers in the seventeenth century would be competent speculative theologians, and we have already noted Huarte de San Juan's explanation of this fact, together with a few remarks indicating the very rudimentary theological training given to diocesan clergy, and even in some of the religious orders.[4] The same pessimistic view is shared by one who was both professional theologian and preacher, Fray Basilio Ponce de León, and who believes he is the exception that proves the rule.[5] Another preacher, Fray Diego Murillo, is so persuaded of the average preacher's inability to discourse authoritatively on doctrinal points, unless very closely guided, that he explicitly sets out his sermons in the vernacular and in great detail, for the benefit

---

[1] Sess. v, cap. 2 (17 June 1546), in Tejada y Ramiro, *Colección de canones*, iv. 47–9. See Jedin, *History of the Council of Trent*, ii. 100–10, esp. 108 n. 1. P. Janelle, *The Catholic Reformation* (London, 1971), p. 75. Also sess. xxv (3–4 Dec. 1563), forbidding *subtiliores quaestiones* in vernacular sermons *apud rudem plebem*; López de Ayala, *El Sacrosanto. . .concilio de Trento*, p. 447 and Tejada y Ramiro, *Collección*, iv. 399.

[2] Fray Pedro de Valderrama, *Exercicios espirituales para los tres domingos de septuagesima, sexagesima y quinquagesima* (Barcelona, 1607), p. 78.

[3] *The Spiritual Exercises of Saint Ignatius*, trans. T. Corbishley, S.J. (London, [1963]), pp. 122–3.

[4] See Ch. I. pp. 22–6.

[5] *Discursos para diferentes Evangelios de Quaresma*, i. 93–4. They are 'dos exercicios entre sí tan diferentes, y que cada uno pide un hombre entero'. Ponce de León held a succession of chairs of theology at Salamanca between 1608 and his death in 1629.

of 'nuevos Ministros de la predicación, que aun no han llegado a tener caudal'.[1] He fears that the inexperienced may fall into error because they cannot 'hablar en Romance de los misterios Divinos con términos proprios, castos, graves y significantes', and continues: 'He visto en esto yerros intolerables, parte nacidos de ignorancia, y parte de bizarría de ingenios gallardos, que con lenguaje profano quieren decir las cosas soberanas y misteriosas, siendo tan grande la desproporción que hay entre lo profano y divino.' The most dangerous ignorance is that which cloaks itself in affectation and Benito Carlos Quintero also roundly censures those preachers who, from a misplaced vanity, deal in the pulpit with 'puntos de Teología tan de asiento, tan porfiadamente, y con términos tan escolásticos, que ni aun los muy entendidos seglares lo alcanzan, aunque para disimular su ignorancia los alaban'.[2]

The only effect they achieve is to 'hacer dudar confusamente al vulgo ignorante y sácanle de un sermón tan cansada la cabeza como de una casa de duendes y fantasmas, sin aprovechamiento ni deleite'. This type of preaching, although it is allied to the *culto* style of neologisms and precious archaicisms, is fundamentally a regression to the worst abuses of the scholastic preachers, and as such may be considered by contemporaries not only unedifying but also old-fashioned. This is a reaction similar to that of the eighteenth century towards 'gothic ignorance' and should be approached with care, as should statements by contemporaries which seek to evaluate the spiritual temper of the age. For instance, in François Bertaut, who travelled around Spain in 1659, we have one of the earliest propagators of the *leyenda negra* when he attributes Spain's theological 'backwardness' to Inquisitorial repression: 'Dans les colleges les Estudians ne voyent guère que les vieux Glossateurs et les plus mechans livres: car en Espagne ils n'oseraient lire ni avoir pas un Autheur qui parle un peu librement.'[3] There is no evidence to suppose that our preachers were brought up under such a strict regime, and in fact the first quarter of the seventeenth century was still reaping the fruits of the Catholic and 'apostolic' reforms of the previous century.

On the other hand, it is just as frequently the ignorance of the congregation which is brought forward as an argument against too much 'theology' in the pulpit. Fray Cristóbal de Fonseca speaks of 'los daños grandes que se siguen de que gente ignorante trate de cosas mayores que las que lleva su capacidad, como la dotrina de la Trinidad, predestinación, el modo inefable con que está Dios en el sacramento'.[4]

---

[1] *Discursos predicables [Christo]*, Prólogo al lector.
[2] *Templo*, fos. 45–45^V. Also Terrones, *Instrucción*, pp. 136–7.
[3] *RH* xlvii (1919), 245.
[4] *Quarta parte de la Vida de Christo*, p. 23. Núñez Delgadillo also counts Predestination among those subjects which 'no son para púlpito', *Minas*, fo. 228. We shall see below how he observes this in practice.

When these topics are introduced into sermons, as they quite frequently are at this period, it is in deliberately simple language. For example, P. Jerónimo de Florencia simplifies Aquinas's exposition of the doctrine of the Trinity by adding a paraphrase after the 'technical' version, with the words: 'la cual Teología reducida a púlpito quiere decir. . .'[1] Preachers see their role as popularizers, rather than as dogmatic theologians, and in this chapter we shall note how the faith of the Counter-Reformation is mediated and accommodated to the 'simple faithful'. The sermons, as one might expect, tell us more about what the rank and file in the Church thought, or were conditioned to think, than about the current theological problems and academic controversies. The controversies we do find in the sermons are those which often took to the streets and showed forth as processions and demonstrations of loyalty to one or the other faction.[2] Nevertheless, the boundaries of Spanish Catholicism are defined and fortified by the preachers' refutation, in sermons at *autos-de-fe* or to promote the Bull of the *Cruzada*, of the Protestant heresies of Northern Europe.[3] This refutation often consists of a reaffirmation of the 'official line' taken by the Council of Trent on the following tenets of the faith.

JUSTIFICATION[4]

The prevalent position taken up by our preachers on the tricky relationship between Faith and Works, Grace and Free Will in the process of man's justification is a prudent one, which holds both extremes in check and points to a middle way. As Fray Diego Murillo puts it succinctly: 'para salvarse, entrambas cosas se han de juntar, gracia de Dios y diligencias nuestras',[5] and his co-religionist, Fray Diego de la Vega, is even more epigrammatic: 'no sea todo alas, haya manos también'.[6] This stress on the co-operative effort required from man, as an adjunct not a cause of salvation, could be interpreted as a

---

[1] *Marial*, ii. 47–8.

[2] Most of the controversies at this period were between religious orders: Dominicans and Franciscans debate the Immaculate Conception, Dominicans and Jesuits wrangle over *De Auxiliis*, and the Augustinians vie with all comers over the antiquity of their foundation. The question of the Co-Patronage of Spain divided supporters of Santiago against those of Sta Teresa; see T.D. Kendrick, *St. James in Spain* (London, 1960), Ch. iv.

[3] Fray Basilio Ponce de León, *Sermón en la fiesta de la Naval de Lepanto* (Salamanca, 1620); Fray Tomás Ramón, *Conceptos extravagantes* (Barcelona, 1619), pp. 1–42 and 93 ff.

[4] Sess. vi (13 Jan. 1547). López de Ayala, *El Sacrosanto. . .concilio de Trento*, pp. 36–74; Tejada y Ramiro, *Colección*, iv. 51–66; Jedin, *History*, ii. 166–96, 239–310.

[5] *Discursos predicables [Quaresma]*, i. 155.   [6] *Parayso*, ii. 94 and 255.

counterblast to the Lutheran heresy. We are frequently told, for example,
that 'fe sin obras' is 'fe del demonio'.[1] We have only to read a few
sermons of the period to find this theme reiterated, often in strong,
homely language: 'No es buena cuenta: "predestinado estoy, quiero
meter las manos en el seno y echarme a dormir", sino que habéis de
ganar [el cielo] por vuestros pulgares . . . porque el efecto de la predestinación no se consigue sino mediante las obras.'[2]

The question is, however, rather more complicated and its com-
plexity is catered for by several of our preachers. One might expect
that the different religious orders would take different sides on the
matter, and particularly that the Dominicans and Augustinians would
concur in favour of infused grace while the Jesuits maintained the
importance of the active co-operation of the will. However, the two
positions are not so easily polarized and the Carmelite, Fray Agustín
Núñez Delgadillo leads us gently through what had become, for the
professional theologian, a knotty maze, despite the clarification of the
Tridentine decree:

Preguntan los teólogos ¿si mira Dios nuestras obras naturales y nuestra
disposición natural para darnos su gracia excitante? ¿para llamarnos a
la penitencia? La sentencia que yo siempre seguí, y sacaré a luz, si
Dios fuere servido, es que las obras naturales buenas no son méritos, ni
disposiciones próximas o remotas, para la gracia excitante, mas son
de importancia, porque el sujeto está menos impedido para la conversión y auxilio cuando las ejercita, y así quitan nuevos estorbos. . .
Digo, pues, que Dios, por su bondad (no porque las obras buenas
naturales merezcan, o dispongan al pecador para la gracia) toma ocasión
de las buenas obras naturales para originar mi salvación, porque quiere,
cuando quiere.[3]

The decree on Justification had mentioned the necessity of a good
disposition and of perseverance towards the goal of salvation, but had
left unclear the working distinction between universal and efficient
grace.[4] Núñez Delgadillo, while still leaving much unexplained, steers
a course between the reefs of Pelagianism and Calvinistic Predeter-
mination and the discussion is, in any case, a step beyond the simple
precepts given in the first couple of examples quoted, which tend to
advise obedience at the expense of free inquiry.

Two of our Augustinian preachers, Fonseca and Valderrama, adhere

---

[1] Avendaño, *Sermones del Adviento*, pp. 170–1.
[2] Vega, *Empleo*, i. 340–1.
[3] *Minas*, sermon xxiv.
[4] Sess. vi, cap. 5. This was still being fought out in the *De Auxiliis* controversy, which lasted until Paul V decreed (5 Sept. 1607) that neither side should
pronounce the contrary teaching heretical; cf. Cross, *Dictionary of the Christian
Church* (Oxford, 1957), p. 380 and A. Bonet, *La filosofía de la libertad en las
controversias teológicas del siglo xvi y . . . xvii* (Barcelona, 1932).

very closely to the doctrine of their founder, a doctrine popular among the 'Evangelical' Catholics of the 1540s in Spain and Italy before it was reformulated by the followers of Jansenius.[1] According to this position, *opera humana* are in no sense meritorious in themselves and every good impulse is God-given:

Desde el primer paso que da el hombre en la conquista del cielo, hasta el último en que viene a gozarle y poseerle, todos son tan de Dios que aun el querer ir alla nace de la voluntad divina, y compone de suerte Dios su gracia con nuestras obras que, no haciendo cosa sin su favor, se pone el galardón a cuenta de nuestro merecimiento.[2]

Fray Pedro de Valderrama warns that:

aunque hagáis muchas obras, sino las acompaña la divina gracia, y esa os previene, alumbra y trae.. .no os aprovechará cosa ninguna para la vida eterna.. .lo cierto es, que si El no alumbra y llama, aunque seáis más diligente que un Delfín, más discreto que un Mercurio, amigo de paz, guardador de las leyes humanas, si las misericordia de Dios no os alumbra con su gracia eficaz, y os sigue y va delante y detrás de vos, como paje, no haréis nada.[3]

This stress on man's helplessness is frequently found in the sermons, but is just as frequently balanced by reminders that man is distinguished from the rest of creation by his free will. Fray Diego de la Vega puts it in characteristically blunt words:

No por esto tampoco quiero que nadie entienda que atropelle Dios el uso del libre albedrío, ni que lleva a nadie forzado y de las greñas al cielo, que siempre Dios a nuestra voluntad le guarda sus imunidades y fueros; sino lo que decimos es que aquellos que tiene Dios escogidos para su gloria los llama a sí y los atrae con llamamiento eficaz, y los lleva mansamente y al amor del agua, aunque algunas veces bien agua arriba de sus inclinaciones.[4]

God moves in a mysterious way, and, as the preacher-*pícaro* Guzmán de Alfarache says, albeit cynically in relation to his renegade father, '¿Qué sabe nadie de la manera que toca Dios a cada uno?'[5] Conversion was a popular subject in Counter-Reformation art, and popular devotion loved to dwell on the tears of St. Peter, the anguished attitudes of the penitent Magdalene or the unlikely conversion of the Good Thief on the Cross. Saints could be found on the city streets or among the

[1] See O.M.T. Logan, 'Grace and Justification: some Italian views of the 16th and 17th centuries', *Journal of Ecclesiastical History* xx (1969), 67–78. Also Jedin, *History*, i. 364–70.

[2] Fonseca, *Quarta parte de la Vida de Christo*, p. 51. In a Lenten sermon, however, Fonseca points out that, although grace is gratuitously given, it is only given to him who wants and longs for it passionately ('al que revienta por ella, como por la Corona del Estadio'): *Discursos predicables*, fo. 118.

[3] *Exercicios espirituales [Santos]*, p. 531.   [4] *Parayso*, ii. 141.

[5] *Guzmán de Alfarache*, I. i. 1 (ed. cit. i. 58).

cooking-pots as well as in the desert, and this was a powerful incentive
to a lay apostolate, working the will of God in their everyday lives.
Fray Hortensio Félix Paravicino brings home the 'ordinariness' of
conversion: '¿De dónde sacó a Mateo? de un cambio; ¿al Ladrón?
de una horca; ¿a Madalena? de unos amores; ¿a Francisco? de una
puerta de Guadalajara. ¿Por qué no os podrá sacar a vos de la Calle
Mayor, o de la de Atocha, a este Hábito mío, o al de un Cartujo más
aspero? Sí, podrá, sino que vos no queréis.'[1] The main obstacle to
conversion is man's obstinacy, not any unfortunate circumstances of
birth or situation in life. Fray Basilio Ponce de León seems to echo
Erasmus in his exhortation to his congregation to seek salvation in their
worldly state or calling, however, humble it may be: 'No hay llegar a
Dios a pedir gloria a título de Apóstol, de Profeta, Doctor o Catedrático,
Príncipe, Oidor, Juez, Fraile o Monja, sino a título de que en este
estado obráis y vivís como debéis.'[2] The occasions of repentance and
conversion are very often unexpected and seemingly trivial, as Fray
Agustín Núñez Delgadillo illustrates with an *exemplum*:
la conversión de un pecador la origina Dios de acciones de suyo tan
desproporcionadas a tan alto fin, que parecen niñerías respeto de un si
grande sobrenatural. . .Váis acaso a casa de un amigo vuestro, con
intento que los dos os váis a tomar el sol un rato al campo. Entráis,
halláisle con unos versos en las manos.—¿Qué es eso?—Aquí estoy
leyendo este verso, que lo he repetido dos o tres veces, y siempre hallo
nueva admiración en el y lo que encierra: *Loco debo de ser pues no soy
santo*. . .reparáis en las palabras, quedáis confuso; este verso basta para
sermón; no quiero ser más loco. Salís con deseo de hacer vida nueva. . .[3]
Salvation is not, however, arbitrary but predestined, and whereas it
may be vouchsafed in unexpected places there are no shortcuts, as an
illustration from Fray Diego de la Vega makes plain. He is speaking
about the righteous or 'justified' man (*justus*) in terms of an aristocracy
of heaven, recognizable by certain signs which can be equated, within
the terms of a homiletic *comparación*, to the distinctive dress and
bearing which reveal a nobleman in the world. The contrast, between an
uncouth peasant and a refined courtier, springs easily from Isaiah's
prophetic words about Christ: 'Erit iustitia singulum lumbrorum eius'
(11:5). I quote it in full to show how a preacher may elaborate a
doctrinal point in a style accommodated to every level of his congregation
and which draws on their familiar experience:

[1] *Oraciones Evangélicas [Christo]*, fo. 33^V.
[2] *Discursos para diferentes Evangelios*, ii. fo. 324. The Erasmian refrain
Cucullus non facit monachum: monacatus non est pietas ('no porque tuvo hábito,
velo, borla, cathedra, sino por las buenas obras') is no longer a novelty and is
already incarnated in the newer religious orders; cf. H.O. Evennett, *The Spirit of
the Counter-Reformation* (Notre Dame and London, 1970), pp. 73–7.
[3] *Minas*, sermón xxiv, fo. 323.

Hay diferencia entre la gente cortesana y la rústica, que la gente rústica y villana ni ciñe justo, ni calza justo tampoco. Veréis un pastor de Sayago, o criado allá en las Asturias, desabrochado y desceñido, con el pecho todo de fuera, lleno de vello, que parece un oso o salvaje. En sus pies unas abarcas, hechas de un cuero de vaca tan holgadas, que dentro de ellas trae una espuerta de tierra y de piedras. Este ni viste justo, ni calza justo tampoco. Pero un hombre curioso, criado en corte, viste y calza muy de otra manera. Viste justo y tan apretado que le revienta el vestido. Un zapato tan justo y tan a la medida del pie que una chinita, por más pequeña que sea, le dé fatiga, y no la puede sufrir, hasta que se va a su casa y se descalza y échala fuera. Esta diferencia hay entre la gente villana y rústica, que está prescita para el infierno, y la gente ilustre, criada para ser cortesanos del cielo. Que aquéstos calzan abarcas en la conciencia, andan a lo holgado, y viven a sus anchuras. Acontecerá traer en la consciencia cargas de basura y de tierra, de pecados y culpas y pasan por todo. Pero aquéllos que Dios tiene predestinados para su gloria, calzan justo; son gente apretada, un pelo que tienen en la consciencia les da mucha pena, y no paran hasta echarle fuera por la confesión y dolores de sus culpas.[1]

This passage also serves as a commentary on cap. 10 of the decree on Justification (*De acceptae justificationis incremento*) which speaks of the household of God and how righteousness is increased, day by day, in those who walk in the right path: 'El que es justo continua justificándose'.[2] The importance of the sacrament of Penance is also stressed, in this connection,[3] as the preachers are anxious to relate all discussion of redemption to the sacramental life of the Church. Nevertheless, while they maintain that external observances are essential for the maintenance of faith ('porque lo ceremonial es lo que defiende lo esencial y que provoca los hombres a levantar sus corazones a la consideración de las cosas divinas'[4]), the same preachers often add a rider that works are useless without Faith and Charity and that, moreover, *lo interior* is most important of all ('las almas puras y las conciencias limpias son unos templos de marfil', ibid.). This last phrase hints strongly of Erasmianism. Fray Cristóbal de Avendaño relates a sad tale of a man who for fifty years had led an exemplary life of good works, attendance at the sacraments, fasting, and alms-giving, only to

---

[1] Vega, *Parayso*, i. 304. See Cervantes, *El licenciado vidriera* (Clásicos Castellanos, 1952), pp. 60–1 and N. Salomon, *Recherches sur le thème paysan* (Bordeaux, 1965), p. 52. Another Franciscan, Fray Diego Murillo, distinguishes between 'hombres carnales' and 'hombres espirituales', following St. Paul, in *Discursos predicables [Quaresma]*, ii. 31.

[2] López de Ayala, *El Sacrosanto . . . concilio de Trento*, pp. 51–2.

[3] See Fonseca, *Discursos predicables*, fo. 199, who quotes from the Council of Trent, sess. xiv.

[4] Fray Antonio Feo, *Tratados quadragesimales y de la Pascua* (Valladolid, 1614), p. 244.

miss salvation on his deathbed, 'que se halló en pecado mortal, sin caridad y amor de Dios'. His pious practices were counted for nothing then.[1]

THE EUCHARIST[2]

The Eucharist is, of course, the chief sacrament of post-Tridentine Catholicism and the subject of sermons, preached not only on the traditional feast of Corpus Christi but also at the 'modern' service of benediction and the forty hours' exposition of the blessed sacrament.[3] We find a number of printed sermons on the Eucharist in *Santoral* collections[4] but also, more predictably, in Fray Diego Murillo's *Discursos predicables sobre todos los Evangelios que canta la Iglesia en las Festividades de Christo* (Saragossa, 1607). Many of these sermons are closely modelled on the individual chapters of the decree on the Eucharist: the Real Presence, the Insitution of the sacrament, Transubstantiation, Veneration, Reservation, Preparation and Reception of the sacrament.[5] Fray Diego de la Vega explains that the Eucharist subsumes the Creation, the Incarnation, and the Redemption and therefore is the most excellent of all the sacraments of the Church.[6] He uses images of light and heat to convey the workings of Divine Love within the human heart (*candela-tizón-asqua-centellas*), and from page 19 onwards he expounds the doctrine of Transubstantiation clearly and soberly. He attempts the same task in more strikingly figurative language in a sermon from another collection, where he illustrates the nature of Christ's presence in the sacramental species with the *exemplum* of Cleopatra disolving a priceless pearl in vinegar.[7]

Fray Pedro de Valderrama uses more conventional, yet fervent, language to convey the mystery, and this particular passage underlines a recognizably Counter-Reformation tendency to present the Eucharist as a divine food in which Christ is given to each individual:

El efecto del sacramento de la Eucaristía, que todo es amoroso, es transformar al amante en la cosa amada, y hacer que el uno esté en el pecho y corazón del otro, y así lo dijo: *In me manet et ego in eo*, yo me entraré en su pecho, debajo de las especies de pan y vino, *y le*

---

[1] *Sermones del Adviento*, p. 563.

[2] Council of Trent, sess. xiii (11 Oct. 1551).

[3] Much popularized by the Capuchins and the Jesuits, the *Quarantore* was first held in Milan in 1527; cf. Evennett, *Counter-Reformation*, p. 38.

[4] Cristóbal de Avendaño gives five in *Otro tomo de sermones de Santos* and Diego de la Vega includes a couple in the second volume of the *Parayso*.

[5] López de Ayala, *El Sacrosanto. . .concilio de Trento*, pp. 129–44.

[6] *Parayso*, ii. 1 ff.

[7] *Empleo*, ii. 1. The same illustration is used by Du Perron in a sermon preached at Evreux in 1597, according to F.A. Yates, *The French Academies of the Sixteenth Century*, p. 195.

comunicaré mi gracia, y mil dones, y él morará en mí y estará en mi pecho por unión de caridad y gracia, y participación de mi espíritu divino.[1]

Alongside the development of new pious practices connected with the reserved sacrament, there is renewed emphasis on the Eucharist as Mass and as meal, joined with encouragement to the laity, as well as those vowed to the religious life, to communicate more frequently. P. Jerónimo de Florencia wrote a tract entitled *Práctica de la frecuencia de la sagrada comunión* which was dedicated to Queen Isabel, first wife of Philip IV, and published in 1622, and we find Fray Agustín Núñez Delgadillo defending the practice in these words:

Y de camino responderé a una duda, o objección que ponen algunos contra las frecuentes comuniones:—Señor, ¿es el seglar sacerdote? ¿es la mujer sacerdote, que ha de comulgar cada día? Respondo lo primero, que de comuniones no hay [que] dar regla cierta que hable con todas personas, sino gobernarse por un confessor docto, prudente, deseoso del aprovechamiento de las almas. Lo segundo digo, que si el seglar hace lo que el sacerdote (no en decir Misa), si le imita en la vida, en el recogimiento, en la humildad, en la mortificación, en el amor de Dios, en el menosprecio del mundo, no es contra razón que le imite en la frecuencia de recibir a nuestro Señor.[2]

The Franciscan Fray Diego Murillo suggests that the most devout members of the community are the lower classes, who fulfil those pious obligations that the aristocracy neglect:

Decidme (hermanos míos) ¿quién oye los sermones? ¿Quién frecuenta los sacramentos? ¿Quién trata de devoción y oración, sino solamente la gente común? ¿Hay Caballero que trate de oír sermones entre año? ¿Hay noble que trate de confesar a menudo? ¿Hay rico que se acuerde de cumplir las obras de misericordia?[3]

However, more and more of the laity were following 'la vie dévote', under the guidance of a spiritual director, and religious practices were becoming private and personal rather than simply communal. Just as the individual confessional box is beginning to replace public confession by the 1630s, so the private oratory and the conducted retreat come to supplement considerably the weekly parish mass. It is in this context that the printed collections of sermons in Spanish can be seen in another important light: for the use of the laity as much as for apprentice preachers.

THE SAINTS, HELL, AND PURGATORY[4]

While what is known as the Counter-Reformation may properly be

---

[1] *Exercicios espirituales [Santos]*, p. 420.

[2] *Minas*, fo. 112^V.

[3] *Discursos predicables [Quaresma]*, i. 243. Also Fonseca, *Discursos para la Quaresma*, fo. 83.

[4] Sess. xxv (3–4 Dec. 1563). López de Ayala, *El Sacrosanto. . .concilio de Trento*, pp. 446–54 and Tejada y Ramiro, *Colección*, iv. 399 ff.

traced back to the beginnings of Catholic renewal in the mid-fifteenth
century (in Spain and Italy as well as in Cologne and Windesheim),[1]
the canons and decrees of the Council of Trent, together with the lists
of anathematized propositions that accompany them, are a monument
to a direct and embattled confrontation with Protestantism. In Spanish
sermons of the late sixteenth and early seventeenth centuries it is
possible to find both aspects of the Counter-Reformation: the revival
of an inner spirituality alongside a restatement of those doctrines
which are traditionally and visibly Roman Catholic.[2] The doctrine of
Purgatory is a case in point. Fray Tomás Ramón explicitly refutes
Luther and Calvin who seek to deny the saints' power of intercession,
and a similar defence of the Catholic practice of invoking the aid of the
saints is found in Fray Hernando de Santiago and many other preachers.[3]
However, Ramón, for one, adds a rider, in a later collection of sermons,
to the effect that man must co-operate himself in the work of redemption by a sincere repentance. Superstitious practices are those performed in the wrong spirit:

¡O quán raros son el día de hoy los que importunando a los Santos que
por ellos intercedan, les dan tiempo en que no impedidos de sus culpas
puedan libremente interceder por ellos! Grande ceguera es por cierto,
y engaño grande, de los que estándose muy a su pie quedo en sus
pecados, con el amancebamiento, con la enemistad &c. piensan que con
la oración del justo en quien se encomiendan, con esa a secas han de
negociar lo que pretenden.[4]

Nevertheless, preachers are quick to seize upon instances in which
the saints may be seen as intervening in history and are eager to foster
devotion to the *milagrero*. 1622 saw the canonization of four new
Spanish saints and Fray Diego de la Vega had commented, in a sermon
on San Idelfonso preached nearly twenty years before, that Spain 'no
es muy santera, pero los Santos que produce sónlo de veras y con
grandes ventajas'.[5] Among these *ventajas* were those attributed to Sta.
Teresa of Avila, doubtless as part of a campaign to promote her canonization but also as a foretaste of the Co-patronage controversy.[6] Fray
Cristóbal de Avendaño, a member of the *carmelitas calzados* but who

---

[1] Evennett, *Counter-Reformation*, pp. 26–8. See also works by M. Bataillon
and V. Beltrán de Heredia in the List of Works Consulted.
[2] 'Los herejes' are constantly being denounced by our preachers, e.g. Murillo,
Discursos predicables [Quaresma], i. 563; Fonseca, *Quarta parte*, p. 695; Ponce de
León, *Sermón en la fiesta de Santa Clara* (Salamanca, 1625), p. 20: 'aquella bestia
infernal de Alemania Martin Lutero . . . que tuvo el hábito desta Orden, pero no
el corazón desta orden'.
[3] *Flores nuevas*, i. 264–6. Santiago, *Consideraciones [Quaresma]* p. 151.
[4] *Puntos escripturales*, p. 20.
[5] *Parayso*, ii [*Adiciones*]. p. 40.   [6] See Kendrick, *St. James in Spain*, Ch. iv.

called the saint 'una bisagra que abraza y traba ambas religiones',[1]
sees significance in the fact that:

El día que el Turco ganó a Chipre y tomó la ciudad famosa de Famagusta,
este día tomó possessión la santa madre del monasterio de San Joseph
de Avila: que si el Turco por aquella parte derriba la Iglesia, y Lutero
y Calvino por la suya, quiere Dios que la santa madre levante y repare
esos portillos y haga gente para el cielo y traiga gente a Dios, que
llegan ya los monasterios a Persia y a las Indias.[2]

Likewise, Fray Basilio Ponce de León points out that:

Cuando la Reina Isabela de Inglaterra, perdiendo la vergüenza a Dios, y
al mundo, se intituló cabeza de la Iglesia, destruyó los templos, y
persiguió los fieles, levantó Dios a nuestra Santa Madre Teresa de Jesús.
Aquella despertó tanta persecución contra la Iglesia el año de 1559,
y esta santa fundó su primer monasterio en el año de 1562. . .oponién-
dose al estrago que los herejes hacían.[3]

He adduces various other parallels, leading up to the conclusions that:

Día de San Bartholomé en el año de 1562 fundó el primer monasterio
de monjas, y en Francia algunas personas principales y graves han
observado, con diligente observación que han hecho, que desde aquel
día y año, en ese mismo día, han alcanzado los católicos grandes
victorias de los herejes, y lo atribuyen todo a la intercessión de esta
Santa, que defiende desde el cielo la Iglesia. (ibid.)

Graphic accounts of Purgatory and Hell are to be found in one of
Fray Luis de Rebolledo's funeral sermons (oración xlv). He speaks of
Purgatory as a 'taller' (in this case 'stonemason's yard') where souls
are hewn into shape.[4] Hell is a 'tierra de miserias' and a 'tierra de
tinieblas', full of horror and confusion, drawn as a composite picture
from cross-references to Sheol in the Old Testament. In an earlier
sermon (xiv) he composes the picture even more dramatically:

Un pozo tan hondo, que llega al centro de la tierra, lleno de fuego y
serpientes (que son los demonios) y con las bocas abiertas, por los deseos
que tienen de nuestra condenación. Y que la boca deste pozo es el
pecado mortal, y que está el pecador en la boca del pozo, colgado de un
cabello, el cual está arrimado a los filos de un agudo cuchillo. Y que
este delgado cabello es la vida, y el cuchillo cortador es la muerte.[5]

Fray Tomás Ramón, basing himself on St. Thomas Aquinas, claims that
Hell and Purgatory are one and the same place, but the suffering in

---

[1] *Sermones del Adviento*, p. 569.
[2] Ibid., p. 553.
[3] *Sermón de Sta Teresa* [preached in Toledo] (1620), p. 23. In 1559 the
return of the Marian exiles forced upon Elizabeth I a more extreme Protestant
settlement (the Acts of Supremacy and Uniformity) than she had either envisaged
or desired: see J.H. Elliott, *Europe divided 1559–1598* (London, 1968), pp.
31–2.
[4] *Cien oraciones fúnebres*, fos. 324–8[V].   [5] Ibid., fo. 106.

Hell is eternal: 'Una sola gota de sudor que un alma de un estudiante que en el padecía echó en la mano a un su maestro se le atravesó como si fuera un rayo y se la quemó.'[1] He then makes a pathetic plea to his audience to give generously to free their nearest and dearest from the terrible fires of Purgatory.

Contrary to what one might expect, Spanish sermons of the early seventeenth century are relatively free from 'fire and brimstone'. The only preachers to give us Last Judgement sermons calculated to inspire terror, which in turn will lead to repentance, are the Franciscans Rebolledo and Fray Diego Murillo (see above, p. 67). This is consistent with the Franciscan style of preaching, little changed since the Middle Ages. However, both Fray Basilio Ponce de León, O.S.A., and Fray Tomás Ramón, O.P., evoke gruesome details of worms and putrefaction ('colchones de polilla y cobertores y colchas de gusanos') after death as an incentive to a swift repentance in this life.[2]

THE IMMACULATE CONCEPTION

The history of the controversies which raged over the dogma of the Immaculate Conception stretches back to the thirteenth century and continues, beyond our period, until the proclamation of the bull *Ineffabilis* (8 December 1854) by Pius IX. A feast in honour of Our Lady's Immaculate Conception had been observed in the Church ever since the twelfth century and popular piety continued to support the *opinión piadosa*, despite the wranglings of the theologians. Moreover, the Virgin Mary's exemption from the universal curse of Original Sin had already been mentioned in session v of the Council of Trent.[3] In seventeenth-century Spain Seville was the centre of a flourishing movement to define and proclaim the Immaculate Conception as a dogma, and public demonstrations took place in 1615–16 between 'immaculistas' and opponents of the belief. In the pulpits this became a verbal battle between Franciscans and Dominicans (see above, p. 116). Domínguez Ortiz reports that certain prelates insisted on the *Ave Maria* being recited as part of the *salutación* of sermons, and debarred from preaching those who would not comply.[4] Indeed, one rarely finds alternative prayers being used in printed sermons at this period, regardless of religious order, whereas the *Veni Sanctus Spiritus* had been another prayer used in this context in the early Middle Ages.[5] In 1618 the University of Salamanca took a vow ('juramento') to defend the dogmas of the Immaculate Conception and Fray Basilio

---

[1] *Conceptos extravagantes*, p. 104.
[2] Lepanto sermon, p. 25 and *Conceptos extravagantes*, pp. 176–8.
[3] Tejada y Ramiro, *Colección*, iv. 35–7.
[4] *La sociedad española*, ii. 98.   [5] See above, p. 46 n. [4].

Ponce de León was prominent among those who promoted this resolution.[1]

Even so, our preachers express themselves with considerable caution on this topic, bearing in mind the decrees of Sixtus IV and Pius V which attempted to damp down the fires of controversy, awaiting a final definition of the dogma. The Franciscan Fray Diego Murillo puts partisan feeling on one side in the interests of obedience when he writes, in his 'Advertencias al pío y cristiano lector', that although he had argued (in his sermon on the 'puríssima concepción') that to doubt the Immaculate Conception of Our Lady was tantamount to doubting the omnipotence, wisdom, or goodness of God, he did not, of course, mean to imply that those who claimed that Our Lady was *not* immaculately conceived *actually* doubted those perfections in which they were obliged to believe as fundamental articles of faith![2] This retraction comes rather too late to prevent the harm being done, but one can sense that pressure was put on Murillo to insert this proviso into the preliminaries to his sermon collection in an attempt to avert a renewed outbreak of hostilities.

Likewise, Fray Pedro de Valderrama adds a note to one of his sermons on the Immaculate Conception to the effect that, while defending 'la pureza de la limpia Concepción', he does not mean to 'tener por mala ni improbable la opinión contraria'.[3] Fray Cristóbal de Avendaño, however, is more whole-hearted: he tells us that he has been asked by some Franciscan preachers to include a sermon on the Immaculate Conception in each of his books, and he is prepared to do so, 'por la devoción que tengo a este misterio y por lo mucho que a los Padres debo y a su Religión'.[4]

It is interesting to note that in many of the sermons of this period which deal with the Immaculate Conception (and there are a great many which do) the dogma is expounded in an extremely 'popular' idiom. We have already seen Avendaño's *exemplum* on the subject,[5] which is hardly more than a traditional joke loosely adapted to a theological purpose, and in two of his sermons on the same point Fray Diego de la Vega illustrates his remarks with references to contemporary social reality. In the first he compares Our Lady's exemption from

[1] *Relación de las fiestas que la Universidad de Salamanca celebró desde 27 hasta el 31 de Octubre del año de 1618 al juramento del nuevo estatuto, hecho en 2 de mayo del dicho año, de que todos los graduados defenderán la pura y limpia concepción de la Virgen* (Salamanca, 1618).
[2] *Vida y excelencias de la Madre de Dios*, sig. ††7.
[3] *Exercicios espirituales [Santos]*, p. 234.
[4] *Sermones de Santos*, Prólogo. In 1618 he preached an 'inmaculista' sermon in the Franciscan church in Valladolid.
[5] See above, pp. 72-3.

Original Sin to a human queen's exemption from common law and taxes like the *alcabala*.[1] He adds more circumstantial details about the kind of *premáticas* which were being issued at the time and which were the equivalent of sumptuary laws: 'que no se traiga seda sobre seda; que no almidonen los cuellos; que no se traiga oro esmaltado'. Here again the queen is exempt, just as the Queen of Heaven is not bound by the common law of human frailty. In the second sermon, which follows directly afterwards in the same volume, he compares the effect of the Fall to the trial of a penitent by the Inquisition:

Cuando en un acto de Inquisición sacan un penitenciado al tablado, con un sanbenito, para que le tenga no más de mientras durare el leer la sentencia, y que luego se le quiten, aunque aquello sea por aquel breve tiempo no más, no por eso deja de quedar por infame, y afrentados sus parientes y deudos: y los privilegios que después vienen no son bastantes para purgar esta deshonra.[2]

The analogy with Original Sin breaks down when one remembers that Baptism can wash away this hereditary stain; however, it does highlight a very topical sense in which the Virgin's Conception was 'limpia' by referring indirectly to the statutes of *limpieza de sangre*.

In conclusion, it would be as well to record that Spain sent numerous delegations to Rome, in 1617, 1618, and 1622 particularly, to press for the definition of the dogma of the Immaculate Conception and this is frequently given as proof of a *national* devotion to Our Lady, as well as a personal devotion on the part of Philip III ('esclavo de María').[3]

THE PAPACY

Although papal infallibility was not declared a dogma of the Church until the first Vatican Council (1869–70),[4] it was already a firmly held belief in Catholic Spain by the early seventeenth century, to judge from passages in a number of sermons of the period.[5] Fray Diego Murillo invokes the authority of *theologi omnes* to prove the point: 'que el

---

[1] *Parayso*, i. 49–50.

[2] Ibid. 68. In his *Marial* (Alcalá, 1616) he also speaks of 'quitar de acuestas [de la Virgen] el sanbenito de la culpa' and of the Immaculate Conception in terms of an 'ejecutoria de hidalguía' (fos. 24ᵛ–25).

[3] See L. Wadding, *Legatio Philippi III et IV . . . ad SS. DD. NN. Paulum PP. V et Gregorium XV, de definienda controversia inmaculatae conceptionis beatae virginis Mariae* (Louvain, 1624). Also S. Arbolí, *La Eucaristía y la Inmaculada: devoción española* (Seville, 1895).

[4] Sess. iv, cap. 4. The text of the decree was submitted to the Council by Pius IX on 6 March 1870 and solemnly proclaimed, despite opposition, on 18 July 1870. See K. Otmar von Aretin, *The Papacy and the Modern World* (London, 1970), pp. 99–104.

[5] Fray Tomás Ramón is under the impression that at the Council of Trent 'se declaró ser suprema la majestad del Pontífice Romano' (*Conceptos*, p. 93) principally as a result of the efforts of Philip II.

Sumo prelado, que es el Pontífice, no puede errar en lo que toca a las determinaciones de Fe y de buenas costumbres'.[1] He elaborates further: 'Y se tiene por cierto, que si el sumo Pontífice quisiese firmar como de Fe alguna proposción errónea, no podría, porque o se le tulliría la mano, o la pluma no administraría tinta al papel, o acaecería otro milagro para estorbar aquel yerro.' He corroborates this with an *exemplum* from the life of St. Basil, who could not be banished because the Emperor's chair broke beneath him and three pens refused to sign the decree of banishment. Murillo, in another sermon, calls the Pope the sun-dial ('relox de sol') by which all human clocks are set and 'que no puede errar, porque le gobierna el movimiento del Cielo, con la asistencia del divino Espíritu'.[2] Pursuing the *comparación*, he speaks of the officers of the Inquisition as 'reloxeros', who set all the clocks of Christendom to Rome time, and correct them when they deviate.

Another Franciscan preacher, Fray Diego de la Vega, in a sermon on Saints Peter and Paul, expounds the same doctrine: 'El juicio y censura del Sumo Pontífice, después de haber hecho lo que es de su parte, y haberlo consultado con Dios, es infalible y certísimo; y así como Dios no puede mentir, así Pedro no puede arrar [las verdades de la fe que ha de recibir y creer la Iglesia].'[3] Related to this question is that of the priesthood: the office is greater than the man, contrary to the erroneous belief of the Protestant heretics. Their contention was that mortal sin deprived the Pope of his pontificate, and of his priesthood in the case of a priest, rendering the sacraments he administered automatically invalid. This heresy is fiercely refuted by Fray Cristóbal de Fonseca.[4]

The Counter-Reformation was responsible for a new flowering of papal supremacy, of an executive rather than a purely academic nature.[5] Although neither his father nor his grandfather had ever fully cooperated with the Supreme Pontiff in political matters,[6] Philip III, from the moment of his accession to the throne in 1598, took a vow of obedience to the Pope, 'reconociéndose humilde y obediente hijo de la Iglesia'.[7] This led to his sending a detachment of troops into the Republic of Venice at the time of the Schism in 1606. The Popes whose pontificates coincided with the reign of Philip III were Clement VIII

---

[1] *Discursos predicables [Quaresma]* i. 462–3.   [2] Ibid., 563.
[3] *Parayso*, ii. 100–1.
[4] *Discursos para la Quaresma*, fos. 147^V–148.
[5] Evennett, *Counter-Reformation*, pp. 92–4.
[6] J.H. Elliott, *Imperial Spain, 1469–1716* (London, 1963; paperback 1970), pp. 100–3, 227–31.
[7] Ana de Castro Egas, *Eternidad del Rey Don Felipe Tercero* (Madrid, 1629), fo. 6.

(1592–1605), Leo XI (1605 for twenty-six days), and Paul V (1605–21). The first was a Renaissance Pope in the grand manner: profligate, a patron of the arts, and with a tendency towards nepotism. He also inclined towards France and obtained the conversion of Henri IV, who in turn hailed his successor as the 'French Pope'.[1] Paul V, on the other hand, seemed to incarnate the strict reforming zeal of the Counter-Reformation and did much to strengthen the prestige of the Papacy. It could be argued that, despite the *Patronato* won in 1486, Philip III himself brought Spain under the influence of the Papacy to a greater extent than either before or since, and therefore the character of the Spanish Church became rather more ultramontane during his reign.

THE AUTHORITY OF SCRIPTURE

Every sermon hangs on at least one biblical text, usually more, and must be seen not just as exposition of the Word of God but exposition adapted to a precise situation, historical, theological, and linguistic.[2] In the words of Karl Barth:

Preaching follows from the command given to the Church to serve the Word of God by means of a man called to this task. It is this man's duty to proclaim to his fellow men what God himself has to say to them by explaining in his own words a passage from Scripture which concerns them personally.[3]

Scripture is interpreted by our preachers according to the fourfold method, with the literal and moral senses being those most favoured in homilies. Fray Agustín Núñez Delgadillo is frequently praised for being 'literalissimo',[4] while Fray Tomás Ramón is commended for 'el sentido espiritual'.[5] The typological or allegorical sense is used by Fray Diego de la Vega, who speaks of 'trazas y borrones' of the Incarnation,[6] and by Fray Diego Murillo, who uses the story of Absalom to 'typify' both Christ and Judas. The former was 'colgado de un árbol' and the latter 'murió ahorcado'.[7]

The preacher's knowledge of Scripture is, therefore, vital if he is to be able to expound it truthfully, and, in order for his proclamation of the Word of God to be truly effective, he has to be able to speak the language of his contemporaries both linguistically and theologically. This means, in seventeenth-century Spain, that if he is not himself a gifted exegete he needs to be able to navigate the sea of Bible

[1] H. Trevor-Roper, 'Spain and Europe, 1598–1621', *The New Cambridge Modern History*, iv (1970). 262–3.
[2] See above, pp. 11–14.
[3] *Prayer and Preaching* (London, 1964), p. 65.
[4] Aprobación to *Minas*, sig. ¶3^V.
[5] Aprobación to *Puntos escripturales*, ii.   [6] *Empleo*, i. fo. 174.
[7] *Discursos predicables [Quaresma]*, ii. 296 and 385.

commentaries and glosses, and if he is a conscientious Catholic he has
to bear in mind that for the post-Tridentine Church revelation embraces
both the written canon of Scripture and the whole legacy of apostolic
tradition. Fray Cristóbal de Fonseca reiterates this position, in refutation
of the Lutheran heresy of *sola scriptura*:

Esa autoridad alegan los Herejes, contra las tradiciones apostólicas y eclesiásticas, contra los decretos de los concilios, no considerando, lo uno, que
no sólo es su palabra lo que Dios dijo, sino lo que reveló. . .lo otro, que no
se ha de añadir ni quitar cosa que haga sentido contrario . . .pero lo que no
tiene contradición, sino mucha conformidad, muy bien se puede añadir.[1]

Conciliar decrees and Papal bulls are, in fact, given as 'authorities' here
and there in the sermons of this period, side by side with Scripture,
and certainly St. Thomas Aquinas carries almost as much weight,
particularly in the sermons of Fray Tomás Ramón, who calls him 'el
divino intérprete de la Voluntad de Dios mi Angélico padre', being
himself a member of the Dominican Order, and in those of Fray Agustín
Núñez Delgadillo who, despite his reputation as a Scripturalist, frequently
has recourse to the theological formulations of the 'Angélico Doctor'.[2]
In scriptural interpretation. St. Augustine reigns supreme and the
proverb 'no hay olla sin tocino, ni sermón sin Agostino' holds good for
the sermons of this period. Fonseca and Vega quote St. Augustine far
more frequently than Aquinas.

As aids to the exposition of Scripture (in addition to study of the
principal preaching Fathers, Augustine, Origen, and John Chrysostom)
Fray Diego de Estella recommends to his apprentice preacher a few
'standard works'. These include Nicholas of Lyra, Alonso Madrigal (El
Tostado) and Dionisius of Ryckel (El Cartujano), while among the
'moderns' he has especial praise for the Portuguese Fray Heitor Pinto
and even Erasmus himself.[3] Pinto and Arias Montano are, indeed,
quite frequently referred to as authoritative exegetes by Fray Cristóbal
de Avendaño, and the latter is several times quoted by Fray Juan
Galvarro in his *Glosa moral* (Sanlúcar de Barrameda, 1622). Fray Basilio
Ponce de León gives verbatim, and with a marginal acknowledgement, a
passage from Fray Luis de León's translation of the Song of Songs,[4]
and as for Erasmus, he often recurs in the works of our preachers,
offering an alternative reading to the Vulgate.[5] Fray Diego de la Vega

[1] *Discursos para la Quaresma*, fo. 248. See the Council of Trent, sess. iv.
(8 Apr. 1546), in López de Ayala, *El Sacrosanto... concilio de Trento*, pp. 12–19.
[2] See *Flores nuevas*, i. 248 and *Minas*, fo. 228.
[3] *Modo de predicar*, ii. 15–17. He refers specifically to Erasmus' *Paraphrases
in Novum Testamentum* (Basle, 1516).
[4] *Discursos de los Evangelios de Quaresma*, i. 282–3 and 285. In another
collection he quotes from *De los Nombres de Christo*, 'Rey' (*Discursos para
diferentes Evangelios*, ii. fo. 423).
[5] Avendaño, *Sermones del Adviento*, p. 78 and Vega, *Marial*, fo. 81[V].

refers to Erasmus in a suitably guarded way, carefully qualifying the praise he bestows on the defender of *bonae litterae*: 'Erasmo Rotherdamo, casi contemporáneo y vecino nuestro, y que si como fue benmérito de la elocuencia lo fuera de la piedad christiana, no tuviera tantos quejosos, a vueltas de otras cosas que dijo bien dichas, dijo también una admirable sententia: *Ingens onus magna fortuna*.'[1] Although this is a reference to the *Adagia*, it is clearly Erasmus the biblical scholar who is present in most of the other passages where his name is mentioned in the sermons, and Erasmus was explicitly scornful of the Vulgate, which in 1546 was instated as the official version of the Bible, with the words 'longo tot saeculorum usu in ipsa ecclesia probata est'.[2]

Nevertheless, this 'canonization' of the Vulgate came at a time when the philological and humanistic methods of scriptural translation and interpretation were at last being accepted by Catholics and Protestants alike, and when a moral victory had been won by Reuchlin and his followers over the obscurantists.[3] The Catholic Church had seemed ready for a return to the original languages, and in Spain the movement was already further advanced than elsewhere in Europe. Cisneros' founding of the University of Alcalá for precisely this purpose proved a natural continuation, and legitimation, of the medieval schools of Jewish exegesis which had flourished in the kingdoms of 'Los Reyes de las tres religiones'.[4] The earliest vernacular translations of the Bible that circulated openly in the first decades of the sixteenth century (and surreptitiously later in the century) were made directly from the Hebrew Old Testament and were intended for use among the large Jewish community. The conciliar decree and various rulings by the Spanish Inquisition[5] sought to prohibit, or at least control, these vernacular versions, as much because they were *judaizantes* as because the promulgation of Scripture in the language of the people was a central tenet of 'un heresiarca perdido y desalmado, que ahorcó los hábitos de la Religión, que sacó la monja del recogimiento, que se casó con ella, y acabando la vida tristemente, dio en la muerte prendas claras de su infierno'.[6] There were, of course, partial translations, accompanied by marginal notes, of which the most famous and often reprinted was Fray Ambrosio Montesino's *Epístolas y Evangelios de los*

[1] *Parayso*, ii (*Adiciones*). p. 10.
[2] Sess. iv. See López de Ayala, *El Sacrosanto. . .concilio de Trento*, p. 16.
[3] W. Schwarz, *Principles of Biblical Translation* (Cambridge, 1955).
[4] See M. Morreale, 'The vernacular scriptures in Spain', *Cambridge History of the Bible* (Cambridge, 1969), ii. 473-4. Also Bataillon, *Erasmo y España*, pp. 10-24, 339-45, 549-58.
[5] In the Index of 1551 (*Tres Índices expurgatorios de la Inquisición española en el siglo xvi*, Madrid, 1952) and thereafter throughout our period.
[6] Fonseca, *Quarta parte de la Vida de Christo*, fo. 695.

domingos y fiestas de todo el año (Toledo, 1512),[1] and the whole question of the Bible in the vernacular was much debated in the second half of the sixteenth century.

The Sandoval Index of 1612, in addition to prohibiting the vernacular Bible 'con todas sus partes impressa' (Regla iv, p. 3), also banned the Talmud, together with its glosses and commentaries, and 'los libros de Rabbinos, o de otros qualesquier Hebreos, o Judíos, o de Moros. . .cuyo principal argumento es contra nuestra santa fe christiana'. It adds, however, that a licence will be given *in scriptis* 'solamente a varones píos y doctos, para leer y tener algunos de los dichos Rabbinos que escribieron sobre la divina Escritura, cuando nos parezca no hay inconveniente'.[2] Several of our preachers have been able to avail of this dispensation, to judge by the references to well-accredited Rabbinical sources: Maimonides (Rabi Moysen),[3] Abraham ibn Ezra (Rabbi Abenzerra or Aben Ezrah),[4] Rabi David,[5] Rabi Solomon ben Isaac of Troyes,[6] Rabi Jonathan (Jonatas),[7] and the Targum.[8] This does not, I feel, amount to any marked relaxation in the imposition of orthodoxy, but it does underline what has already been suggested by many historians of the period, namely that the *leyenda negra* of Spanish Counter-Reformation Catholicism has been exaggerated, and that in fact at certain levels the sterner rulings of the Council of Trent were modified to preserve long-standing traditions.[9]

There are, however, signs that doctrinal orthodoxy is still being formally maintained and even the most prudent preachers—those who exhort their congregations to denounce heretics to the Inquisition and who see fire as the 'único remedio' against pernicious opinions[10] —find some of their published sermons listed in the 'Second Class' of the *Index Lusitanae* of 1624.[11] Certain propositions are singled out for

---

[1] The sermons were clearly separated from the scriptural passages and could be read independently, which may account for the work's inclusion in the 1559 Index.

[2] *Index librorum prohibitorum et expurgatorum . . . D. Bernardi de Sandoval et Roxas* (Madrid, 1612), p. 2.

[3] Avendaño, *Sermones del Adviento*, p. 94.

[4] Ibid., p. 553; Vega, *Empleo*, i. 293. Also González, *Consideraciones*, fo. 1[V].

[5] Vega, *Parayso*, ii. 16; Ramón, *Conceptos*, p. 578.

[6] Vega, *Empleo*, i. 293; Ramón, *Conceptos*, pp. 50 and 578.

[7] Santiago, *Consideraciones*, p. 9.

[8] Vega, *Parayso*, ii. 16.

[9] The Rabbinic strains in Spanish biblical scholarship have often been confused with Erasmianism and made to seem more 'modern' than they in fact are, as E. Asensio points out in 'El erasmismo y las corrientes espirituales afines', *RFE* xxvi (1952), 44–56.

[10] Murillo, *Discursos predicables Quaresma*, i. 555.

[11] Works by Murillo, Vega, Ramón, Valderrama, and Avendaño. Diego de la Vega's *Parayso de la Gloria de los Santos* also appears for correction in the Sandoval Index (p. 36.).

censure and it is possible to find mutilated or expurgated copies of *sermonarios* from which doubtful passages have been removed.[1] Obviously the preacher had to be careful, particularly in his printed works but also in the pulpit (see above, p. 113). Perhaps the strongly worded *Protestación* which the Franciscan Fray Diego de Arce prints at the front of one of his collections of sermons testifies to a climate of opinion in which even the clergy might feel uneasy. Addressing himself to his 'sanctissima madre Iglesia Católica, apostólica, Romana' he says: 'maldigo a todos tus enemigos, anathemizo a Luthero, abomino a Calvino, escupo a Melanchtón, doy mil higas a Beza y a todos los Herejes pasados, presentes y que están por venir'.[2] This is reminiscent of the reported 'public retraction of errors' preached by the famous Capuchin Fray Alonso Lobo in Rome in 1562.[3] Without knowing the circumstances, this case would seem to be an extreme one and, despite the fierce language of some of our Franciscan and Dominican preachers on occasions in the Church's year which called for it (i.e. on Passion Sunday or when preaching the Bull of the *Cruzada*), sermons at the turn of the sixteenth century normally reflect pastoral rather than polemical concerns. The theological message of the sermons is couched in the language of popular piety and promotes the sacramental life of the Church rather than speculation or even private prayer.

---

[1] The works of Fray Cristóbal de Avendaño appear to have suffered particularly badly, since in two editions (Valladolid, 1619 and Valencia, 1623) of the *Sermones del Adviento* a sermon is expurgated. A *Letanía* is expurgated from the *Sermones de Santos* (Madrid, 1625) and a passage in the first volume of *Sermones de la Quaresma* (Madrid, 1622) is censored, albeit according to rulings of 1641 and 1707, which indicates a longer period of readership than might otherwise be assumed.

[2] *Miscelánea primera de oraciones eclesiásticas*, sig. B6.

[3] MS. Salazar N. 32 (Real Academia de la Historia, Madrid), p. 145. See Nicolás Antonio *Nova* I, 32.

CONCLUSION

An initial survey of so vast an area as preaching in Spain, even within the limiting framework of a single reign and a handful of preachers, must of necessity be inconclusive. Again and again one becomes aware of the different currents which flow together in the formation of each preacher, if not each sermon, and which all demand to be followed back to their source. These include the Pauline and patristic tradition of preaching to which sermons in the Spanish Golden Age belong, regardless of more ephemeral fashions; the special character and traditions of each of the major preaching orders; the movement of spiritual renewal which is not entirely spent by the end of the sixteenth century, but which is orientated towards different aspects of the Christian life; and, perhaps, a legacy of eloquence and wisdom, *sententiae* and *exempla*, which preaching has received and holds in trust from the medieval miscellanies. Printed sermon literature in the Spanish Golden Age, particularly in its *sermonario* form—comprehensive but often inconsequential—is the true heir to the miscellanies and proposes, as a defining principle, to be *Para Todos*:

Hallarán en estos libros los Predicadores sermones; el Teólogo Escolástico, los puntos dificultosos que se ventillan en las escuelas declarados; el Teólogo positivo, muchos lugares de la Sagrada Escritura, expuestos con diversas traslaciones y con doctrina de los Santos Padres; el Humanista, diversidad de historias; el buen Christiano, doctrina moral para la salvación de su alma. Comida es guisada para todos, cada cual coma lo que viere le fuere de más provecho.[1]

The sermons represent a vast repository of ideas (old rather than new), scriptural glosses, social observations, art theory, humanistic erudition, and *conceptos* often based on the *Natural History* of Pliny or the medieval bestiaries. The temptation of the researcher is to gather together curious or amusing passages from different preachers, concentrating on those which seem to bear some relation to contemporary secular literature, or which allude to events and customs which recognizably belong to the Spanish Golden Age. In so far as this temptation has been resisted in the present study, it is possible to find certain topics explored more systematically: for example, the debate over the use of the vernacular and the much older debate over the use of *humanidades* and profane arts of eloquence in sermons. The 'staging' of the sermon has been examined, although not exhaustively, and some attempt has been made to separate literary topoi and historical evidence,

---

[1] Almenara, *Pensamientos literales y morales*, Prólogo al lector.

which is always difficult when the former are so prevalent and the latter so scarce.

A constant feature has been the persona and rhetoric of the preacher as man of letters, and even publisher: his prefaces to the reader echo and parallel those of his secular counterparts. Preaching does, indeed, seem to run in parallel to other forms of literature: it has its own precepts, its own controversies, but these are usually situated within the more general critical preoccupations of the age. It is not necessary to establish any clear relation of mutual influences between, say, preaching and the Spanish picaresque novel, in order to be aware that both spring from the same historical, cultural, and religious context and are aimed at the same 'congregation'. I feel it is more accurate to consider coincidences of style and taste rather than conscious emulation or 'contamination' (to adopt the loaded language of the Decadence theory of preaching referred to in the Introduction). The essential premisses of the preaching situation have not changed much down the ages and Welsh Nonconformist ministers of the twentieth century have much more in common with seventeenth-century Spanish Franciscans or Dominicans when it comes to composing and delivering a sermon than might at first be imagined. The sermon form itself, although it retains the constants of Biblical exposition and the division of texts, is intrinsically flexible, and easily becomes a vehicle to mediate not only the Word of God but also a set of cultural assumptions from preacher to people: hence its interest for the social historian and, even more, for the literary historian.

LIST OF WORKS CONSULTED

1. TREATISES ON PREACHING AND RHETORIC

Aquaviva, Claudio, 'Epistola . . . ad Provinciales Societatis . . . formandis concionatoribus accommoda', in *Epistolae praepositorum generalium ad patres et fratres Societatis Iesu* (Roeselare, 1909), vol. i.

Augustine, St., *De doctrina christiana libri iv* (Paris, 1861), Migne, *PL* xxxiv.

Bonifacio, Juan, *De sapiente fructuoso* (Burgos, 1589; trans. F.G. Olmedo, Madrid, 1938).

Borja, San Francisco, *Tratado breve. . .para los Predicadores del Santo Evangelico* (Madrid, 1592), in P. Pedro de Ribadeneyra, *Vida de San Francisco de Borja* (Madrid, 1591), iii. 19 ff.

Borromeo, San Carlo, [authorized by] *Instructiones Praedicationis verbi Dei* (Barcelona, 1588).

Borromeo, Federigo, *De concionante episcopo libri tres* and *De sacris nostrorum temporum oratoribus libri quinque* (Milan, 1632–3).

Cascales, Francisco, *Cartas filológicas* (Murcia, 1634; 3 vols., Clásicos Castellanos, 1930–41). 'Carta al licenciado Andrés de Salvatierra, sobre el lenguaje que se requiere en el púlpito', Década tercera, vi. 125–46.

Caussin, Nicolas, *Eloquentia sacra ac prophana parallela, xvi libri* (La Flèche, 1619).

Erasmus, Desiderius, *Ecclesiastiae, sive de ratione concionandi, libri iv* (1535; ed. F.A. Klein, Leipzig, 1820).

Estella, Diego de, *Modus concionandi* Salamanca, 1576). Modern edn., with Estella's own Spanish version: *Modo de predicar*, ed. P. Sagüés Azcona (2 vols., Madrid, 1951).

García Matamoros, Alfonso, *De arte concionandi* (Alcalá, 1570).

García del Valle, Francisco, *Evangelicus Concionator et Novi Hominis Institutio, ex doctrina Verbi Dei* (Lyons, 1622).

Gerardus, Andreas, (alias Hyperius of Marburg), *De formandis concionibus sacris, seu de interpretatione scripturarum popularum libri ii* (Dortmund, 1555). [Transmitted in Spanish by Lorenzo de Villavicencio, q.v.].

Gracián, Baltasar, *Agudeza y arte de ingenio* (Huesca, 1648; ed. A. del Hoyo, Madrid, 1960).

Granada, Luis de, *Ecclesiasticae Rhetoricae, sive de ratione concionandi libri sex* (Lisbon, 1576). Spanish trans. *Retórica Eclesiástica* (1770). Edn. used: *BAE* iii (Madrid, 1863).

Guzmán, Juan de, *Primera parte de la Rhetorica dividida en catorze combites de oradores* (Alcalá, 1589).

Jiménez Patón, *see* Ximénez Patón

Márquez, Juan, 'Del modo de predicar a los Príncipes', in *C de D* xlvi (1898), 172–87, 259–71. *See* Blanco García, P.F.

Panigarola, Francesco, *Rhetorica ecclesiastica, sive de modo componendae concionis libellus* (Cologne, 1605).
Il Predicatore (Venice, 1609).
Pérez de Montalbán, Juan, 'Discurso del predicador: De la lección y elección de los libros', in *Para Todos* (Madrid, 1632), día v. Edn. used: Seville, 1756.
Pérez de Valdivia, Diego, *De sacra ratione concionandi* (Barcelona, 1588).

Quintero, Benito Carlos, *Templo de la elocuencia castellana* (Salamanca, [1629]).

Ramón, Tomás, *Nueva premática de Reformación, contra los abusos de los afeytes, calçado, guedejas, guardainfantes, lenguaje crítico, moños, trajes y exceso en el uso del tabaco* (Saragossa, 1635).
Regius, Carolus, *Orator Christianus, in quo de concionatore ipso, tum de concione, demum de concionantis prudentia et industria agitur* (Cologne, 1613).
Rodríguez de León, Juan, *El Predicador de las Gentes, San Pablo* (Madrid, 1638) (Palau attributes to León Pinelo, Juan).

Salucio, Agustín de, *Avisos para los predicadores del Santo Evangelio*, ed. A. Huerga (Barcelona, 1959).
Sánchez, Pedro Antonio, *Discurso sobre la Eloquencia sagrada en España* (Madrid, 1778).
Soares, Cipriano, *De arte rhetorica libri tres ex Aristotele, Cicerone et Quintiliano deprompti* (Coïmbra, 1561). Edn. used: Salamanca, 1577.
Suárez de Figueroa, Cristóbal de, *El Passagero. Advertencias utilissimas a la vida humana* (Madrid, 1617; Madrid, 1914).

Terrones del Caño, Francisco, *Instrucción de predicadores* (1st edn., posthumously, Madrid, 1617; ed. F.G. Olmedo, 1946).
Tesauro, Emanuele, *Il Cannocchiale Aristotelico* (1654; 5th edn., Turin, 1970).

Valades, Diego, *Rhetorica Christiana* (Perugia, 1579). For use on foreign missions.
Villavicencio, Lorenzo de, *De formandis sacris concionibus seu de interpretatione Scripturarum populari libri iv* (Antwerp, 1564).

Ximénez Patón, Bartolomé, *Eloquencia española en arte* (Toledo, 1604).
    El perfecto predicador (Baeza, 1612).

2. SIXTEENTH- AND SEVENTEENTH-CENTURY SERMONS
   Unless otherwise indicated, reference is to the first edition.

Aguilar de Terrones, *see* Terrones del Caño
Alemán, Mateo, *Oración fúnebre, see* Bushee, A. (5) Preached in Mexico
    c. 1611.
Almenara, Miguel de, *Pensamientos literales y morales sobre los Evan-
    gelios de las Dominicas después de Pentecostes* (Valencia, 1619).
Arce, Diego de, *Miscelánea primera de oraciones ecclesiásticas, desde el
    Domingo veinte y cuatro después de Pentecostes hasta la vigilia de
    Navidad* (Murcia, 1602). Edn. used: Murcia, 1606.
    Sermón de la Cruz y del Ladrón (Murcia, 1607).
Avendaño, Cristóbal de, *Sermones del Adviento, con sus festividades y
    Santos* (Madrid, 1617). Also: Valladolid, 1619.
    Segunda parte (Madrid, 1625). Together: Barcelona, 1630.
    Tomo primero sobre los Evangelios de la Quaresma (Madrid, 1622).
    Tomo segundo (Madrid, 1623).
    *Sermones para algunas festividades de las más solemnes de los
    Santos* (Madrid, 1625). Edn. used: Valladolid, 1628.
    *Libro intitulado Otro tomo de sermones para muchas festividades
    de los Santos* (Valladolid, 1629).
    *Marial de las fiestas ordinarias y extraordinarias de la Madre de
    Dios señora nuestra, con sermones al fin de sus celestiales padres*
    (Valladolid, 1629).
Avila, San Juan de, *Dos pláticas hechas a sacerdotes* (Cordoba, 1595).
    Obras completas, ed. L. Sala Balust (2 vols., Madrid, 1952–3).
    Sermones del Espíritu Santo, ed. Julio Simancas (Madrid, 1957).

Cabrera, Alonso de, *Libro de Consideraciones sobre los Evangelios,
    desde el Domingo de Septuagésima, y todos los domingos y ferias de
    la Quaresma* (2 vols., Barcelona, 1602).
    Sermones, ed. M. Mir, *BAE* iii (Madrid, 1906; 2nd edn. 1930)
    [Predicadores de los siglos xvi y xvii].
Capilla, Andreas de, *Libro de la oración en que se ponen consideracio-
    nes de los Domingos del Año y de todas las ferias de Quaresma*
    (Lérida, 1572). Also trans. into Catalan and French.
Cavo, Ilario, *Predica del Molto Rever. P.D. Ilario Cavo Genovese
    Chierico Regolare sopra l'autenticatione della Dottrina di S. Tommaso
    d'Aquino* (Venice, 1618).

Feo, Antonio, *Tratados quadragesimales y de la Pascua* (Valladolid,
    1614).
Florencia, Jerónimo de, *Sermón . . . en el entierro y cuerpo presente de
    don García Loaysa y Gyrón* (Alcalá, 1599).

Florencia, Jerónimo de, (cont'd)

Sermón en las honras de la Sacra Cesarea Magestad de la Empera-triz Doña María (Madrid, 1604).

Sermón en las honras. . .a la serenissima Reyna Dª Margarita (Madrid, 1611).

Sermón segundo . . . en las honras . . . de la serenissima Reyna doña Margarita (Madrid, 1612).

Sermón. . .en la Beatificación de la B.M. Teresa de Jesús (Madrid, 1615).

Sermon preached on the Assumption of Our Lady in October 1616 in Toledo (*see* Herrera).

Sermón. . .en las honras del Rey Felipe III (Madrid, 1621).

Sermón. . .en las honras del Duque de Monteleón (Madrid, 1622).

Sermón. . .en las honras del Conde de Lemos (Madrid, 1622).

Marial que contiene varios sermones de todas las fiestas de Nuestra Señora (2 vols., Alcalá, 1625).

Fonseca, Cristóbal de, *Quarta parte de la vida de Christo S.N. que trata de su doctrina y contiene los Evangelios de los Santos y Domingos del año y extravagantes* (Madrid, 1611).

Discursos para todos los Evangelios de la Quaresma (Madrid, (1614). Trans. into English by James Mabbe as *Devout Contem-plations expressed in Two and Fortie Sermons upon all ye Quadra-gesimall Gospells* (1629).

Sermon on the Birth of the Virgin Mary preached in Toledo in 1616 (*see* Herrera).

Galvarro y Armenta, Juan de, *Glosa moral sobre los Evangelios de Quaresma* (Sanlúcar de Barrameda, 1622).

González, Cristóbal, *Consideraciones sobre el Psalmo ciento y treinta y tres. Para los seis Domingos de Quaresma en la tarde* (Madrid, 1609).

Guevara, Antonio de, *Libro primero de las Epístolas familiares* (Valla-dolid, 1539; ed. J.M. Cossío, 2 vols., Madrid, 1950–2).

Herrera, Pedro de, *Descripción de la Capilla de N^a S^{ra} del Sagrario que erigió en la Santa Iglesia de Toledo el Illmo. Sr Cardenal D. Bernardo de Sandoval y Rojas* (Madrid, 1617), (contains sermons preached for the occasion by Florencia, Fonseca, and others).

Labata, Francisco de, *Apparatus concionatorum, seu loci communes ad conciones ordine alphabetico* (3 vols., Lugduni, 1615–21).

Lanuza, Jerónimo Bautista de, *Tractatus evangelici continentes discur-sus et conceptus literales, morales et allegoricis* (Saragossa, 1612).

López de Andrade, Diego, *Primera parte de los Tratados sobre los Evan-gelios de Quaresma* (Madrid, 1615).

Segunda parte (Madrid, 1617).

Primera parte de los Tratados sobre los Evangelios. . .en las festi-vidades de los Santos (Pamplona, 1620).

Segunda parte (Pamplona, 1621).

Manrique, Angel, *Meditaciones para los días de la Quaresma* (Salamanca, 1612).
    Discursos predicables para todas las fiestas de Nuestra Señora (Salamanca, 1620).
Murrillo, Diego, *Sermón fúnebre para las honras del . . . Rey Don Philippe. . .I deste nombre* (Saragossa, 1599). Philip II was Philip I of Aragón.
    Discursos predicables sobre todos los Evangelios que canta la Iglesia, assi en las Ferias como en los Domingos, desde la Septuagesima hasta la Resurrección del Señor (Saragossa, 1601). Edn. used: augmented in 2 vols. (Saragossa, 1605). Quoted as *Discursos predicables [Quaresma]*.
    Discursos predicables para los quatro Domingos de Adviento y fiestas (Saragossa, 1603). Edn. used: Saragossa, 1610.
    Discursos predicables sobre todos los Evangelios que canta la Iglesia en las festividades de Christo Nuestro Redemptor (Saragossa, 1607).
    Vida y excelencias de la Madre de Dios, i (Saragossa, 1610); ii (Saragossa, 1614).
    Sermón. . .en la Beatificación de la B.M. Teresa de Jesús. . .predicado en Çaragoça [1614] (pub. in a collection of sueltos, Madrid, 1615, *see Sermones*).

Nadal, Jerónimo, *Pláticas espirituales en Coïmbra*, ed. M. Nicolau (Granada, 1945).
Núñez Delgadillo, Agustín, *Sermón en la Beatificación de la B.M. Teresa de Jesús* (Madrid, 1615) (*see Sermones*).
    De la Victoria de los Justos Celebrada por David en el Psalmo 17 (Granada, 1618).
    Minas Celestiales descubiertas en los Evangelios de Quaresma (Madrid, 1629).

Paravicino, Hortensio Félix, *Oraciones evangélicas de Adviento y Quaresma* (Madrid, 1636).
    Oraciones evangélicas en las Festividades de Christo (Madrid, 1638).
    Oraciones evangélicas y panegíricos funerales (Madrid, 1641).
    Obras póstumas divinas y humanas, ed. J. Ibarra (Madrid, 1766).
Pineda, Juan de, *Sermón a Jueces y otros ministros de Justicia . . . último día de Pascua de Navidad, haciendo fiesta votiva del Espíritu Santo la congregación de su avocación* (Seville, 1612).
Ponce de León, Basilio, *Primera parte de discursos para todos los Evangelios de la Quaresma* (Madrid, 1605). Edn. consulted: *Discursos para diferentes Evangelios del año* (Salamanca, 1608) (same sermons).
    Segunda parte: Salamanca, 1609.

  * Sermones de la Purísima Concepción de la Virgen y de la S.M. Teresa de Jesús, y del Santo F. Thomas de Villanueva* (Salamanca, 1620).

Ponce de León, Basilio, (cont'd)
* *Sermón en la fiesta de la Naval de Lepanto* (Salamanca, 1620).
* *Sermón predicado. . .en las honras de la Magestad Católica de Felipe III* (Ciudad de Toro, 1621).
* *Sermón en la fiesta de Santa Clara de Monte Falco* (Salamanca, 1625).
* *Sermón predicado en la fiesta de S. Augustín en Salamanca a 28 de Agosto 1628* (Salamanca, 1628).
* *Relación y sermón en las Honras de F. Augustín Antolínez* (Salamanca, 1629) [preached 1626].
* Bound together as *Sermones varios* in BNM (3—13925).

Ramón, Tomás, *Flores nuevas, cogidas del vergel de las divinas y humanas letras* (2 vols., Barcelona, 1611—12).
Puntos escripturales de las divinas letras y Santos Padres (2 vols. Barcelona, 1618).
Conceptos extravagantes y peregrinos, sacados de las divinas y humanas letras y Santos Padres (Barcelona, 1619).
Nuevas y divinas Indias de las altissimas virtudes de María, y doce soberanissimos privilegios suyos: figurados en las doce estrellas de su Imperial Corona (Saragossa, 1624).
Vergel de plantas divinas las más bellas y que más campean en el campo de la Iglesia (Barcelona, 1629).
Rebolledo, Luis de *Primera parte de cien oraciones fúnebres, en que se considera la vida, y sus miserias: la muerte, y sus provechos* (Seville, 1600). Edn. used: Madrid, 1600.
Sermón en las honras del Conde de Chinchón (Toledo, 1606).

Santiago, Hernando de, *Consideraciones sobre todos los Evangelios de los Domingos y Ferias de la Quaresma* (Salamanca, 1597). Edn. used: Madrid, 1606. *See also* under Pérez, Quintín (5).
Sagrameña, Antonio de, *Sermón en las honras del R.P. Agustín Núñez Delgadillo* (Madrid, 1631).
Semple de Tovar, Andrés, *Miserere en discursos predicables para las tardes de Quaresma* (Madrid, 1644).
Sermones predicados en la Beatificación de la B.M. Teresa de Jesús Virgen fundadora de la Reforma de los Descalços de N. Señora del Carmen, colegidos por orden del padre fray Joseph de Jesús María (Madrid, 1615).

Tamayo y Porres, Francisco de, *Sermón en la festividad del glorioso príncipe de los apóstoles San Pedro, sacado de memoria y puesto en verso castellano. . .Predicóle el R.P.F. Antonio Morato, capellán de su Magestad, en la Capilla y Convento Real de N. Señora de la Merced. . .de Barcelona. Año 1627* (Barcelona, 1630).
Tapia de la Camara, Dr., *Discursos predicables de diversos tratados, de la Passión de Christo N.S., de las siete Palabras de la Soledad de Nuestra Señora, Misterios de la Cruz, del Mandato, y de los quatro novissimos* (Madrid, 1604).

Terrones del Caño, Francisco, *Sermón en las Honras de Felipe II* [Madrid, 1598].

Truxillo, Tomás, *Conciones quadragesimales quadruplices* (Barcelona, 1591).

Valderrama, Pedro de, *Sermón en las honras de don Diego López de Haro* (Cordoba, 1599). Repr. in *Teatro de las Religiones* (q.v.).
Sermón en la canonización de San Raymundo de Peñafort (Seville, 1601).
Exercicios espirituales para todos los días de la Quaresma (Seville, 1602). Edn. used: corrected reprint Seville, 1603.
Segunda parte (Madrid, 1604).
Tercera parte (Madrid, 1605).
Exercicios espirituales para todas las festividades de los Santos (3 vols., Lisbon, 1606). Edn. used: Barcelona, 1607. Each of the three parts is by a different printer: (i) Sebastian Cormellas, (ii) Gabriel Graells y Giraldo Dotil, (iii) Jayme Cendrat. Same with 16 sermons on the feasts of Our Lady and 8 on the Eucharist (Madrid, 1608).
Exercicios espirituales para los tres domingos de septuagesima, sexagesima y quinquagesima (Lisbon, 1607). Edn. used: Barcelona, 1607.
Sermón primero de la Concepción de Nuestra Señora. . .en la fiesta de Sanlucar de Barrameda (Seville, 1609).
Sermón en la fiesta de la beatificación de San Ignacio de Loyola (Seville, 1610). Repr. in *Teatro de las Religiones*.
Sermón. . .en las. . .exequias del muy Reverendo Padre Maestro Fray Diego de Avila (Seville, 1611).
Teatro de las Religiones (posthumous, Seville, 1612).

Vázquez, Dionisio, *Sermones*, ed. Félix G. Olmedo (Clásicos Castellanos, 1943).

Vega, Diego de la, *Conciones vespertinae quadragesimales, super septem poenitentiales psalmos* (Alcalá de Henares, 1595).
Quadragesimale opus pro omnibus Dominicis, et feriis. . .a Septuagesima usque ad feriam secundam Resurrectionis (Toledo, 1600).
Parayso de la Gloria de los Santos. Donde se trata de sus prerogativas y excelencias (2 vols., Toledo, 1602). Edn. used: Medina del Campo, 1604 (also contains *Adiciones*).
Empleo y Exercicio Sancto sobre los Evangelios de las Dominicas de todo el año. Tomo primero (Toledo, 1604) *Tomo segundo* (Madrid, 1607). Edn. used: Valladolid, 1608.
Discursos predicables sobre los Evangelios de todos los días de la Quaresma (Alcalá de Henares, 1611).
Prerogativas y Excelencias de la Virgen Nuestra Señora, fundadas sobre los Evangelios que se predican en sus Festividades, por otro nombre Marial (Alcalá, 1616).

Vieira, Antonio, *Sermão de sexagésima e Carta a D. Afonso VI*, ed. J. de Almeida Lucas (Lisbon, [1964]).

3. OTHER PRIMARY SOURCES

Alciati, Andreas, *Emblematum liber* (edn. of Lyons, 1550), trans. B. Daza as *Los emblemas* (Lyons, 1549).

Aldana, Cosme de, *Inuectiva contra el vulgo y su maledicencia* (Madrid, 1591).

Alemán, Mateo, *Guzmán de Alfarache* (Madrid, 1599 and Lisbon, 1604; ed. S. Gili y Gaya, Clásicos Castellanos, 1927–36).

ANON., *El Cancionero Antequerano* (recogido por Ignacio de Toledo y Godoy), ed. D. Alonso and R. Ferrers (Madrid, 1950).

La vida de Lazarillo de Tormes, ed. R.O. Jones (Manchester, 1963).

Aranda, Juan de, *Lugares comunes de conceptos, dichos y sentencias* (Seville, 1595).

Azpilcueta, Martín de, *Tractado de alabanza y murmuración. En el qual se declara quando son mérito, quando pecado venial y quando mortal* (Valladolid, 1572).

Bertaut, *see* Cassou, F. (5)

Capilla Real—con observancias proprias de la del Rey Catolico N.S.D. Felipe IV el Grande (por D. Vicencio Tortoreti y Nápoles) (Madrid, 1630).

Carballo, Luis Alfonso de, *Cisne de Apolo* (Medina del Campo, 1602; ed. A. Porqueras Mayo, 2 vols., Madrid, 1958).

Castro Egas, Ana de, *Eternidad del Rey Don Felipe Tercero. . .discurso de su vida y santas costumbres* (Madrid, 1629).

Erasmus, Desiderius, *The Praise of Folly* [1511], trans. Betty Radice, ed. A.H.T. Levi (Harmondsworth, 1971).

Fonseca, Cristóbal de, *Primera parte de la Vida de Christo* (Barcelona, 1597).

(Franciscans) *Un tractado muy provechoso llamado Manual de las cosas essentiales a que son obligados los frayles menores por su regla* (Coïmbra, 1571).

Opuscula Sancti Patris Francisci Assisiensis sec. Codices MSS. Emendata et Denuo Edita (Quaracchi, 1904) [Bibliotheca Franciscana Ascetica Medii Aevi, i].

Furió Ceriol, Fadrique, *Bononia, sive de libris sacris in vernaculam linguam convertendis* (Basle, 1556; Leyden, 1819).

Garcilaso de la Vega, *Obras. . .con anotaciones de Fernando de Herrera* (Seville, 1580).

Gavin, Antonio, *A Master-key to Popery* (Dublin, 1724).

Giovio, Paolo, *Dialogo dell' Imprese Militari et Amorose* (Rome, 1555).

González Dávila, Gil, *Historia de la vida y hechos del ínclito monarca amado y santo D. Felipe Tercero. Obra póstuma* [1619], pub. as vol. iii of Salazar de Mendoza, *Monarquía de España* (Madrid, 1770−1).

Gracián, Baltasar, *El criticón* (1651, 1653, and 1657), in *Obras completas*, ed. Arturo del Hoyo (Madrid, 1960).

Gracián, Jerónimo (de la Madre de Dios), *Obras*, ed. Silverio de Santa Teresa (3 vols., Burgos, 1933).

Granada, Luis de, *Vida del Venerable Maestro Juan de Avila* [1588] (*BAE* iii, Madrid, 1863).

Herrera, Tomás, *Historia del convento de S. Augustín de Salamanca* (Madrid, 1652).

Horozco y Covarrubias, Juan, *Emblemas morales* (Segovia, 1589).

Huarte de San Juan, Juan, *Examen de Ingenios para las Ciencias. Edición comparada de la príncipe* [Baeza, 1575] *y la sub-príncipe* [Baeza, 1594], ed. Rodrigo Sanz (2 vols., Madrid, 1930).

(Index) *Index librorum qui prohibentur* (Valladolid, 1559) [Valdés].
    Index librorum prohibitorum et expurgatorum Illmi ac Rmi DD. Bernardi de Sandoval et Roxas (Madrid, 1612).
    Tres Índices expurgatorios de la Inquisición española en el siglo xvi [facsimile reprint of two 1551 Índices and the Valdés Index] (Madrid, 1952).

Isla, José Francisco, *Historia del famoso predicador Fray Gerundio de Campazas* (Madrid, 1758; ed. Russell P. Sebold, Clásicos Castellanos, 1960).

(Jesuits) *Ratio atque Institutio Studiorum Societatis Iesu* (Rome, 1606). See also *Institutum Societatis Iesu* (Rome, 1870).

Joly, see Barrau-Dihigo (5)

Ledesma, Alonso de, *Conceptos espirituales* (Madrid, 1602; ed. E. Juliá Martínez, 3 vols., Madrid, 1969).

León Pinelo, Antonio de, *Anales de Madrid de León Pinelo en el reinado de Felipe III* [BNM MS. 1255], ed. R. Martorell Téllez-Girón (Madrid, 1931).

López de Ayala, Ignacio, *El Sacrosanto y ecuménico concilio de Trento* (Madrid, 1785).

López Pinciano, Alonso, *Philosophia antigua poetica* (Madrid, 1596; 3 vols., Madrid, 1953).

Luján, Pedro de, *Coloquios matrimoniales* (Seville, 1550; Madrid, 1943).

Luque Fajardo, Francisco de, *Razonamiento grave y devoto que hizo el padre M.F. Pedro de Valderrama . . . muy cercano a la Muerte, con más un breve Elogio de su vida y predicación* (Seville, 1612).

Malón de Chaide, Pedro de, *Libro de la Conversión de la Magdalena* (Barcelona, 1588; ed. Félix García, Clásicos Castellanos, 1947).

Malvezzi, Virgilio, *Historia. . .que comprehende sucessos de el reynado de Don Phelipe Tercero*, in J. Yañez, *Memorias para la historia de Don Felipe III* (Madrid, 1723).

Manningham, John, *The Diary of John Manningham* [1602–3], ed. John Bruce (London, 1868) [Camden Society Texts, 99].

Manrique, Angel, *Socorro que el Estado Eclesiástico de España podía hacer al Rey en el aprieto de Hacienda que hoy se halla, para mejor provecho suyo y del Reino* (Salamanca, 1624).

Mayans y Siscar, Gregorio, *El orador christiano* (2nd edn., Valencia, 1786).

Mexia, Pedro, *Silva de varia lección* (Antwerp, 1544; 2 vols., Madrid, 1933–4).

Navarra, Pedro de, *Diálogos de la diferencia del Hablar al Escribir* and *Diálogos de la diferencia que hay de la vida rústica a la noble* (Toulouse, ?1565).

Pacheco, Francisco, *Libro de descripción de verdaderos retratos de illustres y memorables varones . . . En Sevilla, 1599* [must be later than 1627] (reproduction in photochromotype, 1881–5, of MS. pub. in 1870 by J. Mª Asensio).

Pérez de Moya, Juan, *Comparaciones o símiles para los vicios y virtudes* (Alcalá, 1584).
  Philosophia secreta, donde debajo de historias fabulosas se contiene mucha doctrina provechosa a todos estudios, con el origen de los Idolos o Dioses de la Gentilidad (Madrid, 1585).

Pinheiro da Veiga, T., *La Fastiginia* [*c.* 1605] see García Mercadel, J. (5).

Quevedo, Francisco de, *Obras completas: prosa*, ed. L. Astrana Marín (Madrid, 1932).

Ramón, Tomás, *Cadena de oro, hecha de cinco eslabones y por diálogo para confirmar al Christiano en la Santa Fe católica* (Barcelona, 1610). Edn. used: Barcelona, 1612.

(Regla) *Regla del Coro y cabildo de la Santa Iglesia Metropolitana de Sevilla, y memoria de las processiones y manuales que son a cargo de los señores Dean y cabildo della* (Seville, 1658).

(Relación) *De la fiesta que se ha hecho en el convento de Santo Domingo de la Ciudad de Zaragoza a la Canonización de San Hyacintho* (Saragossa, 1595).
  Relación de las exequias que Zaragossa ha celebrado por el rey don Philipe (Saragossa, 1599), ed. J. Martínez.
  Relación de la venida de los Reyes Católicos al Collegio Inglés de Valladolid (Madrid, 1600), ed. A. Ortiz.

(Relación) (cont'd)
> *Relación de la fiesta de la beatificación de San Ignacio de Loyola* (Seville, 1610), ed. Luque Fajardo.
> *Solemnísimas Fiestas que la insigne ciudad de Toledo hizo a la Inmaculada Concepción de nuestra Señora, hallándose presente a ellas la Católica Magestad del Rey don Felipe* (Toledo, 1616), ed. C. de Castillo.
> *Relación de la fiesta que el colegio mayor de Santa María de Jesús, Universidad de la Ciudad de Seville hizo en la publicación de un Estatuto, en que se juró la Concepción limpísima de Nuestra Señora* (Seville, 1617), in Gayangos. BNM (R. 12677).

Ribadeneyra, P. Pedro de, *Flos Sanctorum o Libro de las Vidas de las Santos* (2 vols., Madrid, 1599–1601; 2 vols. in Latin: Cologne, 1630).

Rufo, Juan, *Las seiscientas apotegmas* (Toledo, 1596; ed. A.G. de Amezúa, Madrid, 1923).

Sambuco, Johannis, *Emblemata* (Antwerp, 1564).

Santoro, J.B. (trans.), *Prado espiritual de Sophronio Patriarcha de Hierusalem* (Saragossa, 1578).

Suárez, Francisco, *Operis de Religione pars segunda* (Lyons, 1625).

Suárez de Figueroa, Cristóbal, *Plaza universal de todas ciencias y artes* (Perpignan, 1630).

Teresa de Avila, Sta, *Obras completas* (2nd rev. edn., *BAC*, Madrid, 1967).

Texeira, Pedro de, *Topographia de la Villa de Madrid* (Madrid, 1656; facsimile reprint, Madrid, 1965).

[Trent, Council of] *Catechism of the Council of Trent for Parish Priests* [1566], trans. J.A. McHugh and C.J. Callan (11th printing, New York, 1949).

Valdés, Alonso de, *Diálogo de las cosas ocurridas en Roma* [1527] (Clásicos Castellanos, 1956).
> *Diálogo de Mercurio y Carón* [*c.* 1531] (Clásicos Castellanos, 1929).

Vega, Lope de, *Epistolario*, ed. A. González Amezúa (4 vols., Madrid, 1935–43).
> *El castigo sin venganza*, ed. C.A. Jones (Oxford, 1966).

Vitoria, Baltasar de, *Teatro de los Dioses de la Gentilidad* (2 vols., Salamanca, 1620; Madrid, 1676).

4. IN MANUSCRIPT

Sermons   (a) Quaresma (before 1612) TCD MS.A.5. 25–7 (144) [in different hands].
           (b) Quaresma (Baltasar López) TCD MS.A.6.1 (145).
           (c) Quaresma y Santos   TCD MS.C.2.20 (283).

Las reglas e constituciones que suelen ser guardadas en la Capilla
[Real] (undated)   El Escorial MS.& II.7.
Actas Capitulares de la Seo (Saragossa) 1593–1610; 1611–1617.
Actas Capitulares (Toledo)   1598–1614.
Autos Capitulares (Seville)   1580–1610.
Etiquetas reales de Phelipe III   Biblioteca del Palacio
                                             11/3052.
Clero (Dominicos, Saragossa)   Archivo Histórico Nacional
                                             MS.3817, leg. 2479.
    (Carmelitas calzados,   Ibid., leg. 7812–14.
    Valladolid, Medina del Campo)
Censuras inquisitoriales   Archivo Histórico Nacional.
    (Núñez Delgadillo)   MS.4.444, no. 45.
    (Avendaño)   MS.4.461, no. 25.
Papeles del P. Méndez, O.S.A. año de 1770 ⎱ Real Academia de la
                                             ⎰ Historia, MS.9.5395,
Gaceta y nuevas de la Corte de España   ⎰ leg. 1. Ibid., fos.
desde el año 1600   ⎰ 221–4.

5. SECONDARY SOURCES AND GENERAL CRITICISM

Alarcos Llorach, E., 'Los sermones de Paravicino', *RFE* xxiv (1937),
    162–97, 249–319.
Allen, D.C., *Mysteriously Meant: the Rediscovery of Pagan Symbolism
    and Allegorical Interpretation in the Renaissance* (Baltimore and
    London, 1970).
Alonso, D., *Poesía española: ensayo de métodos y límites estilísticos*
    (4th edn., Madrid, 1962).
    Del Siglo de Oro a este siglo de las siglas (Madrid, 1962).
Alonso Cortés, N., *Noticias de una corte literaria* (Madrid and Vallo-
    dolid, 1906).
    El falso 'Quijote' y Fray Cristóbal de Fonseca (Valladolid, 1920).
    'Acervo biográfico. Fray H.F. Paravicino', *BRAE* xxx (1950),
    219–20.
Andrés Martín, M., *Historia de la teología en España, 1470–1570*,
    vol. i: *Instituciones teológicas* (Rome, 1962) [Publicaciones del
    Instituto Español de Historia Eclesiástica Monografías, vii].
Andrés Puente, H., *La reforma tridentina en la orden agustiniana*
    (Valladolid, 1965).
Anson, P., *The Building of Churches* (London, 1964) [The New Library
    of Catholic Knowledge, x].
Arbolí, S., *La Eucaristía y la Inmaculada : devoción española* (Seville,
    1895).
Arco y Garay, R., 'Notas inéditas acerca de la famosa biblioteca de
    Don Vicencio Juan de Lastanosa', *BRAH* lxv (1914), 316–42.
von Aretin, K. Otmar, *The Papacy and the Modern World* (London,
    1970).
Armstrong, A.H. and R.A. Markus, *Christian Faith and Greek Philo-
    sophy* (London, 1960).

172 LIST OF WORKS CONSULTED

Arriaga, G. de, *Historia del Colegio de San Gregorio de Valladolid* (augmented and corrected, ed. M. de Hoyos, 3 vols., Madrid, 1928–40).

Asensio, E., 'El erasmismo y las corrientes espirituales afines', *RFE* xxxvi (1952), 31–99.

Asensio y Toledo, J. Mª, *Francisco Pacheco, sus obras artísticas y literarias* (Seville, 1876).

Astraín, A., *Historia de la Compañía de Jesús en la asistencia de España* (7 vols., Madrid [*Razón y Fe*], 1902–5).

Auerbach, E., *Literary Language and its public in late Latin Antiquity and in the Middle Ages* (in German, 1958; London, 1965).

Aulén, G., *The Drama and the Symbols* (in Swedish, 1965; London, 1970).

Barrau-Dihigo, L., 'Voyage de Bartolomé Joly, OSB., conseiller et aumônier du Roy', *RH* xx (1909), 459–618.

Barth, K., *Prayer and Preaching* (London, 1964).

Baselga y Ramírez, M., 'El púlpito español en la época del mal gusto', *Revista de Aragón*, iii (1902), 64–5, 129–34, 211–14, 317–21, 402–5, 510–14.

Bataillon, M., 'De Savanarole à Louis de Grenade', *RLC* xvi (1936), 23–9.

—— *Erasmo y España* (2nd Spanish edn., Mexico, 1966).

Batllori, M., 'La Agudeza de Gracián y las retóricas jesuíticas', in *Actas del Primer Congreso Internacional de Hispanistas* [Oxford, 1962] (Oxford, 1964), pp. 57–71.

—— and C. Peralta, *Baltasar Gracián en su vida y en sus obras*, in *BAE Obras completas*, i (Madrid, 1969).

Baxandall, M., *Painting and Experience in Fifteenth Century Italy* (Oxford, 1972).

Beltrán de Heredia, V., *Las corrientes de espiritualidad entre los dominicos de Castilla durante la primera mitad del siglo xvi* (Salamanca, 1941).

—— 'La formación intelectual de clero según nuestra antigua legislación canónica', *Escorial*, vii (1941), 289–98.

—— 'Los comienzos de la reforma dominicana en Castilla, particularmente en el convento de San Esteban de Salamanca y su irradición a la provincia de Portugal', *Archivum Fratrum Praedicatorum*, xxviii (1958), 221–62.

Bethell, S.L., 'Gracián, Tesauro and the Nature of Metaphysical Wit', *Northern Miscellany of Literary Criticism*, i (1953), 19–40.

Bettenson, H. (ed.), *Documents of the Christian Church* (Oxford, 1946; 2nd edn. 1967).

Biéler, A., *Architecture in Worship* (in French, Geneva, 1961; trans. London, 1965).

Binns, J.W. (ed.), *Ovid* (London, 1973) [Greek and Latin Studies: Classical Literature and its Influence].

Blamires, D., 'Eckhart and Tauler: a comparison of their sermons on *Homo quidam fecit cenam magnam* (Luke 16:16)' *MLR* lxvi (1971), 608–27.

Blanco García, P.F., 'Un manuscrito inédito del P. Márquez: "Sobre el modo de predicar a los príncipes" ', *C de D* xlvi (1898), 172–87, 259–71.

Blench, J.W., *Preaching in England in the late fifteenth and sixteenth centuries* (Oxford, 1964).

Boggs, R.S., *Index of Spanish Folktales classified according to Anti Aarne's 'Types of the Folktale'* (Helsinki, 1930) [Folklore Fellows' Communications, xc].

Bolgar, R.R., *The Classical Heritage* (Cambridge, 1954; New York, 1964).

Bonet, A., *La filosofía de la libertad en las controversias teológicas del siglo xvi y primera mitad del xvii* (Barcelona, 1932).

Bonnefoy, J.F., 'Sevilla por la inmaculada en 1614–1617', *A I–A* xv (1955), 7–33.

Bossy, J., 'The Counter-Reformation and the People of Catholic Europe', *Past and Present* xlvii (1970), 51–70.

Bourdeau, F., 'Les Origines du sermon missionaire sur la mort', *Vie spirituelle* cviii (1963), 319–38.

Bouyer, L., *Liturgy and Architecture* (Univ. of Notre Dame, Indiana, 1967).

Bremond, H., *Histoire littéraire du sentiment religieux en France* (Paris, 1916), i: *L'Humanisme dévot, 1580–1660*.

Bushee, A. (ed.), 'Oración fúnebre del contador Mateo Alemán', *RH* xxv (1911), 407–21.

Cambridge History of the Bible: vol. ii, ed. G.W. Lampe: *The West from the Fathers to the Reformation* (Cambridge, 1969); vol. iii, ed. S.L. Greenslade: *The West from the Reformation to the Present Day* (Cambridge, 1963).

Cantel, R., *Les Sermons de Vieira: Étude de style* (Paris, 1959).

Caplan, H., 'Rhetorical invention in some medieval tractates on preaching', *Sp* ii (1927), 284–95.

'The Four Senses of Scriptural Interpretation and the Medieval Theory of Preaching', *Sp* iv (1929), 282–90.

'Classical Rhetoric and the Medieval Theory of Preaching', *Classical Philology* xxviii (1933), 73–96.

Medieval Artes Praedicandi: a Handlist (New York, 1934; suppl. 1936) [Cornell Studies in Classical Philology].

and H. King, 'Spanish treatises on preaching: a book-list', *Speech monographs* (Cornell, 1950), 161–70.

Cassou, F., 'Voyage d'Espagne de François Bertaut [1659]', *RH* xlvii (1919), 1–317.

Cave, T., *Devotional poetry in France c. 1570–1613* (Cambridge, 1969).

Cayuela, A.M., 'La retórica y la predicación sacra' [review of F.G. Olmedo's edn. of *Instrucción de predicadores*], *R y F* cxxxv (1947).

Cereceda, F., 'El nacionalismo religioso español en Trento', *Hispania* v (1945), 236–85.

Chadwick, H., *Early Christian Thought and the Classical Tradition* (Oxford, 1966).

Chadwick, O., *The Reformation* (Harmondsworth, 1965).

Chandos, J., *In God's Name: examples of preaching in England 1534–1662* (London, 1971).

Chapman, J.A., 'Juan Ruíz's learned sermon', in *Libro de Buen Amor Studies*, ed., G.B. Gybbon-Monypenny (Tamesis, 1970), pp. 29–51.

Charland, Th.-M., *Artes praedicandi: Contribution à l'histoire de la rhétorique au Moyen Age* (Paris and Ottawa, 1936) [Publications de l'Institut d'Études Mediévales d'Ottowa].

Charmot, F., *La Pédagogie des jésuites* (Paris, 1951).

Chueca Goitia, F., *Arquitectura del siglo xvi* (Madrid, 1953) [*Ars Hispaniae*, xi].

Clark, A.M., *Studies in Literary Modes* (Edinburgh, 1946).

Clark, G., *The Seventeenth Century* (Oxford, 1929; 2nd edn. 1947).

Clements, R.J., *Picta Poesis: Literary and Humanistic Theory in Renaissance Emblem-Books* (Rome, 1960) [*Temi e Testi*, vi].

Correa Calderón, E., *Baltasar Gracián: vida y obra* (Madrid, 1961).

Coster, A., *Baltasar Gracián, 1601–1658* (New York and Paris, 1913).

Costes, R., *Antonio de Guevara, sa vie* (Bordeaux, 1925–6) [Bibliothèque de l'École des Hautes Études Hispaniques, facs. x, 1, and 2].

Cox, J.C., *Pulpits, Lecterns, Organs* (Oxford, 1915).

Crane, T.F., *Italian Popular Tales* (London, 1885).

The Exempla (or Illustrative Stories from the Sermones Vulgares) of Jacques de Vitry (London, 1890) [Folklore Society Texts, xcix].

Medieval sermon-books and stories (1917, repr. from *Proceedings of the American Philosophical Society*).

Croce, B., *I predicatori italiani del Seicento e el gusto spagnuolo* (Naples, 1899).

Cros, E., *Protée et le gueux: Recherches sur les origines et la nature du récit picaresque dans 'Guzmán de Alfarache'* (Paris, 1967).

Curtius, E.R., *European Literature and the Latin Middle Ages* (German edn., 1948; trans. New York, 1953).

Daniel-Rops, H., *The Catholic Reformation, 1500–1622* (trans. from French, 1962).

Dargan, E.C., *A History of Preaching* (2 vols., New York, 1905–12).

David-Peyre, Y., *Le Personnage du médecin et la relation médecin-malade dans la littérature ibérique de xvie et xviie siècle* (Paris, 1971).

Davies, G., *A poet at court: Antonio Hurtado de Mendoza (1586–1644)* (Oxford, 1971).

Delumeau, J., *Le Catholicisme entre Luther et Voltaire* (Paris, 1971).

Deyermond, A.D., [review of Owst's book] in *Estudios lulianos* vii (1963), 233–5.

The Middle Ages (London, 1971) [*A Literary History of Spain*, ed. R.O. Jones, vol. i].

Dickens, A.G., *The Counter Reformation* (London, 1968).

Domínguez Carretero, E., 'La escuela agustiniana de Salamanca', *C de D* clxix (1956), 638–85.

Domínguez Ortiz, A., *La sociedad española en el siglo xvii* (2 vols., Madrid, 1963–70), ii: *El estado eclesiástico*.

Crisis y decadencia de la España de los Austrias (Barcelona, 1969).

Donovan, R.B., *The Liturgical Drama in Medieval Spain* (Toronto, 1958).

Duncan, E., *The Story of the Carol* (London, 1911).

Dunn, P., 'Honour and the Christian background in Calderón', *BHS* xxxvii (1960), 90–105.

Eguía Ruiz, C., *Cervantes, Calderón, Lope, Gracián: nuevos temas crítico-biográficos* (Madrid, 1951) [*Cuadernos de literatura*, anejo viii].

Eliot, T.S., *For Lancelot Andrewes: Essays on Style and Order* (London, 1928; reissued 1970).

Elliott, J.H., *Imperial Spain, 1469–1716* (London, 1963; paperback, 1970).

Europe divided 1559–1598 (London, 1968) [Fontana History of Europe].

Entrambasaguas, J. de., *La biblioteca de Ramírez de Prado* (2 vols., Madrid, 1943).

Evennett, H.O., *The Spirit of the Counter-Reformation* (Notre Dame and London, 1970).

Farrar, F.W., *A History of Interpretation* (London, 1886).

Farrell, A.P., *The Jesuit Code of Liberal Education: development and scope of the Ratio Studiorum* (Milwaukee, 1938).

Flecniakoska, J.L., *La Formation de l' "Auto" religieux en Espagne avant Calderón, 1550–1635* (Montpellier, 1961).

Fletcher, A., *Allegory: the theory of a symbolic mode* (Cornell and New York, 1964).

Fortunatus a Iesu [with Beda a SS Trinitate (Fr. Bede Edwards)] *Constitutiones carmelitarum discalceatorum, 1567–1600* (Rome, 1968).

Fraser Mitchell, W., *English Pulpit Oratory from Andrewes to Tillotson: a study of its literary aspects* (London, 1932).

Gagnebin, B., *L'Incroyable Histoire des sermons de Calvin* (Geneva, 1956) [Extrait du *Bulletin de la Societé d'Histoire et d'Archéologie de Genève*, x (1955)].

Galbraith, G.R., *The Constitution of the Dominican Order, 1216–1360* (Manchester, 1925).

García Berrio, A., *España e Italia ante el conceptismo* (Madrid, 1968) [Anejo de la *RFE* lxxxvii].

García Mercadel, J. (ed.)., *Viajes de extranjeros por España y Portugal* (Madrid, 1959), ii: *siglo xvii.*

García Villoslada, R., *Manual de la Historia de la Compañía de Jesús* (Madrid, 1941).

Garrido, P., 'El magisterio espiritual de Santa Teresa de Jesús entre los Carmelitas españoles', *Carmelus* xviii (1971), 91–7.

Gemelli, A., *Il Francescanesimo* (Milan, 1932), trans. H. Hughes: *The Franciscan Message in the World* (London, 1934).

Gibbs, J., *Vida de Fray Antonio de Guevara, 1481–1545* (Valladolid, 1960).

Gilman, S., 'An Introduction to the Ideology of the Baroque in Spain', *Symposium* i (1946), 82–107.

Gilson, E., 'Michel Menot et la technique du sermon mediéval', *Les Idées et les Lettres* (Paris, 1932), pp. 93–154.

Glaser, E., '*Convertentur ad vesperam*: on a rare Spanish translation of an Inquisitorial sermon by Frei João de Ceita', in *Collected studies in honour of Américo Castro's 80th year*, ed. M.P. Hornik (Oxford, 1965), pp. 137–74. [The Richard Kronstein Foundation for the promotion of Jewish and cognate studies, Lincombe Lodge, Oxford].

Gombrich, E.H., *Norm and form: studies in the art of the Renaissance* (London, 1966).

González de Amezúa, A., Introduction to edition of Cervantes, *El casamiento engañoso* (Madrid, 1912). *See also* under Vega, Lope de, *Epistolario* (3).

González de la Calle, P.U., 'Documentos inéditos acerca del uso de la lengua vulgar en los libros espirituales', *BRAE* xii (1925), 258–73, 470–97, 652–73.

Gray, H.H., 'Renaissance Humanism: the pursuit of eloquence', *Journal of the History of Ideas* xxiv (1963), 497–514.

Green, O.H., 'On the attitude towards the *vulgo* in the Spanish *Siglo de Oro*', *Studies in the Renaissance*, iv (New York, 1957).
    '*Se acicalaron los auditorios*: an aspect of the Spanish literary baroque', *HR* xxvii (1959), 413–22.

Griselle, E., *Bourdaloue, histoire critique de sa prédication d'après les notes de ses auditeurs et les témoignages contemporains* (3 vols., Paris, 1901–6; facsimile reprint, Geneva, 1971).

Guibert, J. de., *The Jesuits, their Spiritual Doctrine and Practice* (in French, 1953; Chicago, 1964).

Gutiérrez, C., *Españoles en Trento* (Valladolid, 1951).

Gutiérrez, D., 'Del origen y carácter de la escuela teológica hispano-agustiniana de los siglos xvi y xvii', *C de D* cliii (1941), 227–55.
    'Ascéticos y místicos agustinos de España, Portugal e Hispano-américa', in *Sanctus Augustinus vitae spiritualis magister*, ii (Rome, 1959), 147–238.

Gutiérrez, D., (cont'd)
  Los agustinos desde el protestantismo hasta la restauración católica
  (Rome, 1971).

Hafter, M.Z., Gracián and Perfection (Harvard, 1966).
Hagstrum, J.H., The Sister Arts (Chicago, 1958).
Hale, J.R., Renaissance Europe, 1480–1520 (London, 1971) [Fontana History of Europe].
Harris, V., 'Allegory to Analogy in the Interpretation of Scriptures', Philological Quarterly, xlv (1966), 1–23.
Hefele, Ch.-J., Histoire des Conciles (Paris, 1917), x.
Herr, A.F., The Elizabethan Sermon: a survey and a bibliography (Philadelphia, 1940; facsimile, 1970).
Herrera Puga, P., Sociedad y delincuencia en el Siglo de Oro: aspectos de la vida sevillana en los siglos xvi y xvii (Granada, 1971).
Herrero, F., Aportación bibliográfica a la oratoria sagrada española (Madrid, 1971) [Anejos de Revista de Literatura, 30].
Herrero García M., 'Nueva interpretación de la novela picaresca', RFE xxiv (1937), 343–62.
  Sermonario clásico: con un ensayo sobre la oratoria sagrada (Madrid and Buenos Aires, 1942).
  'La literatura religiosa', in Historia General de las Literaturas Hispánicas, ed. G. Diaz-Plaja (Barcelona, 1953), iii. 17–26.
Highet, G., The Classical Tradition (Oxford, 1949).
Hill, C., Puritanism and Revolution (1st edn., London, 1958; paperback, 1968).
  The World Turned Upside Down (London, 1972).
[Hospital Real] Privilegios de la antigua fundación del Hospital Real y General de Nuestra Señora de Gracia de Zaragoza (Jaca, 1944) [Comunicación iii, Semana de Estudios de Derecho aragonés].
Howell, W.S., Logic and Rhetoric in England, 1500–1700 (Princeton, 1956).
Huerga, A., Predicadores, alumbrados e inquisición (Madrid, 1973).

Jammes, R., Études sur l'œuvre poétique de Don Luis de Góngora (Bordeaux, 1967).
Janelle, P., The Catholic Reformation (Bruce, 1963; London, 1971).
Jedin, H., History of the Council of Trent (2 vols., London, 1957–61).
Jones, R.F., 'The Attack on Pulpit Eloquence in the Restoration', in The Seventeenth Century: studies in the History of English thought and literature from Bacon to Pope (Stanford, 1951), pp. 111–42.
Joseph, B.L., Elizabethan Acting (2nd edn., Oxford, 1964).

Kahrl, S.J., 'Allegory in Practice: a study of narrative styles in medieval exempla', Modern Philology lxiii (1965–6), 105–10.
Kane, E.K., Gongorism and the Golden Age (Columbia, 1928).
Kendrick, T.D., St. James in Spain (London, 1960).

Kernan, A.P., *The Plot of Satire* (Newhaven and London, 1965).

Krailsheimer, A.J., *Rabelais and the Franciscans* (Oxford, 1963).

Kristeller, P.O., *Renaissance Thought: the Classic, Scholastic and Humanist Strains* (Harvard, 1955; New York, 1961).

La Fuente, V. de, *Historia de las Universidades, colegios y demás establecimientos de España* (4 vols. bound as 2, Madrid, 1884–9).

Lanson, G., *Histoire illustrée de la littérature française* (Paris and London, 1923).

Lázaro Carreter, F., 'Sobre la dificultad conceptista', in *Estudios dedicados a Menéndez Pidal*, vi (Madrid, 1956), 355–86.

Leeman, A.D., *Orationis Ratio: the stylistic theories and practice of the Roman Orators, Historians and Philosophers* (2 vols., Amsterdam, 1963).

Leyburn, E.D., 'Notes on Satire and Allegory', *Journal of Aesthetics and Art Criticism* vi (New York, 1958), 323–31.

Logan, O.M.T., 'Grace and Justification: some Italian views of the 16th and 17th centuries', *Journal of Ecclesiastical History* xx (1969), 67–78.

López, A., 'Notas de bibliografía franciscana', *A I–A* xxvi seqq.
'Introducción bio-bibliográfica sobre el P. Fr. Diego Murillo', *Revista Bibliográfica y Documental*, v (1951), 179–216.

López Santos, L., 'La oratoria sagrada en el seiscientos (un libro inédito del P. Valentín Céspedes)', *RFE* xxx (1946), 353–68.

Lukács, L. (ed.), *Monumenta Paedagogica Societatis Iesu*, i [1540–56] (Rome, 1965).

Lynch, J., *Spain under the Hapsburgs* (2 vols., Oxford, 1964–9).

Maclure, M., *The Paul's Cross Sermons, 1534–1642* (Toronto, 1958) [University of Toronto Department of English Studies and Texts, vi]

Mâle, E., *L'art religieux de la fin du xvie siècle, du xviie siècle et du xviiie siècle* (Paris, 1951).

Márquez Villanueva, F., *Espiritualidad y literatura en el siglo xvi* (Madrid and Barcelona, 1968).

Martí, A.M., 'La retórica sacra en el Siglo de Oro', *HR* xxxviii (1970), 264–98.
La preceptiva retórica española en el Siglo de Oro (Madrid, 1972).

Martín Hernández, F., *Los seminarios españoles. Historia y pedagogía, 1563–1700* (Salamanca, 1964).

Martínez Vigil, R., *Orden de predicadores, sus glorias en santidad, apostolado, ciencias, artes y gobierno de los pueblos. Seguidas del Ensayo de una Biblioteca de dominicos españoles* (Madrid, 1884).

Martz, L., *The Poetry of Meditation* (Yale Univ. Press, 1954; rev. edn. 1962).

May, T.E., 'Gracián's idea of the *concepto*', *HR* xviii (1950), 15–41.

Mazzeo, J.A., *Renaissance and Seventeenth Century Studies* (New York, 1964).

Menéndez y Pelayo, M., *Orígenes de la novela*, *NBAE* (4 vols., Madrid, 1905–15).

Menéndez y Pelayo, M., (cont'd)
Historia de los heterodoxos españoles (8 vols., Buenos Aires, 1945).
Historia de las ideas estéticas en España (Madrid, 1881; rev. edn. 1947).
Meseguer Fernández, J., 'Fr. Francisco Ortiz en Torrelaguna: notes para su biografía', *A I–A* viii (1948), 479–525.
'Estatutos del P. Francisco Zamora para el Estudio de Teología de San Juan de los Reyes', *A I–A* xxvi (1966), 31–9.
Michelot, M., *Les Systèmes sténographiques* (Paris, 1959) [Que sais-je?, no. 790].
Mir, M., *Predicadores de los siglos xvi y xvii*, i: *Fray Alonso de Cabrera* [discurso preliminar], (*BAE*, Madrid, 1906).
Monasterio, I., *Místicos agustinos españoles* (2nd edn., El Escorial, 1929).
Moorman, J., *A History of the Franciscan Order from its origins to the year 1517* (Oxford, 1968).

Nicolau, M., *Jerónimo Nadal, 1507–1580* (Madrid, 1949).
Pláticas espirituales en Coïmbra (Granada, 1945) [Biblioteca Teológica Granadina, i. 2].
'Espiritualidad de la Compañía de Jesús en la España del siglo xvi', in *Corrientes espirituales* (*see* Trabajos).
Nolting-Hauff, I., *Visión, sátira y agudeza en los "Sueños" de Quevedo* (Madrid, 1974).

Olmedo, F.G., 'Decadencia de la oratoria sagrada en el siglo xvii', *R y F* xlvi (1916), 310–21.
'Restauración de la oratoria sagrada en el siglo xviii', *R y F* li (1918), 460–72.
'Predicadores célebres', *R y F* lvi (1919), 334 and 486; lvii (1920) 76–87.
'Santa Teresa de Jesús y los predicadores del Siglo de Oro' *BRAH* lxxxiv (1924), 165–75 and 280–95.
Juan Bonifacio, 1538–1606, y la cultura literaria del Siglo de Oro (Madrid and Santander, 1938).
Ong, W.J., 'Wit and Mystery: a revaluation in medieval Latin hymnody', *Sp* xxii (1947), 310–41.
O'Reilly, T., 'Saint Ignatius Loyola and Spanish Erasmianism', *Archivum Historicum Societatis Iesu* xliii (1974), 301–20.
Oroz Reta, J., *La retórica en los sermones de S. Agustín* (Madrid, 1963).
Ortega, A., *Las casas de estudios en la provincia de Andalucía* [extracto del *A I–A* iv, v, vii–xvii, xix, and xx] (Madrid, 1917).
Osgood, C.O., *Boccaccio on poetry* (Princeton, 1930).
Owst, G.R., *Preaching in Medieval England: an Introduction to sermon manuscripts of the period c. 1350–1450* (Cambridge, 1926).
Literature and Pulpit in Medieval England: a neglected chapter in the history of English people (1933; rev. 1961; repr. Oxford, 1966).

Palomera, E.J., *Fray Diego Valades, O.F.M., Evangelizador humanista de la Nueva España, su obra* (Mexico, 1962).

Parker, T.H.L., *Supplementa Calviniana: an account of the manuscripts of Calvin's sermons now in course of preparation* (London, 1962).

Pascoe, L.B., 'The Council of Trent and Bible Study', *Catholic Historical Review*, liii (1967), 18−38.

Pastor, L. von, *The History of the Popes, 1305−1585*, trans. from German (Freiburg i. Br., 1886−1925) by F.I. Antrobus and R.F. Kerr (from vol. vii) (20 vols., London 1891−1930).

Paulson, R., *The Fictions of Satire* (John Hopkins, 1967).

Paz y Melia, A., *Sales españoles, o agudezas del ingenio nacional* (Madrid, 1890; 2 vols., ed. R. Paz Remolar, Madrid, 1964).

    Papeles de Inquisición (2nd edn., 2 vols., R. Paz, Madrid, 1947).

Peers, E.A., *Studies of the Spanish Mystics* (3 vols., London, 1927−60).

    Handbook of the Life and Times of St. Teresa and St. John of the Cross (London, 1954).

    (ed.) *The Complete Works of St. John of the Cross* (rev. edn., London, 1953).

Pennington, D.H., *Seventeenth Century Europe* (London, 1970).

Pérez, J., 'Moines frondeurs et sermons subversifs en Castille pendant le premier séjour de Charles-Quint en Espagne', *BH* lxvii (1965), 5−24.

Pérez, Q., *Fray Hernando de Santiago* (Santander, 1929) [anthology].

    Fray Hernando de Santiago (Madrid, 1949) [Anejo de la *RFE* xliii].

Pérez Bustamante, C., *Felipe III: semblanza de un monarca y perfiles de una privanza* (Madrid, 1950).

Pérez Goyena, A., 'Un episodio de la historia de la teología española, *R y F* xxxiv (1912), 334−444; xxxv (1913), 30−42.

Pevsner, N., *An Outline of European Architecture* (1943; Harmondsworth, 1963).

Pfandl, L., *Introducción al Siglo de Oro. Cultura y costumbres del pueblo español de los siglos xvi y xvii* (Madrid, 1929).

Pike, R., *Aristocrats and Traders; Sevillian Society in the Sixteenth Century* (Cornell and London, 1972).

Pollard, A., *Satire* (London, 1970) [Methuen Critical Idiom, vii].

Polman, A.D.R., *The Word of God according to St. Augustine* (in Dutch, 1955; London, 1961).

Praz, M., *Studies in Seventeenth Century Imagery* (1939; 2nd rev. and aug. edn., Rome 1964) [Sussidi Eruditi, xvi].

Prentice, A.N., *Renaissance Architecture and Ornament in Spain*, ed. H.W. Booton (London, 1970).

Preston, G., 'Wrestling with the Word−1', *New Blackfriars* li (1970), 117−25.

Preto-Rodas, R.A., 'Anchieta and Vieira: drama as sermon, sermon as drama', *Luso-Brazilian Review* vii (1970), 96−103.

Pring-Mill, R.F., 'Some techniques of representation in the *Sueños* and the *Criticón*', *BHS* xlv (1968), 270−84.

Quinn, D., 'Donne's Christian Eloquence', *Journal of English Literary History* xxvii (1960), 276–97.

Rahner, H., *Greek Myths and Christian Mystery* (Zurich, 1957; London, 1963).

Recio, A., 'La Inmaculada en la predicación franciscano-española, *A I–A* xv (1955), 99–200.

Reglá, J., *Historia social y económica de España*, iii (Barcelona, 1957) [General editor J. Vicens Vives].

Reichenberger, A., 'The uniqueness of the *comedia*', *HR* xxvii (1959), 303–16.

Rennert, H.A., *The Spanish Stage in the time of Lope de Vega* (New York, 1909; Dover facsimile reprint, 1963).

Ricard, R., 'Notes et matériaux pour l'étude du "socratisme" chrétien chez Sainte Thérèse et les spirituels espagnols', *BH* xlix (1947), 5–37, 170–204; l (1948), 5–26; li (1949), 407–22.

Estudios de la literatura religiosa española (Madrid, 1964).

Riley, E.C., *Cervantes's theory of the novel* (Oxford, 1962).

'Aspectos del concepto de *Admiratio* en la teoría literaria del Siglo de Oro', in *Homenaje a Damaso Alonso*, iii (Madrid, 1963), 173–83.

Rodríguez Marín, F. (ed.), *Rinconete y Cortadillo*, discurso preliminar (2nd edn., Madrid, 1920).

Rodríguez-Moñino, A., 'Construcción crítica y realidad histórica en la poesía española de los siglos xvi y xvii', *Acta of the 9th Congress of FILLM* (2nd edn., Madrid, 1968).

Rotunda, D.P., *Motif-Index of the Italian Novella in Prose* (Bloomington, 1942).

Russell, P.E., 'A Stuart Hispanist: James Mabbe', *BHS* xxx (1953), 75–84.

'English Seventeenth-Century Interpretations of Spanish Literature', *Atlante*, i (1953), 65–77.

Ruthven, K.K., *The Conceit* (London, 1969) [Methuen Critical Idiom, iv].

Sainz de Robles, F.C., *Madrid, crónica y guía de una ciudad impar* (Madrid, 1962).

Salomon, N., *Recherches sur le thème paysan dans la "comedia" au temps de Lope de Vega* (Bordeaux, 1965).

San José, V. de, 'Apuntes sobre la prosa carmelitana hasta el siglo xix', *El Monte Carmelo* liii (1949), 3–109.

Santa Teresa, S. de, *Obras del P. Jerónimo Gracián de la Madre de Dios* (3 vols., Burgos, 1933).

Procesos de Beatificación y Canonización de Sta Teresa de Jesús (3 vols., Burgos, 1935).

Historia del Carmen Descalzo en España, Portugal y América (Burgos, 1937).

Schwarz, W., *Principles of Biblical Translation: some Reformation controversies and their background* (Cambridge, 1955).

Sergio, A., *Ensaios* (Coimbra and Lisbon, 1934—49).
Shearman, J., *Mannerism* (Harmondsworth, 1967).
Shepard, S., *El Pinciano y las teorías literarias del Siglo de Oro* (Madrid, 1962).
Shergold, N.D., *A History of the Spanish Stage* (Oxford, 1967).
Sierra Corella, A., *La censura de libros y papeles en España y los Índices y catálogos españoles de los prohibidos y expurgados* (Madrid, 1947).
Simón Díaz, J., *Historia del Colegio Imperial de Madrid* (2 vols., Madrid, 1952).
Simpson, E.M., 'Donne's Spanish Authors', *MLR* xliii (1948), 182—5.
Smalley, B., *The Study of the Bible in the Middle Ages* (Oxford, 1941; 2nd edn. 1952).
Smyth, C., *The Art of Preaching* (London, 1940; rev. edn., 1964).
Soria Ortega, A., *El Maestro Fray Manuel de Guerra y Ribera y la oratoria sagrada de su tiempo* (Granada, 1950) [Anejos del *Boletín de la Universidad de Granada*, iii].
Spingarn, J.E., *A History of Literary Criticism in the Renaissance* (New York, 1899).
      Critical Essays of the Seventeenth Century (3 vols., Oxford, 1908—9).
Spitz, L., *The Religious Renaissance of the German Humanists* (Cambridge, Mass., 1963).
Stinglhamber, L., 'Baltasar Gracián et la Compagnie de Jésus', *HR* xxii (1954), 195—207.
Street, G.E., *Some account of Gothic architecture in Spain* (London, 1865).
Strowski, F., *Saint François de Sales: Introduction à l'histoire du sentiment religieux en France au dix-septième siècle* (Paris, 1898).

Tavard, G.H., *Holy Writ or Holy Church* (London and New York, 1959).
Tejada y Ramiro, J., *Colección de canones de la Iglesia española, publicada en latín* (4 vols., Madrid, 1849—53).
Thomas, L.-P., *Le Lyrisme et la préciosité cultistes en Espagne* (Halle, 1909) [*Zeitschrift für romanische Philologie*, xviii].
Thompson, S., *Motif-Index of Folk-Literature* (2nd rev. edn., 7 vols., Copenhagen, 1955—7).
Ticknor, G., *History of Spanish Literature* (3 vols., London, 1849; rev. edn. 1863).
Trabajos del ii Congreso de Espiritualidad (1956) *Corrientes espirituales en la España del siglo xvi* (Barcelona, 1963).
Trevor Davies, R., *The Golden Century of Spain, 1501—1621* (London, 1937).
Trevor-Roper, H.R., *Religion, the Reformation and Social Change* (1956); London, 1967).
      'Spain and Europe, 1598—1621', *The New Cambridge Modern History*, iv. (Cambridge, 1970).

Truchet, J., *La Prédication de Bossuet: Étude de thèmes* (2 vols., Paris, 1960).
Tubach, F.C., 'Exempla in the decline', *Traditio* xviii (1962), 407–17.
Tuve, R., *Elizabethan and Metaphysical Imagery* (Chicago, 1947).

Vatican II—*Concilio Vaticano II: constituciones, decretos, declaraciones, legislación posconciliar, BAC* (6th edn., Madrid, 1968).

Walsh, J., 'St Thomas on preaching', *Dominicana* v (1921), 6–14.
Walz, A.M., *Compendium Historiae Ordinis Praedicatorum* (Rome, 1933).
Watkin, E.I., *Catholic Art and Culture* (London, 1942).
Weinberg, B., *A History of Literary Criticism in the Italian Renaissance* (2 vols., Chicago, 1961).
Welter, J.-Th., *L'Exemplum dans la littérature religieuse et didactique du moyen âge* (Paris and Toulouse, 1927).
Whinnom, K., 'El origen de las comparaciones religiosas del Siglo de Oro: Mendoza, Montesino y Román', *RFE* xlvi (1963), 263–85.
White, H.C., *English Devotional Literature (Prose) 1600–1640* (Madison, 1931).
Willey, B., *The Seventeenth Century Background* (London, 1934; Harmondsworth, 1962).
Williamson, G., *The Senecan Amble: a study in prose form from Bacon to Collier* (London, 1951).
Wilson, E.M., 'Spanish and English Religious Poetry of the Seventeenth Century', *Journal of Ecclesiastical History* ix (1958), 38–53. *Some aspects of Spanish Literary History* (Oxford, 1967) [Taylorian Lecture, 1966].
Wind, E., *Pagan Mysteries in the Renaissance* (London, 1958; rev. edn., Harmondsworth, 1967).
Woods, M.J., 'Sixteenth Century Topical Theory: some Spanish and Italian views', *MLR* lxiii (1968), 66–73.
'Gracián, Peregrini, and the Theory of Topics', *MLR* lxiii (1968), 854–63.

Yates, F.A., *The French Academies of the Sixteenth Century* (London, 1947) [*Studies of the Warburg Institute*, xv].
The Art of Memory (London, 1966; Harmondsworth, 1969).
Young, R.F., *Comenius in England* (London, 1932).

Zawart, A., 'A History of Franciscan preaching and Franciscan preachers', in *The Franciscan Educational Conference*, ix (New York and Washington, 1927), 242–587.

6. BIBLIOGRAPHIES, DICTIONARIES, AND CATALOGUES

Alcocer y Martínez, M., *Catálogo razonado de obras impresas en Valladolid, 1481–1800* (Valladolid, 1926).
Alonso, M., *Enciclopedia del Idioma* (3 vols., Madrid, 1958).

Antonio, N., *Bibliotheca Hispana Nova, sive Hispanorum scriptorum qui ab anno MD ad MDCLXXXIV floruere notitia* (2 vols., Madrid, 1783–8).

Backer, Augustin de and Alois de Backer, *Bibliothèque de la Compagnie de Jésus. Première partie: Bibliographie*, ed. C. Sommervogel (10 vols., Brussels and Paris, 1890–1909).
Bellarmine, R., *De scriptoribus ecclesiasticis* (Rome, 1613).
Bustamante y Urrutia, J-Mª. de, *Catálogo de la Biblioteca Universitaria* [de Santiago de Compostela], iii: *Impresos del siglo xvii* (Santiago, 1945).

Capmany, A. de, *Teatro histórico-crítico de la Eloquencia Española* (Madrid, 1786–94), iv and v.
Catalina García, J., *Ensayo de una tipografía complutense* (Madrid, 1889).
Cejador, J., *Historia de la lengua y literatura castellana* (14 vols., Madrid, 1915–27).
Covarrubias, S. de, *Tesoro de la lengua castellana* (Madrid, 1612; ed. M. de Riquer, Barcelona, 1943).
Cross, F.L. (ed.), *The Oxford Dictionary of the Christian Church* (Oxford, 1957).

Dagens, J., *Bibliographie chronologique de la littérature de spiritualité et de ses sources, 1501–1610* (Paris, 1952).
Diccionario de Autoridades (3 vols., Madrid, 1765; facsimile, 1963).
Dictionnaire d'histoire et de géographie ecclésiastiques, ed. A. Baudrillart (Paris, 1909–).
Diccionario de historia eclesiástica de España, ed. Q. Aldea, T. Marin Martinez, and J. Vives Gatell (Madrid, 1973).
Dictionnaire de spiritualité, ascétique et mystique, ed. M. Viller (Paris, 1932–).
Dictionnaire de théologie catholique, ed. A. Vacant, E. Mangenot, and E. Aman, (13 vols., Paris, 1902–35).

Escudero y Perosso, F., *Tipografía Hispalense, anales bibliográficos de la ciudad de Sevilla. . .hasta fines del siglo xviii* (Madrid, 1894).

Gallardo, B.J., *Ensayo de una biblioteca española de libros raros y curiosos, formado con los apuntamientos de B.J.G.–, coordinados y aumentados por D.M. Zarco del Valle y D. J. Sancho Rayón* (4 vols., Madrid, 1863–89).
García Peres, D., *Catálogo razonado biográfico y bibliográfico de los autores portugueses que escribieron en castellano* (Madrid, 1890).

Hatzfeld, H., *Bibliografía crítica de la nueva estilística aplicada a las literaturas románicas* (Madrid, 1955).
Herrera, T., *Alphabetum Augustinianum* (2 vols., Madrid, 1644).

Hurter, H., *Nomenclatur literarius recentioris theologiae catholicae* (3 vols., Innsbruck, 1892).

Jiménez Catalán, M., *Ensayo de una tipografía zaragozana del siglo xvii* (Saragossa, 1925).

Latassa y Ortín, F. de, *Biblioteca nueva de los escritores aragoneses*, ii: *1600–1640* (Pamplona, 1799).

Ossinger, J.F., *Bibliotheca Augustiniana historica, critica et chronologica in qua mille quadrigenti Augustiniani ord. scriptores inveniuntur* (Ingolstadt, 1768).

Palau y Dulcet, A., *Manual del librero hispano-americano; inventario bibliográfico de la producción científica y literaria de España y de la América desde la invención de la imprenta hasta nuestros días* (7 vols., Barcelona, 1923–7; 24 vols., Barcelona and Oxford, 1948– [incomplete]).

Penney, C.L., *List of Books printed 1601–1700 in the Library of the Hispanic Society of America* (New York, 1938) [Hispanic Notes and Monographs, lxxxiii].

Pérez Pastor, C., *La imprenta en Toledo* (Madrid, 1887).
  Bibliografía madrileña (3 vols., Madrid, 1891).
  La imprenta en Medina del Campo (Madrid, 1895).

Quétif, J. and J. Echard, *Scriptores Ordinis Praedicatorum recensiti, notisque historicis et criticis illustrati* (2 vols., Paris, 1719–21).

Rezabel y Ugarte, J. de, *Biblioteca de escritores que fueron individuos de los seis Colegios Mayores* (Madrid, 1805).

Ribadeneyra, P., with P. Alegambe, and N. Southwell, *Bibliotheca Scriptorum Societatis Iesu* (Rome, 1676; facsimile, Gregg, 1969).

San Antonio, J. de, *Bibliotheca universa franciscana, sive alumnorum trium ordinum S.P.N. Francisci* (3 vols., Madrid, 1732; facsimile [reduced], Farnborough, 1966).

Santiago y Vela, G. de, *Ensayo de una Biblioteca Ibero-Americana de la Orden de San Agustín. Obra basada en el catálogo bio-bibliográfico agustiniano del P. Bonifacio Moral* (6 vols., Madrid and El Escorial, 1913–25).

Sbaralea, J., *Supplementum ad Scriptores Lucae Waddingi* (Rome, 1908).

Simón Díaz, J., *Bibliografía de la literatura hispánica* (10 vols., Madrid, 1950– [incomplete]).

Thomas, H., *Short-title catalogues of Spanish, Spanish-American and Portuguese Books printed before 1601 in the British Museum* (London, 1921; photographic reprint, 1966).

Villiers, C., *Bibliotheca Carmelitana, notis criticis et dissertationibus illustrata: cura et labore unius e Carmelitis provinciae Turoniae collecta* (2 vols., Orleans, 1752).

Vindel, F., *Manual gráfico-descriptivo del bibliófilo hispano-americano, 1475—1850* (12 vols., Madrid, 1930—4).

Wadding, L., *Legatio Philippi III et IV...ad SS. DD. NN. Paulum PP. V et Gregorium XV, de definienda controversia inmaculatae conceptionis beatae virginis Mariae* (Louvain, 1624).

Scriptores Ordinis Minorum (Rome, 1650; rev. edn. 1906).

Zamarriego, T. (ed.), *Enciclopedia de Orientación Bibliográfica* (Barcelona, 1964), i: *Religión.*

INDEX